GLOBAL BARGAINING

GLOBAL BARGAINING

UNCTAD and the Quest for a
New International Economic Order

Robert L. Rothstein

Princeton University Press
Princeton, New Jersey

To my own Geneva "Group"

Contents

Preface

In this book I have sought to examine North-South relations from the perspective of the international bargaining system through which each side seeks to achieve its goals and protect its interests. I argue that this bargaining system has characteristics and consequences that are not always appreciated by participants or observers, that these characteristics and consequences have an important effect on outcomes, that prevailing doctrines and approaches do not provide very reliable explanations of the patterns of behavior within this system, and that only major reforms of institutions, procedures, and concepts (and perhaps beliefs) are likely to lead to the negotiation of mutually acceptable agreements. I illustrate the origins of these propositions in Part One by means of a detailed case study of commodity negotiations in UNCTAD; in Part Two, I analyze these and other propositions in much greater depth and suggest a number of reforms designed to diminish or eliminate existing deficiencies. My intent is thus both analytic and prescriptive.

I do not mean to imply that the international bargaining system has a completely independent or determinative effect on outcomes in the North-South arena. What happens at the national level or in other bargaining arenas is hardly irrelevant or unimportant. But the international bargaining system is important both in and of itself and in its effect on the questions considered and the answers reached in other arenas. Indeed, much of the focus of what follows will center on the interrelationships between different levels or arenas of decision. Moreover, as we move toward an international system in which more and more issues require some form of cooperative decision making, the ability of the international bargaining system to produce consistent and timely decisions is likely to become an increasingly crucial issue for both national and international leaders. Successful outcomes will require more than simplistic injunctions to expand the bargaining process and more than facile analogies with domestic bargaining patterns in pluralist systems. In other words, it is time to think very deeply about how we can bargain in a particularly difficult environment and about what we can legitimately expect from the settlement process in this environment.

I could not have written this book without the support of a very generous grant from the Rockefeller Foundation's Program on Conflict in International Relations. This grant permitted me to spend a year and a half in Geneva, Paris, and Nairobi closely studying the negotiating process at UNCTAD, and it facilitated comparisons with other negotiating processes in other arenas such as the Conference on International Economic Cooperation. I want particularly to thank my friend Dr. John Stremlau of the Foundation not only for many kindnesses during the period of my grant but also for many useful and interesting discussions of North-South relations. This book repays only some small part of my debt to the Rockefeller Foundation, for the educational experience that the grant permitted was invaluable.

I would not have been able to finish this book as quickly as I have without the support of another grant from the Office of External Research of the Department of State. This grant permitted me more than just the time to write (although it certainly did that), for it also facilitated a great deal of contact with many of the officials directly concerned with North-South relations. This contact did not change the substance or thrust of the book, but it was of great indirect help in alerting me to the significance of some factors that seemed less important from the Geneva perspective and in providing me with a sophisticated and interested audience on which to test my ideas. I would like to thank Mr. Daniel Fendrick of the Office of External Research for being very helpful throughout and Dr. Ray Platig, Director of the Office of External Research, for a number of useful comments on my manuscript and for his efforts to diffuse some of my conclusions through publication of several External Research Studies.

Charles R. Frank, Jr., formerly Deputy Assistant Secretary of State in the Bureau of International Organization Affairs, first suggested and then strongly supported my application to the Office of External Research. I am very grateful for this support, but I want also to thank him for a number of conversations and discussions of these issues that made me reconsider or think more clearly about my own arguments.

Professor Raymond Hopkins of Swarthmore College read my manuscript with great care and suggested a number of changes in substance and style that have made this a better book. As with my previous book and our continuing discussion of so many issues and ideas, I am once again greatly in his debt. Professor Henry Nau of George Washington University, who seems to have transcended without difficulty the limitations of an early exposure to my ideas in his days as a graduate student, also commented in great detail and with great discernment on my manuscript. Again, I am grateful. I should also like to thank Professor Bela Balassa of Johns Hopkins University and the World Bank for his comments on my interpretation of the economics of commodities.

Many of the participants in the bargaining process were of great help to me, and some indeed have become good friends. I cannot mention all of them—and given the nature of what follows, not all would like to be mentioned—but I would feel ungrateful if I could not register my thanks to a few who were especially helpful. Dr. John Cuddy of the UNCTAD staff made a valiant effort to expand my knowledge of commodity economics, to explain the UNCTAD position in great detail, and to discuss the issues on many occasions. His careful reading of Chapters 2, 3, and 4 was especially helpful. On all these counts I am greatly indebted.

Several American officials who served as delegates to UNCTAD were very helpful. I want to thank especially Michael Boerner and Edith Bruce, with whom I exchanged ideas, arguments, and speculations—always to my benefit. I should also like to thank Robert Allen of the American Mission in Geneva, who did much to facilitate my stay. Finally, I would like to thank two Nordic friends, Torill Oftedal Sjaastad of Norway and Rolf Akesson of Sweden, for comments on an earlier draft of my study and for numerous discussions of the issues.

To avoid unnecessary misunderstandings, I want to emphasize several points. First, none of the official participants mentioned are in any way responsible for my views, and all agreed and disagreed in various proportions. Second, the fact that an agency of the U.S. Government financed a year of writing does not imply either approval or any control by the government over what I have written. I was left entirely alone to say exactly what I wanted to say—a good part of which, as will shortly become clear, is highly critical of U.S. policies. Third, in a few places in the case study I may appear to speak ex cathedra, but I have done so only to protect persons who requested anonymity or on the basis of my own observations. None of these instances, however, are very important and all relate primarily to details, not to design or direction.

I have written the prescriptive chapters on reforms primarily from the point of view of what the developed countries, particularly the United States, might do to improve the bargaining process and UNCTAD. Nevertheless, I believe that much of the argument is also directly relevant to the efforts of the Third World to devise its own policies on these issues. This is especially true because institutional, structural, and conceptual reforms in the international system are likely to be successful only if all sides can agree on what needs to be done. I hope that my sharp criticism of some of the actions of UNCTAD and the Group of 77 is not used to obscure this more general point: my reform proposals are meant to be mutually beneficial. I should note also that in my analyses I have done my best to be fair and to avoid oversimplifications of either side's intentions or policies. I am aware, however, that some of my comments will be painful to a number of participants—on both sides—and for this I am genuinely sorry. But I cannot see that it would be in either side's interest (although it might be in the short-run interest of a few individuals) to avoid or obscure criticisms that I believe justified.

I was generously supported in researching and writing this book, and would like to thank all those whose cooperation helped to make it possible. Whatever errors, omissions, or misinterpretations remain are entirely my responsibility.

Robert L. Rothstein

Washington, D.C.
September 1978

List of Abbreviations

CIEC	Conference on International Economic Cooperation
ECA	Economic Commission for Africa
ECLA	Economic Commission for Latin America
EEC	European Economic Community
FAO	Food and Agriculture Organization
GATT	General Agreement on Tariffs and Trade
GSP	General System of Preferences
IFAD	International Fund for Agricultural Development
ILO	International Labor Organization
IMF	International Monetary Fund
IPC	Integrated Program for Commodities
ITO	International Trade Organization
NIEO	New International Economic Order
OECD	Organization for Economic Cooperation and Development
UNCTAD	United Nations Conference on Trade and Development
UNDP	United Nations Development Program
UNESCO	United Nations Educational, Scientific, and Cultural Organization
UNIDO	United Nations Industrial Development Organization

GLOBAL BARGAINING

Introduction

The attempt to negotiate a new commodity order within the United Nations Conference on Trade and Development (UNCTAD) was the central issue on the North-South agenda from mid-1974 to late 1977. These negotiations could be justifiably perceived as the first major effort to give substantive meaning to the Third World's desire to construct a New International Economic Order (NIEO). In a less controversial sense, they might also be perceived as the first major attempt to deal with the resource universe in the aftermath of OPEC's radical reorientation of our political, economic, and psychological perceptions. In short, these were critically and intrinsically important negotiations.

The negotiations reflect all of the dimensions implicit in the effort to create "the" New International Economic Order—as the developing countries would have it—or merely "a" new order, if only a reformed old order—as the developed countries would have it. Politically, the demands of the developing countries for an increased role in international decision making were represented in force; economically, the demand for a greater share of the income and wealth derived from commodity production and trade provided the primary rationale for the negotiations; and psychologically, the entire negotiating process was permeated by the developing countries' new sense of power and status. Conversely, the response of the developed countries to these demands and perceptions provides significant evidence not only of their views of commodity trade but also of their interpretations of the entire North-South arena.

The commodity negotiations that I shall describe and analyze in Part One (Chapters 2, 3, and 4) have not come to an end, and they may again become a central issue of high controversy in the years ahead. Nevertheless, my analysis will concentrate on the initial three-year period and even more intensively on the period from mid-1974 to the Nairobi Conference—UNCTAD-IV—in May 1976. This is inevitably arbitrary, since it is self-evidently clear that judgments of success or failure in relation to the earlier years of the negotiating process may well be invalidated by subsequent developments.[1] Indeed, since there is no conceivable way in which the negotiations that I shall discuss could be described as successful, I would hope very much—personally—that ongoing and future commodity negotiations result in very different outcomes. In this sense, what follows could be interpreted as something of a cautionary tale; more pessimistically, it may also illustrate why North-South negotiations have been so difficult and why they are likely to continue to be so.

At any rate, I shall limit my comments to the early years of the negotiations for three reasons. The first is because it now seems probable that they have entered a new and less public phase and that other issues (debt, trade liberalization, transfer of technology) will dominate the near-term North-South agenda. The second is that my own direct observation of the negotiations is limited to the earlier years. And finally, since I intend more than an analysis of a particular set of negotiations (as I shall shortly indicate), the generalizations I want to make and the lessons and reforms that I want to emphasize can be easily extrapolated from the events that occurred between 1974 and 1977.[2]

My intention in Part One is to describe, to analyze, and to interpret in some detail a major attempt to restructure the commodity order. I hope to provide a fair and honest description and analysis of the factors that affected the negotiations, the dynamics of the bargaining process, and the results that ensued. But, as noted, I also intend in a number of places to provide interpretations or judgments of what happened.

---

[1] Also, of course, the choice of any set of dates for an ongoing process is arbitrary. Thus, even if the negotiations are more successful in the future, that success might prove to be short-lived—and so on.

[2] I should note one point of style. I shall use the past tense throughout the case study, not—obviously—to indicate that the commodity negotiating process has come to an end, but rather to set off the period that I shall analyze from subsequent developments.

These are necessary to clarify what otherwise might be obscure (for example, the influence of OPEC on the negotiations), or to justify a number of arguable assertions on my part about what might have happened if other choices had been made (for contrary to many opinions I believe that other choices were possible). Still, I hope that the line between my judgments and the descriptive and analytical statements is sufficiently clear so that disagreement with my judgments does not diminish the utility of the case study itself.

The material in Part Two provides perhaps the most important justification for the interpretations and judgments that appear in Part One. Commodities are important enough for both developed and developing countries to justify—or indeed necessitate—a detailed analysis. However, in a specific sense they are incidental to my broader concerns in this book. If other issues had been prominent during my stay in Geneva, the subject matter of my case study would have been considerably different, but I doubt that the factors in play, the nature of the bargaining process, or the type of outcome that resulted would have been much different.[3] What is clearly implied here is that I am seeking a second and deeper level of meaning from the commodity negotiations: I want also—and primarily—to understand the factors that inhibit the negotiation of viable North-South settlements and the factors that encourage delay, misunderstanding, and mistrust. Perhaps above all and from a practical perspective, I want not only to analyze these factors in greater depth but also to suggest reforms that diminish their effect. This more general attempt to understand the North-South bargaining system thus has some effect (but an additional, not a distorting effect) on the questions raised and the issues pursued in Part One. We shall be primarily concerned with why things happened, not merely with what happened, and with the persisting effect of structural and institutional factors on the negotiating process. Commodity economists may consider these concerns a distraction, and students of the bargaining process or of North-South relations may consider the analysis of commodities a distraction, but effective reform of the bargaining process

---

[3] I shall argue this in more detail at the end of Chapter 4.

depends on a greater understanding of the interaction between technical aspects of the specific issues on the agenda
and the wider political and institutional context in which they
must be negotiated. If in the abstract this may seem a commonplace, in fact it is not so, as evidenced by the strong
tendency—particularly among the developed countries—to
treat the negotiations in very narrow terms and by the general
unwillingness to consider broader issues.

Chapters 2 and 3 in Part One are particularly affected by
the more general concerns in Part Two. Chapter 2 establishes
the background and context of the commodity debate and
has a degree of importance that extends well beyond its immediate subject matter. The broader implications concern the
effect of the original decision on the rest of the debate. The
negotiating system between North and South—and within
North and South—is not very flexible: once set in train, it is
very difficult to deflect or adjust more than marginally. Structural, institutional, and ideological factors bear primary responsibility for this, but the ponderous relearning or rethinking process for governments—especially poor governments
with limited analytical capacities—also shares some part of the
responsibility. There is need to keep this factor (which may be
somewhat obscured by specifics) thoroughly in mind, for a
relatively inflexible negotiating process may require both
sides to reconsider what constitutes appropriate behavior in
the early and ostensibly probing stages of a negotiation.

Chapter 3 discusses the technical aspects of the commodity
debate, but it does so from an unusual perspective. I cannot
resolve complex technical disputes over issues like price
stabilization or the viability of buffer stocks, and it is not my
purpose to do so. It needs to be remembered that the subject
matter of the debate is the economics of commodities (or,
sometimes, the fairness of the existing order), but that the
bargaining process that must settle whatever the technicians
(or the theologians) of both sides cannot settle is essentially
political. Consequently, when I cite an UNCTAD argument
and then cite objections to it by developed country experts,
my point is not that one or the other side is "right": what I am
seeking to do is to indicate that technical conflicts did exist

and that it is oversimplification to contend—as the UNCTAD hierarchy persistently did—that only the absence of "political will" prevented agreement on a new commodity order. There are, in short, complex technical issues that might well prevent or delay agreement even *if* the will to agree is strong.[4] Thus I am more concerned with the political implications of technical conflict, or perhaps with the implications of deliberate attempts to obscure such conflict, than I am with the merits of the technical conflicts themselves.

There is another point implicit in the discussion in Chapter 3 that deserves a brief comment. There are genuine technical problems with many of the demands in the NIEO that are not limited to commodities, and these indicate why it is very simplistic to attempt to assess the condition of the North-South dialogue by tracing the degree to which the North has accepted the South's demands.[5] Several of the South's proposals are problematic for *both* sides. To take it as a sign of virtue that the North has become more amenable to a proposal that may not be workable, or that may benefit the wrong groups, or that reflects misplaced priorities is to substitute emotional commitment for analysis. I trust that the significance of these comments will become apparent in Chapter 3,

[4] The Carter administration, which came to power with a generalized desire to "do more" for the developing countries, may illustrate the proposition: current policies can hardly be considered more than minor variations of themes from the previous administrations. There are indeed some experts who feel that current policies are more conservative than earlier policies of the Nixon and Ford administrations. I do not know whether I would go that far, but previous administrations were at least more honest in openly saying no. The persisting effect of Congress, or images of Congress, in forestalling genuinely new approaches ought not to be underestimated in the process of comparison.

[5] This seems to me a major weakness of the analysis in Branislav Gosovic and John Gerard Ruggie, "On the Creation of a New International Economic Order: Issue Linkage and the Seventh Special Session of the UN General Assembly," *International Organization* 30, no. 2 (Spring 1976): 309-345. I do not believe that procedural progress (a presumed willingness to negotiate that is not new and is more accurately described as a willingness to discuss) can be sensibly treated apart from a parallel analysis of the substance of the negotiation: emphasis on the former alone creates illusions of movement or misunderstanding of what is being offered.

but there is a more general point here about criteria of judgment within the North-South context that needs much deeper consideration.[6]

The chapters in Part Two do not require extended comment. Chapter 5 analyzes the structural and institutional factors that have impeded bargaining, and Chapter 6 considers a number of reform proposals. Chapter 7 discusses a different kind of reform that focuses on patterns of thought in the North-South bargaining arena, and it concludes by assessing the possibility of devising effective negotiating rules within a context of conflicting values and interests. In intellectual terms this is the most important chapter in the book, since progress in reforming structural and institutional impediments is unlikely to yield significant results unless *both* sides think again about the long-run consequences of persisting in present patterns of behavior. My analysis is clearly inadequate, for the gap between what seems necessary and what seems possible is extraordinarily difficult to bridge. But the effort itself is imperative.

[6] I shall discuss this again in Chapter 7.

Chapter 1

The Quest for Settlements
in the North-South Arena

This is a book about commodities, about bargaining between unequal partners, and about institutions. On a deeper level, it is a book about the process of change within the international system. Ultimately, however, it is a book about the decisional system in one important part of the international system. Whatever goals we seek, they cannot be achieved unless the integrity of the decisional system is established and maintained. In this sense the political is clearly prior to the economic. There is no doubt that the decision-making process in the North-South arena is badly flawed, and some of the defects seem irremediable, while all seem difficult. Nevertheless, we cannot prudently rest content with the "lesson" that successful decision making is impossible or that only meaningless verbal formulas to disguise disagreement are possible. The commodity negotiations, for example, were never very likely to end in "victory" for either side or perhaps even in a compromise that both sides could accept, but this is not to argue that progress short of agreement was impossible, that limited agreements were impossible, or that more serious efforts to build a foundation for later agreements were impossible. Here the best—or each side's vision of the "best"—was the enemy of the possible. In short, in terms of both sides' interests, a better outcome was difficult but possible.

Obstacles to Bargaining

Bargaining seems the only way to resolve or diminish the conflicts that currently divide North and South. Stanley Hoffman, for example, has argued that "there is no substitute for global bargaining—issue by issue, deal by deal—for colossal expansion of diplomacy, resembling the constant maneuvering and coalition-building of domestic politics."[1] This widely shared judgment seems particularly true for North-South issues: the use of traditional instruments of force seems inappropriate (or ineffectual) in this context, and the analogy with the domestic bargaining process seems especially appropriate.

What principles are to guide this bargaining process? Presumably power and interest—the great guidelines of the classic Realist statecraft—are insufficient. We have been offered in exchange, however, primarily slogans and aspirations: "planetary bargaining," "global compacts," "world order politics," "mutual accountability," "the New International Economic Order." These are surely well-meant and they may even be correct intimations of necessary or desirable ends, but they provide no guidance for resolving conflict, nor do they have any self-evident meaning that all share. The central question of how we are to achieve or approximate these goals in the face of an extraordinary range of practical problems that have impeded the negotiation of viable North-South settlements remains unresolved.

Most of the factors that make a generalized call to the bargaining table problematic are familiar. The difficulties of negotiating substantive agreements between mistrustful and unequal protagonists who pursue divergent goals by conflicting tactics are readily apparent. Different visions of past and future and indeed different visions of the meaning of the present also intrude; in particular, they generate different interpretations of how much needs to be or can be changed and different tactical emphases on the priority between negotiating (or renegotiating) principles or negotiating practices first. The need to maintain unity within each coalition and the structural and institutional difficulties this creates provides an additional dimension of difficulty. The impact of these factors will be examined in some detail in succeeding chapters.

The external environment within which the negotiating process goes on also exerts significant influence on both per-

[1] Stanley Hoffman, "Groping Toward a New World Order," the *New York Times*, 10 January 1976.

ceptions and outcomes. Rising levels of interdependence have
enormously increased awareness of the need to consult other
countries or to act jointly with them before making national
decisions.[2] In the context of North-South relations in which
interdependence has historically been primarily a euphemism
for asymmetrical dependence, the oil crisis and fears of potential resource conflicts may seem to have created the basis
for a more symmetrical—a less unequal—bargaining relationship. The stronger side now seems more in need of the
weaker side's cooperation not merely because of resource
fears but also because many global issues cannot be resolved
without the cooperation of all sides. On these issues—both the
global issues and a number of narrower issues (resources, access to markets and supplies, the viability of the institutional
structure)—each side has something of a veto but not the
power to compel; only consensus increases—but does not
guarantee—the likelihood of stable agreements.[3] The developing countries also are more assertive and more skillful in
manipulating the few assets they possess, especially the power
of unity. As a result, the potential for a genuine bargaining
relationship in which one side is not always benefactor and

---

[2] For a very good quantitative study of interdependence, see Arthur Stein
and Richard N. Rosecrance, "Interdependence: Myth or Reality?" *World Politics* 26, no. 1 (October 1973): 1-27. The degree to which the developing countries have lagged behind the general trend, both in reference to the developed countries and to each other, is important in understanding developing
country reactions to interdependence: for example, in fears of being increasingly shut out of the world economy and in the desire to increase ties within
the Third World (the movement, mostly rhetorical thus far, toward "collective self-reliance"). The problem that the developing countries must deal with
is that while they remain dependent on ties with the industrial world, the industrial countries have become relatively less dependent on the developing
countries (as a whole). These declining "terms of trade" in the bargaining relationship might be reversed (or at least slowed) by virtue of resource power
and by the growing importance of some developing country markets for developed country exports. But however these developments work out, their
effects will be very asymmetrical. This is what makes collective self-reliance
potentially important, for benefits might be more widely shared—provided
care is taken to prevent dominance by the richer developing countries.

[3] I discuss these issues in greater detail in Robert L. Rothstein, *The Weak in
the World of the Strong: The Developing Countries in the International System* (New
York: Columbia University Press, 1977), Chapter 1.

the other supplicant may appear to have risen. But there is little evidence in the chapters that follow that the potential has been realized and some evidence that may suggest that it has fallen.

Interdependence may increase the need for an expansion of bargaining, but whether the need can be met is a difficult question. Interdependence is far from the only factor at work in the international system. The complexity of the external environment, which is partly the result of interdependence and partly independent of it, is also consequential: there are many states at many different levels of development; divergent values; confused, conflicting, and overlapping interests; rapid shifts in comparative advantage and the rate of technologic change; and so forth. These complexities generate substantial uncertainties about the outlines of viable solutions, great difficulty in establishing trade-offs either between or within issues, and an increasing probability that the negotiating process will be lengthy and cumbersome and thus increasingly exposed to the dangers of external surprises, waning enthusiasm, or the arrival of new fashions. Increased governmental responsibility for national socioeconomic welfare has made these uncertainties and complexities particularly disabling: weak governments uncertain of where they want to go or where they are going are not willing to put much in play in any negotiation unless they are certain of future benefits or certain that established benefits cannot be sustained. There is a self-evident danger in these circumstances that external trends or developments will make national decision making increasingly ineffective, but this has primarily engendered pleas to slow the pace of interdependence. More innovative responses have been difficult to discern or to implement.

Interdependence as a condition is not difficult to comprehend, but what to do about it in practical terms is problematic. Perceptions of interdependence are superimposed on already existing ideological and economic differences. Moreover, interdependence (as well as the oil crisis and resource fears) does not elicit widely shared normative and practical responses. Realism, by contrast, was far more successful in providing its practitioners with a shared image of what had to be done and a shared repertoire of the means to do it.[4] But now there is only a rather loose consensus that dependence on others seems to be growing in a number of important areas; what follows from this is far from clear. In the commodity negotiations, traditional perceptions of power, interest, and opportunity seemed to dominate most calculations, and neither national nor international bureaucrats acted as if interdependence were much more than a rhetorical fashion.[5] What is implied here is *not* that interdependence was or is irrelevant but that the possibility of dealing with systemic problems—whether created in whole or in part by interdependence or by other factors—by developing effective policy responses was inhibited by uncertainty about proper behavior and by disagreement about values and goals. As a result, at both the national and international level the easiest choice was to act as if nothing much needed to be changed in familiar procedures and policies. Nevertheless, interdependence *had* changed many of the conditions that decision makers had to deal with, and it had diminished the likelihood that the conventional wisdom would continue to provide satisfactory answers. These factors may imply that rethinking will soon become both necessary and possible. It did not become so, however, in the period we shall examine.[6]

The desire to establish some kind of conceptual framework that helps to explain the existing bargaining universe is understandable. Dissatisfaction with the results produced by traditional conceptualizations in international relations (and economics) is growing, but consensus on the nature of existing problems, the questions to be asked, and the goals to be pursued does not exist. Pleas to avoid premature conceptualization may be well-taken in these circumstances, but they are

[4] For extended comments on the meaning and effects of Realism, see Robert L. Rothstein, *Planning, Prediction, and Policymaking in Foreign Affairs: Theory and Practice* (Boston: Little, Brown, 1972), pp. 67-81.

[5] For an informative analysis of the limited effects of interdependence on U.S. bureaucrats, see Raymond F. Hopkins, "The International Role of Domestic Bureaucracy," *International Organization* 30, no. 3 (Summer 1976): 423-425. I have found very similar results in interviews with international bureaucrats in Geneva.

[6] I shall discuss interdependence again in Chapter 7.

also likely to be ignored—and perhaps justly so, since the need for reliable guidelines to navigate through current complexities is clear. Elegant and precise conceptualizations that adequately comprehend all the forces in play are well beyond the state of the art in either politics or economics; slowly accumulating insights, a clearer sense of prevailing patterns and preferred directions, and more awareness of what questions need to be asked and which questions can be answered is probably the most that can be expected. But even if it were possible, the achievement of these more limited ends in any reliable or convincing fashion will take much time and effort.

One shortcut through the existing complexities that seems to be increasingly fashionable ought to be avoided or at least used with great caution. This is the effort to rely on an analogy with the model of domestic bargaining in pluralist political systems. The analogy may be premature in the sense that it undervalues the persistence of many of the traditional factors that differentiate international politics from domestic politics. I mean by this more than the absence of a social fabric or of authoritative institutions to articulate, implement, and enforce agreed solutions in the international system, for while these are surely significant differences, there may be other differences that are even more crucial.[7]

Pluralist systems tend to favor the interests of large, powerful groups that can organize effectively. The interests of the poor and weak can easily be left aside. The conventional response to this is that the developing countries have organized themselves into an effective "trade union" of the poor, but I do not find this analogy wholly convincing for both structural and ideological reasons (for a detailed argument, see Chapter 5). In brief, the problems faced and the goals sought by workers in pluralist systems are only partially analogous with the problems and goals of the developing countries. The settled pattern of action that characterizes collective bargaining in stable societies in which agreed rules, a fixed organizational context, and the dominance of expertise over ideology tend

[7] Karl Deutsch makes these points in "Between Sovereignty and Integration: Conclusion," in *Between Sovereignty and Integration*, ed. G. Ionescu (New York: Wiley, 1974), p. 183.

to prevail is not on the international horizon. Pluralist systems also work best when there is general acceptance of the existing order, when the operating rules are established, and when there are sufficient resources (and a legitimate central authority to transfer them where necessary) to defuse crises or to buy off the discontented. In addition, incremental outcomes must be sufficient since the plethora of interests makes agreement on major change extremely difficult, and some means must be found to provide consistent direction since incrementalism without some kind of central guidance tends toward drift, inertia, and the slow accumulation of major problems.[8]

The implied difficulties for the international system are obvious. How can a sensible bargaining relationship be established when the legitimacy of the system itself is at stake, when the operating rules are under attack, when resources are increasingly scarce, when the notion of responsibility for the welfare of others is rapidly diluted beyond national borders, and when the poor demand more than a seat at the bargaining table—which they do demand minimally—and more than meliorative and incremental increases in their share of the pie? The point is not that the international system does not or cannot produce incremental decisions (for surely this is the dominant pattern on socioeconomic issues) but that incremental decisions in the North-South arena are insufficient for some developing countries—and appear unjustified to nearly all of them—and the willingness and the mechanisms to do more barely exist. The international system in this context has only the elements of a failed incremental system in which the capacity for response and adaptation falls increasingly behind demands for change. This suggests the need to think about the alternatives or, given the limitations, to understand more clearly the implications of the absence of more effective alternatives.[9]

Needless to say, governmental decision makers do not have the luxury of delaying action or response until the problems

[8] For these and other critical comments on incrementalism, see Rothstein, *Planning, Prediction, and Policymaking in Foreign Affairs*, pp. 22-31.

[9] See Chapter 7 for further comment.

that we have been discussing are clarified or resolved. Choice is imperative within the context of an extraordinarily unsettled and ambiguous environment. What has seemed necessary to a number of sophisticated observers is not an effort to cut through the environment of mistrust, uncertainty, and self-interest with a grand strategy or a new vision of cooperation but rather a pragmatic emphasis on mutual interests and shared, if limited, gains. Jagdish Bhagwati, for example, very sensibly suggests a number of proposals that provide mutual gains for all with an increased share of the gains for the developing countries.[10] I do not disagree, for we shall shortly see the consequences of insufficiently emphasizing mutual benefits in an unequal bargaining relationship. But I also believe that a sensible, pragmatic response to current disabilities may not be adequate. In the first place, unless there are major structural and institutional reforms in the international policymaking system, we are likely to fall well short of achieving agreement even in areas of common interest, a fact that I shall discuss at length in Chapter 6. In the second place, mutual gains and a seat at the bargaining table may be sufficient for the relatively advanced developing countries, but they are not likely to be sufficient for the great majority. The latter (and indeed perhaps all the developing countries) will require a perception of the North-South arena that incorporates a longer time horizon and criteria of inclusion broader than power and interest. Whether such a vision can ever be more than utopian is decidedly uncertain, but we shall return to the issue in Chapter 7.

Themes

I want to comment briefly on three themes that appear in the following pages. I do so for the first two because they are im-

[10] Jagdish N. Bhagwati, "Introduction," in *The New International Economic Order: The North-South Debate*, ed. Jagdish N. Bhagwati (Cambridge: The MIT Press, 1977), p. 15. The same general point is emphasized by Richard N. Cooper, "A New International Economic Order for Mutual Gain," *Foreign Policy*, no. 26 (Spring 1977), pp. 66-120. Bhagwati's specific proposals include such things as a brain drain tax, agreements on access for both sides, a share

portant but not always apparent; I do so for the third not because it is obscured but because it is probably the most important general issue that we need to think about.

The first theme concerns decision making under uncertainty. This is, of course, a familiar topic, although most discussions of the subject seem to be very abstract. I am concerned, however, only with the practical implications of uncertainty. A careful reading of speeches and documents in the commodity negotiations reveals very little concern with this topic when there should have been much concern. Why the issue was not treated seriously and the effects it exerted are of some importance. In private, many delegates and most experts were aware of the enormous uncertainties generated by UNCTAD's efforts to achieve a comprehensive restructuring of the commodity order. There were uncertainties about the wisdom or reliability of extrapolations from the past, there were even greater uncertainties about what could be safely or sensibly projected about future behavior, there were uncertainties about proper negotiating strategies and tactics, and there were very grave uncertainties about political reactions in the developed countries and about political (and economic) performance in the developing countries. Some were certain that what UNCTAD was attempting to do was wrong and some were certain that what the developed countries wanted to do was wrong, but there were far fewer on either side who were certain about what it was right or prudent to do. The "certain-negatives" generally prevailed over the "certain-positives": criticism of what the other side wanted to do was easier than justification of what one's own side proposed.[11]

---

in the profits of seabed mining, and a food aid program. All could be useful, and most are within the bounds of the possible—but they are not going to create a "new" NIEO.

[11] Some UNCTAD officials would reject this argument, but I believe they mistakenly assume that their own certainty—which may or may not be justified—was convincing to the other side. Also, they underrated the effect of their own decision to delay clarifications until agreement on principles was achieved on the persistence of uncertainty. One official told me that to raise this issue would be "unnecessarily confusing," but I believe that recognition of the confusion was the only way in which it could be diminished.

What would it have been wise to do in response to high levels of uncertainty? For the developed countries, prudence seemed to suggest a variety of tactics: hedging, keeping options open and commitments limited until more could be said with certainty, emphasizing the familiar and the short run in contrast to the new and the long run. All of this necessarily implied incrementalism, the classic policy-making response to a universe of uncertainty.[12] UNCTAD, conversely, was far more sanguine about dealing with uncertainty—perhaps because of recognition of how it might be used by the other side to justify immobility. Instead of prudent tactics to live more effectively with uncertainty, UNCTAD emphasized a "grand design" that would sharply diminish uncertainty by reducing the role of the market, stabilizing price fluctuations, and pooling risks. Neither the attempt to live with uncertainty nor the attempt to overcome it was necessarily right or wrong, nor did the one exclude the other, but a joint decision to pursue either strategy (or an agreed mixture of the two) was preferable to opposition and stalemate. Moreover, somewhere between incrementalism, which may be insufficient, and the grand design, which may be too ambitious, a sensible meeting ground may have existed. As we shall see in the next chapter, both sides had reasons to ignore the issue. As a result, however, they lost an opportunity to build mechanisms into the agreement that would diminish the effects of uncertainty. In regard to the latter point, I have in mind measures to ensure early and steady monitoring of agreements, pilot projects that do not commit all assets to a single approach, government guarantees of risky but necessary measures, more research, and so forth.

But this brings us to the second theme: no more than a handful of people on either side of the commodity debate ever seriously raised questions of implementation, that is, questions about the possibility of creating or fostering conditions that might make individual commodity agreements work.[13] As with uncertainty, the issue was ignored or it was

[12] See especially David Braybrooke and Charles E. Lindblom, *A Strategy of Decision* (Glencoe: The Free Press, 1963).

[13] I asked questions about implementation in both Geneva and Washington, but in Geneva I was told by UNCTAD officials that it was "premature"

simply taken for granted that one or another element of the commodity program would resolve all the practical difficulties. Why was there so little concern with this problem—arguably *the* most critical problem in the entire debate? I have no simple answer, but the problem seems endemic: programs that are agreed to at the international level are frequently unworkable at the local level. This reflects a fundamental weakness of the international policymaking system. There is a gap—not always but too often—between what the issue is in Geneva or Paris or New York and what the issue is in Bogotá or Accra or Jakarta. Perhaps one reason for the gap is the symbolic and hortatory nature of much of the international dialogue on North-South issues. Another reason may be the distance between the global policymaking system and the operating systems for which decisions are made. And, finally, the influence of international secretariats with a global perspective and little practical experience is not irrelevant.

Since the global and the domestic policy process can never mesh perfectly, some part of the gap is inevitable. Even within this constraint, however, more discussion of the conditions to facilitate effective implementation was surely possible. For example, it would have been sensible to reorient some of the debates that we shall examine to shift the emphasis from philosophical arguments about first principles to pragmatic discussions about, say, the means of altering the pattern of incentives and disincentives so that decision makers in poor countries would be more inclined to accept the discipline necessary to make a commodity agreement work. This would have made sense both technically and politically—and for both sides. But it did not happen, and the debate in Geneva continued to focus on issues of principle. Whether it was wise to remain at this level or whether agreement in principle—should it be achieved—can be translated into workable programs are separate and unresolved matters.

Beyond the factors already noted (especially the nature of the international decision-making system), the developing countries' strong emotional commitment to nonintervention

and in Washington that it was probably irrelevant (since agreements were unlikely). Both positions are shortsighted. I have further comments on this issue later.

was also very influential. While this commitment is surely understandable, it is also partially disabling since there is no practical way to discuss implementation without touching on very sensitive domestic matters (for example, elite behavior, distribution of benefits, etc.). Refusal by either side to discuss intervention more forthrightly rather than simply treating it as taboo guarantees that the gap between international programs and domestic performance will grow.[14] It may not be irrelevant to note that the Third World elites on the international development circuit are not much more willing—with a few exceptions—than their domestic counterparts to deal with this issue seriously, perhaps because they benefit so well from existing circumstances.

The distance between what happens in Geneva and what may or may not happen in the "real" world should not be forgotten or ignored. One pernicious result, especially if the gap continues to grow, is increased cynicism among many of the participants in the debate. There is a great danger that the development debate will come increasingly to resemble other UN debates on disarmament or human rights, thus further debasing an already weakened international policy process. The situation may get worse simply because living with an increasingly ceremonial process is much easier than trying to reform it—a complaint that is not meant to exclude any of the participants. And, of course, the most obvious consequences ought to be reemphasized: problems get worse, time is lost, resources are expended. I make some suggestions about possible reforms of this situation in Chapter 6 (and, from a more intellectual and less practical perspective, in parts of Chapter 7). These suggestions may already be too little and too late—but also they may be too much for the existing policymaking system and the elites who run it.

"Who chooses" is a classic political question, but the third theme I want to emphasize concerns what is chosen.[15] What

---

[14] In my *The Weak in the World of the Strong*, pp. 368-371, I have discussed the intervention issue in more detail—but still not sufficiently.

[15] I do not mean to slight the question of "who chooses," since "what" may also be partly a function of the "who." Thus we shall be concerned particularly with the role of international staffs in agenda-setting and with other factors that influence "who" chooses. But I do not believe the issue needs separate treatment at this point.

range of strategies and what range of policies are considered in the process of choice? These are critical questions because there is so little effort to consider them. Strategies are essentially opportunistic and short-range, more imposed by the pressure of events than freely chosen; the choice of policies also reflects a commitment to the familiar and the immediate. This is problematic because it seems unlikely that equitable resolution of North-South conflicts is possible without a long-term perspective and because it inhibits the development of a coherent view of the common goals that ought to be sought within the North-South arena.

Perhaps the clearest illustration of this is in the choice of priority goals by UNCTAD and the Group of 77. Restructuring commodity trade and generalized debt relief have been the central Third World demands of the last few years. But as Jagdish Bhagwati has recently noted in specific reference to these two issues, "it is apparent that the developing countries have chosen to focus on particularly ill-designed measures to translate their objectives into reality."[16] Why has this occurred? There is no single answer, but a number of factors have clearly been influential. One was inertia: deciding that the opportunity for major change was present, UNCTAD and the Group of 77 simply grasped popular items that had been on the North-South agenda for more than two decades. Another factor was institutional, for UNCTAD was hardly likely to emphasize issues that would not enhance its own power and influence in the international system.[17] Finally,

---

[16] Bhagwati, "Introduction," p. 14. Mahbub ul Haq, *The Poverty Curtain—Choices for the Third World* (New York: Columbia University Press, 1976) also criticizes the negotiating priorities of UNCTAD and the developing countries in a number of places in his book. I should add that these criticisms of what is being negotiated are separate from criticisms of how the negotiation process functions—a major theme in what follows. From the latter perspective, the problem is not concern for an issue like commodities but rather an excessive emphasis on a specific aspect of each issue (as with the Common Fund) and a tendency to oversimplify—both of which have been far too prevalent. A sense of proportion is missing.

[17] There is a problem implicit in the Third World's institutional strategy: the developing countries most need and most benefit from viable international institutions, but they frequently place such demands on (and through) these institutions that performance declines and the disaffection of the industrial (and the Socialist) countries grows.

however, the most important factor may have been intellectual. For a number of reasons, including an increasing reluctance to confront domestic problems seriously, changes in the international system were misperceived in terms of the likely benefits they could provide—especially quickly and equitably. The overemphasis on the results that could be expected from systemic change resulted, in part, from a failure to very carefully evaluate the relationship between internal and external change and, as we shall see, from excessive expectations of what benefits commodity reform could produce.[18] The significance of this is that it is very difficult to negotiate sensible compromises when one side expects too much from a negotiation. The negotiations always remain slightly out of focus and very vulnerable to suspicion and misunderstanding. What can be done about this is unclear, but I shall offer a few suggestions in Chapter 7.

What negotiating strategy should the developed countries have chosen in these circumstances? The answer presumably depends on an awareness of the contextual constraints that we have discussed and on a long-range view of the future of North-South relations. But neither side has seemed willing to discuss serious reform of structural and institutional deficiencies, and neither has paid much attention to the long-run. Strategy thus has not differed very much from tactics: both have been essentially ad hoc and short-range. This did nothing to reduce the existing distortions and misunderstandings, and it fed the suspicion that the developed countries were no more interested in establishing the grounds for an effective long-term relationship than the developing countries appeared to be.

In a very broad sense, the outlines of several strategies pursued by the participants could be inferred (or, perhaps, postulated).[19] Three kinds of "peace" strategies seemed to be operating, although a good deal of overlapping occurred.[20]

[18] The comments in this paragraph are treated in detail in Rothstein, *The Weak in the World of the Strong*.

[19] I mean to imply here that I doubt many policymakers consciously chose one or another of these strategies; rather, specific decisions tended to create a trend or at least the appearance of a common trend.

[20] I borrow the notion of three separate peace strategies from Arnold Wol-

Some developing countries (Algeria, Benin, Cuba, Jamaica) and a few of their developed country supporters (the Dutch and the Nordics) seemed seriously intent on creating a new order, which is to say that they believed fundamental change for the benefit of the developing countries was possible. Commitment to the NIEO and its demands for an enhanced decision-making role and a greater share of income and wealth for the developing countries was perceived by these countries in substantive and not merely rhetorical terms. These "radical" countries frequently wavered and seemed willing to approach the millennium by stages. In practical terms, this tended from time to time to put them in a second camp of moderate countries who were pursuing a strategy of steadily removing real greivances and reforming existing institutions and practices.

The differences between the radicals and the moderates concerned perceptions of adequacy and finality: the radicals presumed acceptance of pragmatic reforms was merely a stop along the way to massive restructuring, while the moderates presumed reform was sufficient. Membership in the latter group varied according to issues and perceptions of the possibility of movement, but generally included some of the richer developing countries (especially the "success" stories of the past decade who had benefited from manufacturing exports or a commodity in high demand, for example South Korea, Singapore, Malaysia, Ivory Coast) and many developed countries (especially raw material exporters like Australia and Canada but also on some issues even the most conservative countries). Finally, a third group of conservative developed countries (the United States, Japan, West Germany) appeared to feel economically and ideologically threatened by Third World demands, and they insisted that concessions that might undermine existing rules of the game had to be resisted—unless of course, they could be shown to be in the interest of the conservative countries. As noted, at one time or another these countries joined the moderates, espe-

---

fers, *Britain and France between Two Wars* (New York: Harcourt, Brace and Company, 1940), but of course the use to which I have put the notion is entirely my responsibility.

cially when the effects of a concession could be controlled, but generally they followed a strategy of—to borrow Wolfer's image—trying to keep the lid down on a boiling pot. Tactics included delay, ambiguous verbal concessions, and minimal concessions that might split some of the developing countries away from the others.

Consistent commitment to *any* of these strategies might have worked (even the last) if the most powerful developed countries and the most conservative developing countries had been willing to support it. In fact, vacillation and inconsistency predominated, and it was never very clear which strategy—if any—was in use. This added another crucial level of uncertainty to the negotiations, since it was not possible to foresee likely outcomes without some judgment about the strategies being pursued, and it was never possible to determine whether either side was really committed to a strategy or merely reflecting the latest decision on how to respond to passing opportunities. This was important even in the case of specific disputes within particular negotiations because it is at least arguable that fairly widespread agreement to pursue a less than optimal choice was preferable to sharp disagreement—and thus immobility—in pursuit of the "best" course.

Priorities and their Consequences

As will shortly become clear, I criticize both sides—but especially UNCTAD and the Group of 77—for demanding commitment to principles before clarifying what the principles might mean in practice. Since this kind of criticism might be misunderstood, I want to comment very briefly on what I have in mind.

Any period of rapid change (especially one in which conventional practices do not appear to produce expected outcomes) is likely to see an increased concern with first principles or constitutional principles. Thus, the conflict between the developed countries' attempt to maintain the primacy and the adequacy of traditional principles and the developing countries' attempt to assert the need and the possibility of devising new principles is hardly surprising. This conflict might also be beneficial, producing a new order with enhanced global welfare, if there were some acceptable means to devise equitable settlements between opponents divided by different values, different interests, and different interpretations of past, present, and future. But the means of settlement were clearly absent in this instance, and the fervent and persistent assertion of divergent principles became something of an exercise in futility. Neither side could persuade the other merely by reiterating the power of its own convictions, and neither was able (or willing) to attempt to impose its own views; the result was a costly stalemate.

One needs, however to avoid characterizing as irrational the emphasis on first principles. What needs to be added to the calculus is some understanding of the objectives sought. For the conservative developed countries, especially the United States, a stalemate over principles was clearly preferable to the presumed losses implicit in accepting the principles asserted by UNCTAD and the Group of 77. But whether there were other negotiating tactics that might have avoided the need to cast the debate in simplistic either/or terms and that might also have gained some of the benefits of a revised commodity order is a more open question. As I shall indicate, I believe such tactics did exist and that they should have been tried: stalemate was likely, but it was not inevitable.

The developing countries' initial emphasis on principles was surely understandable and arguably justified. The combination of insufficient benefits from the old order and new possibilities of creating a restructured order generated very strong support for a major challenge to traditional patterns of behavior. Nevertheless, even acceptance of the notion that major changes in the rules of the game were imperative did not necessarily imply that such rules could be imposed by fiat—even by joint fiat. The uncertainties and the complexities are so vast that a new order may have to be built from the ground up, agreement by agreement and step by step. The developing countries have tended to respond to this argument in a familiar fashion: slow but steady change is insufficient and merely perpetuates existing inequities. But massive change for the benefit of the developing countries was never likely, and persistent demands for such immediate changes only guaranteed immobility—the continued dominance of existing principles. Slow but steady change was a good deal better than nothing (charges to the contrary notwithstanding), particularly because it at least kept open the possibility of more significant change down the road.

This argument raises a central question about the relationship between principles and practices. If an initial emphasis on principles were (perhaps) justified, why was the emphasis continued when it became increasingly clear that it was futile and costly? In fact, persistence in original demands not only delayed any progress but also inhibited the creation of potentially useful ties with groups within a number of developed country governments that favored a more forthcoming attitude toward changes in commodity production and trade. Movement (especially within the Group of 77) was prevented, I believe, by structural and institutional obstacles that simply froze initial negotiating postures or made compromise appear more costly than acceptance of stalemate.

Each side believed that its principles were correct and that the other side's were unwise and motivated by self-interest. As previously stated, I do not agree that either was wholly right, for both sets of principles neglected important contextual factors. But the points I want to make here are essentially procedural: even if the principles were correct, they were pursued in the wrong fashion. And while the emphasis on establishing first principles was not in itself irrational—and, in any case, was probably inevitable—what *was* irrational was persistence in that quest after it became clear that it was futile. We shall discuss at length the structural and institutional factors primarily responsible for inducing rigidity and inflexibility. We shall also discuss the nature of the principles in conflict, for what we are primarily concerned with are the consequences of a particular mixture of principles and context, and not either alone. If both have some bearing on the outcome, we shall need also to be concerned with reforms in both realms.

The Context of Assumptions

Discussions of policies and problems in the North-South arena tend to rest on assumptions or values that should be set forth explicitly. In this section I want to comment briefly on a few of my own assumptions and contrast them with some conflicting views.

While the argument is seldom made publicly, a number of practitioners and analysts seem to believe that the developed countries worry far too much about their relationship with the developing countries as a whole—in effect, the relationship of confrontation within the global institutional structure—and are too prone to make unnecessary concessions to essentially rhetorical threats. Bilateral relationships or relationships with small groups of developing countries may indeed be more substantively significant for individual developed countries, especially in the short run, than relationships with the Group of 77, or the nonaligned movement, or any other very large grouping of developing countries. Nevertheless, this is a view that sharply undervalues the stake of the developed countries in a more effective relationship with all or much of the developing world.

Many discussions of the need to make some concessions to the developing countries rest on fears of resource shortages (real or contrived) or fears of increases in terrorism and other deliberately destabilizing tactics.[21] These are not especially persuasive grounds for a new relationship, for the threats are not always credible and, if credible, are more likely to be met by negative and hostile responses from the developed countries. Other factors may be more important. The ability of the Third World to act together to impede global or near global settlements (for example, the oceans, nuclear proliferation, pollution) until Third World demands are at least partially met may become increasingly important. In addition, the ability to use numerical power to undermine the capacity of (and

[21] See especially Mihajlo Mesarovic and Edward Pestel, *Mankind at the Turning Point* (New York: Dutton, 1974). On these fears and the other grounds for seeking a new relationship, see also my *The Weak in the World of the Strong*, Chapter 1.

the already diminishing support for) the existing institutional structure ought to be noted. Although the institutional structure has been much maligned (and in large part justly so), it remains useful if not necessary for many (not all) important tasks. Failure to respond to real Third World needs and real Third World concerns (political and psychological as well as economic) may force increasing reliance on any or all of these tactics, and the costs (financial, economic, political, psychological) could be substantial to both developed and developing countries.[22]

Perhaps another argument may be even more persuasive to developed country officials, especially those who are indifferent to the need to establish and maintain an effective institutional system. The growing economic importance of the developing countries in terms of *developed* country prosperity has become increasingly evident in recent years. For example, in 1976 U.S. exports to *non*-OPEC LDCs constituted about 25 percent of total U.S. exports, and imports from the same countries were about 24 percent of the total import bill. From 1970 to 1975 exports to these countries grew at a faster rate than exports to other developed countries (although this changed in 1976 for various reasons), and U.S. exports to *all* of the developing countries are now larger than U.S. exports to the European community, Eastern Europe, the Soviet Union, and China combined. About 40 percent of the European community's current exports go to the developing countries. In short, the importance of the developing countries in stimulating demand and decreasing inflationary pressures in the developed countries is now much more than empty rhetoric.[23]

There is some danger in inferring too much from these

---

[22] To avoid misunderstandings, I emphasize that I am not suggesting that all the changes must be on the part of the developed countries—it is also imperative that complementary changes, both domestic and international, be made by the LDCs.

[23] For a strong argument in this sense, as well as for the trade figures noted, see John W. Sewell, "Can the Rich Prosper Without Progress by the Poor?" in *The United States and World Development: Agenda 1978* (Washington, D.C.: Overseas Development Council, 1979). Also useful is Jonathan Power, "Bound by Hoops of Steel," the *New York Times*, 2 July 1978, p. 15.

TABLE 1

1977 Trade Figures of U.S. Trading Partners in the Third World
(billions of dollars)

Trading Partners	Exports to U.S.	Imports from U.S.
Mexico	$ 4.7	$ 4.8
Korea	2.9	2.4
Brazil	2.2	2.5
Taiwan	3.7	1.8
Hong Kong	2.9	1.3
Israel	0.6	1.4
Malaysia	1.3	1.3
All Other	10.8	11.3
	$29.1	$26.8

SOURCE: The World Bank.

figures. Sewell, for example, argues that U.S. prosperity is increasingly dependent on the Third World, a position that may overstate the case.[24] Table 1 illustrates one of the dangers of generalizations based on aggregate data: thus seven developing countries provide about 63 percent of the exports and take about 58 percent of the imports. Insofar as there is dependence on the (non-OPEC) developing countries, then, it is primarily a dependence on a handful of key countries, not the whole Third World. Moreover, relative bargaining strengths, particularly on a bilateral basis, hardly suggest that any of the seven are likely to have much leverage against the United States: what dependence there is is very weak, since it can be ended (as yet) without great or equivalent cost. Also, the mere existence of common interests does not guarantee that they can be easily converted into mutually beneficial agreements. The chapters that follow will illustrate just how difficult this conversion task can be.

These comments qualify but do not invalidate the general point that the developed countries have an increasingly important stake in the prosperity of the developing countries. Even the fact that only a few developing countries are currently truly important to the developed countries may change over the next decade, if—and it is a very big if—more devel-

[24] Ibid., p. 21.

oping countries were to begin to prosper. Furthermore, the few developing countries that are important may not be as easy to deal with (or, alternatively, in some cases we may not be at ease in dealing with them) as some analysts believe: as we shall see, the strong emotional ties within the Third World put strong pressure on the more powerful developing countries to use their leverage for the benefit of all. The cross-pressures between defending national interests and maintaining standing and status within the Third World have not led to much national altruism, but this does not mean that the more powerful will willingly split from their weaker partners.[25] And even if the United States and its allies could sever these ties, do the developed countries really want—in moral, political, and economic terms—to stand by idly while many of the poor countries go "down the drain" (to borrow a Kissinger analogy) or are forced into increasingly desperate actions to attract attention to their plight?

Another assumption that runs through the following pages is that the international policy process can (and should) provide a reasonable—but hardly revolutionary—order of benefits to the developing countries (especially those countries capable of grasping external opportunities), and that such benefits are worth seeking since they are not always or everywhere irrelevant, wasted, or misplaced.[26] There are surely reasons to fear that the international policy process is becoming increasingly dysfunctional, and there are also reasons to fear that the benefits produced will become increasingly insufficient for the majority of developing countries, but neither of these outcomes is—at this point—inevitable. Some possibilities of reform do exist, although they will be very difficult to implement, and the results are likely to be beneficial enough to justify the effort. One notes also that the two parts

---

[25] This is because of the strong emotional commitment to unity and because the offers of the developed countries have not been very generous.

[26] I mean by the international policy process here the process by which governments, negotiating groups, and international secretariats come together in various institutional settings to set the international agenda, to debate and adopt policies or resolutions, and to implement and evaluate the results.

of this assumption are connected: if the quest for limited gains were justified, even if it were not completely satisfactory it must be carried out through an international policy process that functions effectively.

The North-South arena is dominated by a complex mixture of cooperation and conflict, of mutual needs and mutual antagonisms. Critics on the right have come increasingly to doubt that cooperative outcomes are possible in these circumstances—that needs can outweigh antagonisms or resolve irreconcilable conflicts—and have suggested that close ties be constructed only with a small number of economically important and politically reliable developing countries. One analyst has even argued that the conflicts are so profound and the political and economic interests of the United States so increasingly engaged in the Third World that the "military option" must again be taken very seriously.[27] Denunciations of this option on moral grounds are unlikely to be very persuasive to those who believe that the rich have a right to armed robbery in defending their standard of living against the demands of the poor. A more compelling response is that under prevailing circumstances force is unlikely to achieve its ends or that it will cost more in material terms than other options open to the developed countries. Moreover, since real interests regarding the Third World are far wider than merely guaranteeing access to one or another resource or market, even "successful" implementation of the military option could have severely negative consequences. At any rate, the assumption that genuine cooperation is not possible or that the military option should be revived has the danger of becoming a self-fulfilling prophecy by inducing hostile attitudes and actions on both sides. It seems more sensible to be less dogmatic about "inevitable" conflict and more serious about seeking effective reforms and policies within the existing context. The latter effort may fail, but the former is almost certain to fail.

The radical left is also likely to disagree sharply with the assumptions in this book. If radical criticism merely emphasized

[27] Steven Rosenfeld discusses a Rand Corporation paper by Guy Pauker that apparently suggests the need to take the military option seriously, in the *Washington Post*, 5 May 1978.

the inadequacy of international change (at least currently feasible levels or rates of change) and the concomitant need for major domestic changes, disagreement would be limited, as any discussion of international change must be taken as partial and incomplete, perhaps less important than domestic change but nonetheless potentially important in and of itself. The radical argument, however, goes considerably further. The contention that Third World elites are closely tied to power structures in the developed world and that they are the primary beneficiaries of most of the measures on the international agenda surely contains a great deal of validity. But it is doubtful that the only solution, as so many radicals aver, is domestic revolution, since revolution is hardly a panacea for very poor and weak countries. Similarly it is doubtful that many revolutions, whatever their justification and whatever their likelihood of success, are about to occur.[28] Indeed the radical argument ends in a counsel of despair: what can be done is insufficient, what needs to be done cannot be accomplished. It seems to me that the argument overstates the case and needs to be considerably qualified. This is true not only in the sense that there are some developing countries that can progress and have progressed by more moderate means and that there are numerous instances of left revolutions that end in near chaos (thus Cuba and China need to be contrasted with Cambodia and Ethiopia) but also in the sense that not all programs that benefit the elites need necessarily be injurious to the masses. In addition, too frequently advocates of revolution merely assert its necessity, but they fail to explain how and why it will lead to more equitable development.[29]

[28] One recent advocate of the revolutionary position is Richard F. Fagen, "Equity in the South in the Context of North-South Relations," in *Rich and Poor Nations in the World Economy*, Albert Fishlow et al. (New York: McGraw-Hill, 1978), pp.163-214.

[29] Frances Stewart and Paul Streeten, "New Strategies of Development: A Comment" (unpublished paper), note that those advocating the revolutionary option "are open to the criticism advanced by an examiner of the development paper in the Oxford Final Honour School: 'Several candidates, having argued convincingly that a revolution would be a necessary condition of economic development, in a certain country, concluded that it would be a

I feel more comfortable, both morally and practically (but not always intellectually), with the position that we (the developed countries) cannot wait to act until all of the intellectual uncertainties are clarified or until the great battle between reformists and radicals is somehow settled: we need at least to achieve what can be achieved now, all the while pushing against the constraints that sustain inaction. One accepts this position knowing full well it may be insufficient—treating the symptoms, not the causes—but in the hope that it will produce more short-run benefits than calls to the barricades. Being insufficient, after all, is not the same as being useless.

Attitudes toward the New International Economic Order also tend to affect interpretations of North-South bargaining. In the developed countries the left tends to believe that the NIEO is necessary and justified but only when it is joined to substantial domestic change. Conversely, the right tends to believe that the NIEO is "bad economics, worse politics."[30] Moderates tend to differ only to the extent that they temper judgments of economic and political feasibility with some sense of the pressures on Third World leaders. In the developing countries, however, support for the NIEO tends to cross the political spectrum, with differences relating primarily to questions of tactics—how much and how soon—and the relationship between particular national goals and general international goals.

These divergences are important not so much for what they say about the NIEO as for the influence they exert on

---

sufficient one' " (p. 23). Michael Lipton's warning ought also to be emphasized: "How to make revolutions, how to ensure that they benefit the rural poor—social scientists neither know these things, nor have the right to sacrifice human life to their ignorance." *Why Poor People Stay Poor—Urban Bias in World Development* (Cambridge: Harvard University Press, 1977), p. 329.

[30] See Nathaniel H. Leff, "The New Economic Order—Bad Economics, Worse Politics," *Foreign Policy*, no. 24 (Fall 1976), pp. 202-217. Other publications with much criticism of the NIEO include Bhagwati, *The New International Economic Order: The North-South Debate*; William G. Tyler, ed., *Issues and Prospects for the New International Economic Order* (Lexington, Mass.: Lexington Books, 1977); and Cooper, "A New International Economic Order for Mutual Gain."

specific negotiating arenas. In this sense the central issue is not really the coherence or the justification of the NIEO or even its immediate political feasibility. The NIEO, which was essentially a response to the opportunities or apparent opportunities created by the oil crisis and its immediate aftermath, grouped together in one package nearly all the demands—political and economic—that had been on the North-South agenda for twenty years or more.[31] Elements of incoherence and inconsistency were thus virtually inevitable. Justifications hardly reflected technically competent or historically "proved" indictments: a strongly felt sense of past and present exploitations seemed to provide a moral basis for demands for radical restructuring of the old order. And questions of feasibility were overwhelmed by perceptions of rising influence—or, simply, by rising needs. Nevertheless, while "bad economics, worse politics" was surely a partially justified response, it was also an inadequate response.

Two key points about the NIEO should have been more widely understood. First, while there were some very provocative statements in the NIEO (and other Third World pronouncements), the NIEO neither was nor is a completely revolutionary program. Cooperation and interdependence were emphasized as much as conflict and radical change, and many or most of the individual economic demands mixed in a great deal of good—for both sides—with the bad. Contemptuous responses to the notable flaws within the NIEO came easily but were insufficient: such responses also tended to perpetuate a rhetorical debate that could not be resolved and to diminish concern for isolating elements that promised mutual benefits. Second, the NIEO's effect on specific negotiations such as the ones we shall analyze was primarily atmospheric. When the negotiations got down to cases, sharp breaks with the past—with the economics and politics of the "old" order—were more apparent than real. I do not mean to suggest that the game in individual arenas was unchanged, since all the participants felt the need for varying degrees of

---

[31] A good collection of documents and articles tracing the origin and evolution of the NIEO can be found in Karl P. Sauvant and Hajo Hasenpflug, eds., *The New International Economic Order* (Boulder, Col.: Westview Press, 1977).

change and all had lost some faith in the conventional wisdom. But despite this, elements of continuity—in problems, perceptions, and proposed solutions—were very strong. This was true even in the commodity arena where initial demands seemed to rest on an unprecedented degree of "global resource management," since beneath the surface close ties with previous attempts at commodity control were apparent. Under these circumstances, the proper question (at least in the UNCTAD context) was not whether the NIEO was coherent, justified, or even feasible but whether and how the effects of the atmospherics might have been diminished and the prospects for negotiating practicalities enhanced.

For a number of reasons I believe that the possibility of movement toward meaningful compromise was always present. One reason was the existence of mutual benefits, albeit mixed in with more one-sided or unjustified benefits. In addition, support for the NIEO varied greatly across countries, issues, and time: the question of how much had to be done how soon was never answered definitively—and probably could not have been. Perhaps more critically and as I have already noted, not all of the specific demands within the NIEO were revolutionary: many demands required modest initial actions that could or had to be undertaken merely to lay the groundwork for later changes. Since both sides also agreed that some changes were necessary, it should not have been impossible to concentrate on these changes and to leave unresolved the issue of whether such changes were building blocks for the NIEO, or an attempt to make bricks from straw, or merely a useful reform of the existing system. The latter were questions worth considering at some point—but not at once and to the exclusion of all other matters. But the developing countries feared losing a major opportunity (or apparent opportunity) to strike for a new order, and the developed countries were in no condition to give much to move the debate away from grand principles or to develop a coherent strategy in the midst of great disorder and uncertainty. As a result, movement on either principles or details was minimal.

In what follows I shall leave the fundamental issues raised by the NIEO in suspension. The need for major changes in the commodity order was apparent to both developed and developing countries, and there were reforms on the agenda that could benefit both. Why these reforms were not achieved is a major theme in what follows; how one chooses to describe these changes and where they might lead in ten or twenty or more years are not irrelevant questions, but in this work they will be secondary to questions about getting any gains at all in existing circumstances.[32]

The arguments in this section have attempted to indicate why failures and inefficiencies in an exceedingly complex negotiating process could become increasingly costly to both developed and developing countries. More is at stake than moral or humanitarian claims, intellectual debates about the responsibility for underdevelopment, or the necessity of reparations for past guilt. While these are surely difficult but important analytical and political issues, there are also other interests—practical, growing, and influential for both sides— at stake. Bargaining between North and South to achieve or protect more of these interests, even common interests, is unlikely ever to be harmonious or conflict-free, for differences are too profound and the variables in play too numerous. But even a reasonable approximation of an effective relationship—a relationship in which common interests are not overwhelmed or obscured by conflict and distrust—is improbable if the patterns of behavior that we shall analyze remain the norm.

[32] Since there is much in this book about institutions, I should perhaps add a comment here about divergent attitudes toward these entities. In brief, I believe institutions in the North-South arena are crucial in a number of ways, particularly in affecting the agenda for discussion, in affecting negotiating strategies and tactics, and in affecting the form and content of proposals. This is not to argue that they determine substance but rather that they have a major effect not merely on how but also on what to do. My views stand in conflict with the prevailing view among many practitioners that such institutions are ineffectual and irrelevant. These issues are discussed at greater length in Chapters 5 and 6.

PART ONE

Commodities and the Quest for a

New International Economic Order

Chapter 2

The Commodity Debate

The struggle to establish a new order in commodity trade has been the central issue in the North-South debate for the past three years. The terms of the debate have been set by UNCTAD's Integrated Program for Commodities (IPC), whose most contentious element has been the Common Fund, a financing mechanism (for buffer stocks and perhaps for "other measures") designed to link—to integrate—a series of individual commodity agreements. The attempt to negotiate the IPC and especially the Common Fund has been beset by history, ideology, a difficult mixture of shared and conflicting interests and values, intellectual uncertainties, tacit and overt fears and suspicions, and institutional and personal rivalries. What has transpired thus reflects the difficulties and complexities of arriving at genuine settlements between North and South.

Negotiations within so unsettled a context tend to generate some rather unusual characteristics. The tactics of nonsettlement, for example, are frequently as important as the tactics of settlement: how to agree to disagree or how to disguise disagreement to permit the game to go on can become the central issue from time to time. This ought not to be mistaken for the "normal" process of substantive conflict and compromise. Moreover, what is not discussed is often as revealing as what is discussed. The silent issues reflect either unspoken fears and suspicions about what the other side "really" means or intends (as we shall see in the discussion of stable and rising prices), or they reflect a tacit agreement not to raise certain troublesome issues (as with the domestic equity effects of commodity agreements). Conflicts of record—what everyone is arguing about at any particular moment—are neither irrelevant nor necessarily less important than subsurface conflicts, but the combination of the two is very critical. The debate on UNCTAD's IPC cannot be understood merely by reading public statements of policy or by analyzing the economics of commodity trade.

Commodity Trade: The Quest for Agreement

Commodity exports, excluding oil, account for almost 60 percent of the export earnings of the developing countries. Nevertheless, commodities have been a lagging sector of LDC foreign trade: manufactured exports have risen sharply in the past decade and now constitute almost 40 percent of total nonoil exports from the developing countries. Indeed, again excluding oil, the largest share of commodity trade is among the developed countries themselves.

Nevertheless, commodity trade remains very important to the developing countries. In part this reflects an historical consideration: unfair exploitation of the terms of trade for commodities has been a staple of analyses of "dependencia" and of the depredations of the "center" against the "periphery."[1] Perhaps more to the (immediate) point, growth in manufactured exports has been primarily limited to a handful of relatively advanced developing countries, and many developing countries are still heavily dependent on the export of a few commodities to a few markets. In addition, about 80 percent of the commodity exports of the developing countries are consumed by the developed countries: domestic consumption in the producing countries is very low, and exports to other developing countries or to the socialist countries are generally insignificant. Consequently, the developing countries may suffer severely—and proportionately more than their developed trading partners—from instabilities in commodity trade, and they normally lack the resources and the flexibility to diversify or to save in the good years in order to cushion the bad.[2]

[1] See, for example, the papers of Raúl Prebisch collected in *Development Problems in Latin America* (Austin: University of Texas Press, 1970).

[2] Although there is substantial debate about how disabling price fluctuations are, there is more general agreement that fluctuations in earnings have very negative effects. See Constantine Glezakos, "Export Instability and Economic Growth: A Statistical Verification," *Economic Development and Cultural Change* 21, no. 4 (July 1973): 670-678; and Constantin S. Voivodas, "The Ef-

The problems that have beset commodity trade are very familiar, and efforts to devise solutions can be traced back to the 1920s and the 1930s.[3] Commodities have tended to be traded where demand fluctuates sharply (usually because of the business cycle), where supply is frequently uncertain (because of natural disasters or political interventions by nationalistic governments), and where market imperfections (export controls, quotas on imports, subsidies for domestic production) are widely prevalent. Trade is also frequently dominated by a few large multinational corporations that control production and/or distribution and marketing—which makes a mockery of the notion that the choice is between a "free" market and a regulated price as distinct from a choice between which countries or which companies regulate the price. The amounts actually traded in the market are also not very important for some commodities (for example, sugar and copper) because most of the available supply is controlled by a variety of long-term contracts (which diminishes the utility of fixing market prices). In most cases "downstream" activities also tend to earn a disproportionate share of the final consumer price: one estimate, for example, notes that of $200 billion spent on commodities, the producers earn only about $30 billion.[4] Finally, beyond the negative effects of sharp instabilities in prices and earnings, the trend in the real value of export earnings for a number of critical commodities (coffee, cocoa, tea, cotton, rubber, jute, sisal) was nearly zero or negative from 1953 to 1972.[5]

---

fect of Foreign Exchange Instability on Growth," *The Review of Economics & Statistics* 56, no. 3 (August 1974): 410-412.

[3] See Alton D. Law, *International Commodity Agreements: Setting, Performance, and Prospects* (Lexington, Mass.: Lexington Books, 1975).

[4] The figures are from a comment by Mahbub ul Haq in *New Structures for Economic Interdependence* (New York: Institute on Man and Science, 1975), p. 22. An interesting analysis of the share that developing country producers receive of the final consumer price for all commodities of interest to the developing countries (except oil) can be found in UNCTAD, *Proportion Between Export Prices and Consumer Prices of Selected Commodities Exported by Developing Countries* (TD/184/Supp. 3), May 1976.

[5] UNCTAD, *Commodities* (TD/184), March 1976, p. 6. From 1955-1972 world trade rose by 7.3 percent per year, but the growth rate for nonfuel primary commodities was much lower: 5.2 percent per year for food and 4.2

Early efforts to deal with these problems by cartels or commodity agreements have been unsuccessful (with the exception of tin).[6] Historically, the major impetus toward cooperation has come from producers confronting persistent surpluses, rising costs, and declining prices. But neither cartels (an organization of producers that seeks to intervene actively in the market) nor commodity agreements (an organization of both producers and consumers that seeks to intervene actively in the market but presumably in a more balanced fashion than a cartel), have been able to overcome the obstacles to cooperation.[7] Commodity agreements might well provide both producers and consumers with substantial benefits: the producers, for example, benefit from a reduction in fluctuations, improved access to markets, a diminution of the threat from substitutes or alternative suppliers, and from some consumer help in policing the agreement against new or outside sources; the consumers benefit from improved conditions of access, a potential decrease in inflationary pressures, and perhaps some increased influence over producer decisions.[8] Nevertheless, the benefits have not appeared substantial enough to keep producers from fighting among themselves about price ranges or production shares or to generate

---

percent per year for raw materials. The increase for developing countries was even lower: 3.2 percent for food and 3.8 percent for raw materials. See Shamsher Singh, "The International Dialogue on Commodities," *Resources Policy*, June 1976, p. 88. Singh is also doubtful that future prospects for commodities are much better, although there may be great individual variation.

[6] See William Fox, *Tin: The Working of a Commodity Agreement* (London: Mining Journal Books, Ltd., 1974).

[7] The definitions are from David L. McNicol, *Commodity Agreements and the New International Economic Order*, California Institute of Technology Social Science Working Paper, no. 144 (Pasadena, 1976), p. 6. There are also producer forums or producer-consumer forums that exchange information and consult regularly but do not involve market interventions. The producer-consumer forum as an alternative to commodity agreements was frequently advocated by the Nixon and Ford administrations and has also recently been advocated by the Carter administration as part of an international agreement on copper.

[8] There are some doubts about how significant some of these advantages are likely to be, but I shall defer discussion until the next chapter.

consumer support for shared financing of measures of stabilization.[9] Moreover, technical disagreements about how significant fluctuations were, or about how profound the benefits of stabilization would be, or about how likely agreement between producers and consumers on a "just and remunerative" price range would be tended to generate the conviction that commodity agreements were either more inefficient or costly than efforts to improve the functioning of the market or that, whatever the potential benefits, the technical, political, or ideological obstacles were too difficult to surmount.[10] At any rate, despite many years of analysis and debate, widespread agreement that the conditions of commodity trade were badly flawed could not be translated into general agreement about either the cause of the malaise or its cure.

The oil crisis of October 1973 and the subsequent price revolution, however, sharply altered perceptions, calculations, and strategies.

The Origins of the IPC

The OPEC phenomenon energized the entire commodity order. A certain amount of euphoria on the part of other commodity producers was probably inevitable—at least until it became more readily apparent that oil was indeed different.[11] Even those without significant commodity exports could be

[9] As indicated, consumers were not usually worried about insufficient supply or denial of access, and thus saw little reason to support measures that seemed likely only to increase prices.

[10] Discussion of these issues from different points of view can be found in Jere R. Behrman, *International Commodity Agreements* (Washington, D.C.: Overseas Development Council, 1977) and McNicol, *Commodity Agreements and the New International Economic Order*. The likely negative attitude of Congress, which should have been a factor in UNCTAD calculations, could have been forecast from *International Commodity Agreements*, A Report of the U.S. International Trade Commission to the Subcommittee on International Trade of the Committee on Finance, United States Senate, November 1975.

[11] A good analysis of the very limited possibilities for other commodity producers to emulate OPEC can be found in Ernest Stern and Wouter Tims, "The Relative Bargaining Strength of the Developing Countries," in *Changing Resource Problems of the Fourth World*, ed. Ronald G. Ridker (Washington, D.C.: Resources for the Future, 1976).

buoyed by the discomfiture of the industrial countries or by the hope that OPEC itself would be charitable to its less fortunate brethren. In any case, the lesson of what unity could bring was very quickly learned—perhaps overlearned.

One immediate result was an escalation of verbal warfare in the General Assembly. Thus the Programme of Action on the Establishment of a New International Economic Order, adopted in May 1974, requested UNCTAD to prepare "an overall integrated programme, setting out guidelines and taking into account the current work in this field, for a comprehensive range of commodities of export interest to developing countries."[12] Another factor was perhaps equally significant, for by the summer of 1974 some of the more detrimental results of recent events were becoming evident to all: the boom in commodity prices that had begun before the oil crisis was clearly peaking, export sales were declining as a result of the recession in the industrial countries, inflation was simultaneously increasing the price of critical imports, and reserves were declining. A massive balance of payments crisis was confronting a substantial part of the Third World. For a variety of reasons, none of the traditional policy responses seemed likely to work: neither increasing exports to the rich countries, nor borrowing in the face of depressed export prospects and rising debt-servicing burdens, nor domestic austerity in the face of rising discontent and potential instability. The temptation to seek external salvation by demands for increased resource transfers was thus bound to increase. This combination of circumstances created a major problem for UNCTAD, since its responsibility was to devise a wide-ranging package of measures to reorder commodity trade in a period when the needs of the developing countries were severe and their hopes very high but when the developed countries were shocked, fearful, uncertain about what to do, and unwilling or unable to justify increased resource transfers.

[12] UNCTAD, *An Over-all Integrated Programme for Commodities* (TD/B/498), August 1974, p. 1. Of course this was not a new demand, as much work had been done previously on commodities at UNCTAD and elsewhere, nor was it "surprising" to UNCTAD, since an effort had been made to ensure that it would be asked only to do what it already wanted to do.

The OPEC phenomenon and deteriorating economic conditions were not the only factors influencing the environment of decision. Another factor was UNCTAD itself. In 1972 in Santiago UNCTAD-III had been a disaster, and in 1968 in New Delhi UNCTAD-II had not been much more successful. The future of UNCTAD thus seemed problematic, not in the sense that it would disappear but rather in the sense that it would continue to atrophy. Consequently, with UNCTAD-IV scheduled for Nairobi in May 1976, the need for an issue that would unite UNCTAD and the developing countries (or the Group of 77 as they are called in UNCTAD) seemed imperative. Moreover, the issue not only had to promise substantial benefits to a great many developing countries but also to provide increased power and influence for UNCTAD itself. This had a double effect, for it significantly influenced the effort to locate commodity negotiations and commodity institutions within UNCTAD's ambit, and it exposed the process of decision on these matters to the very difficult decision-making styles that prevailed within UNCTAD.[13]

The attitudes and aspirations (if not the expectations) engendered by OPEC's success and its continuing hold over the energy situation were clearly the dominant influences on UNCTAD's initial decisions. But one important key to understanding the commodity negotiations is that the OPEC phenomenon as well as rising fears of other resource constraints (reflected in the "limits to growth" debate) were not perceived or understood in the same fashion by the major actors in the negotiations. For the Third World, OPEC was not only an inspiration but also a potential source of new resources. (That OPEC was also a threat to the viability of many developing countries and that whatever resources it offered would hardly compensate for the damage to less fortunate "brothers" were

---

[13] The personal ambitions of various UNCTAD officials may also have had some effect; perhaps the fact that the Secretary-General came from Sri Lanka, a country with "weak" commodities, was not irrelevant. These factors are impossible to document or to weigh accurately, but—whatever their actual effect—most of the participants took for granted that they were influential. However, I believe it would be wrong to assume that such personal factors exerted a major effect.

thoughts proscribed by fear, euphoria, the hope of special treatment for LDC oil importers, or the desire to emulate.) OPEC was always formally offstage during the negotiations but never out of the play, for it represented a tacit threat in the armory of the developing countries: if the developed countries resisted necessary changes, OPEC might finance producer associations (or even cartels) without consumer participation, or it might use the oil pricing issue as leverage to extract concessions toward a "New International Economic Order." Indeed, from UNCTAD's perspective only firm support from OPEC seemed likely to enable the IPC to achieve a major restructuring of the commodity order—something more, that is, than price stabilization and improvement of existing market operations.[14]

How likely was OPEC to support a fundamental challenge to the old order—from which it was extracting spectacular benefits? No one (including OPEC, given its internal disagreements) was quite sure. But for UNCTAD uncertainty about the degree of OPEC support would probably suffice, for the implicit threat could still be manipulated by allusion. At any rate, uncertainty was clearly preferable to rejection, which might have been the most likely outcome of demands for premature commitment of real resources.[15] Conversely, from the perspective of the developed countries, fear of antagonizing OPEC or of providing a rationalization for a new round of oil price increases did have a clear effect on negotiating styles and strategies. Negative responses were frequently fudged, and major efforts were devoted to keeping the

[14] Strong OPEC support was probably not indispensable if the primary goals were only to stabilize prices around the long-term trend and to increase domestic processing and diversification, for these goals were not in dispute; but if the goals were also to include efforts to raise prices above the trend, to transfer resources, and to restructure the market radically, OPEC was indeed critical.

[15] After some early soundings, the Secretary-General clearly decided not to seek a hard commitment of money and political support from OPEC before Nairobi. There is no doubt that a judgment about OPEC's likely response strongly influenced the Secretary-General's decision, the result of which was to leave OPEC, per se, off center stage.

dialogue going (especially so that the energy discussions in Paris were not undermined by stalemate and breakdown in UNCTAD).[16]

Perhaps fortunately, the developing countries clearly felt that increased power and the potential support of OPEC were not the only factors altering the bargaining "terms of trade" in their favor. Equally important were shifts (or presumed shifts) in perception among the industrial countries—shifts that were beginning to alter the conventional wisdom about the utility of restructuring commodity trade. On a very general level, what was at issue were new fears of resource scarcity, not resource surplus. Consumer fears of rising prices were now more salient than producer fears of declining prices. The inflationary impact of rising commodity prices, the potentially dampening effect on industrial activity of fluctuating (that is, *either* up or down) commodity prices, fear of insufficient investment or denial of access to resources by increasingly nationalistic governments that would create supply problems in the future—these factors seemed to indicate much more *joint* interest in commodity agreements.[17] The access problem now looked more symmetrical: if the poor needed access to the markets and the resources of the rich, the rich also needed or might need access to the resources of

[16] Ultimately, the American government apparently decided that concessions at UNCTAD or at the North-South dialogue in Paris were not likely to have much effect on OPEC's pricing decisions. Thus an apparently authentic Kissinger telegram to the U.S. delegation to the Conference on International Economic Cooperation (CIEC) in Paris, which was leaked to the European press (with the Dutch as prime suspects), argued that "in our view, the connection which some OPEC officials have made between CIEC and OPEC is more rhetorical than actual [and] it is unlikely that OPEC countries view CIEC as a major factor in a decision on an oil price increase." The full telegram appeared in the *London Sunday Times*, 12 December 1976. One notes, however, that there was always a "shadow of uncertitude" (as with nuclear arms) about how OPEC would respond to major failures at UNCTAD or CIEC.

[17] On inflationary effects, see Behrman, *International Commodity Agreements*; on the dampening effect, see N. Kaldor, "Inflation and Recession in the World Economy," *The Economic Journal* 86, no. 344 (December 1976): 703-714.

the poor. The elements for fairer bargaining between producers and consumers seemed to be increasingly present.[18]

Tactical considerations—rising Third World power, fears of OPEC, new perceptions on the part of the developed countries—thus seemed to push toward some kind of agreement to restructure commodity trade; differences in degree could be compromised in the bargaining process itself. Other factors, however, pushed toward stalemate and conflict. One, which we shall return to in the next chapter, reflected sharp ideological differences (or posturing) on both sides. Another, considerably underrated (perhaps inevitably, given ideological conflict), reflected genuine intellectual uncertainties about what could or ought to be done with commodities and whether so much emphasis on changes in commodity trade were justified or would benefit the right groups and the right countries. This too we shall discuss in a later chapter. But I want here to briefly note two questions that are related to but not identical with questions about immediate reactions to the OPEC phenomenon—their effects are more intangible and psychological. How permanently had recent developments altered the resource universe? How much did these developments necessitate changes in prevailing patterns of behavior?

Initially the oil crisis elicited an extraordinary range of responses, from hysterical justifications of military action to naive or simplistic pleas for an end to growth. As time passed, however, and as adjustments occurred and fears of imminent resource shortages diminished, the notion that the old order could be patched together again began to prevail—particularly among conservative political leaders in the Nixon and Ford administrations. While some changes might be necessary to pacify OPEC for a few years and to facilitate some adjustments to potential shortages, nothing had invalidated the basic principles on which the old order had been built. On the other hand, the developing countries believed

[18] UNCTAD stressed the developed countries' interest in commodity agreements in many documents. For example, see UNCTAD, *Report of the Advisory Committee to the Board and to the Committee on Commodities on its Ninth Session* (TD/B/519), July 1974, p. 7.

or wanted to believe that a new order was now both necessary and possible. Both sides agreed on the existence of a crisis, but one side saw it as reflecting cyclical factors that would shortly return (more or less) to "normal," while the other saw it as the signal for global transformation. There is no objective way in which such sets of beliefs and desires can be judged definitively right or wrong. In any case, neither side was much interested in encouraging analyses that might clear some of the fog away. Still, the point to be kept in mind is that these divergent views had a persistent effect not only on atmospherics but also on the choice of negotiating strategies. Valuations of time were also significantly affected: for different reasons, each side thought that it would benefit from delay and was willing to bear the costs of stalemate (on the assumption, of course, that the deadlock would ultimately be broken in its favor).

The strategy that UNCTAD (or, more precisely, the Secretary-General and the handful of people he consulted) chose to follow was neither modest nor prudent. The end in view was "global resource management in the interests of the development process."[19] The means used were "to encompass the totality of the commodity problem from production to consumption."[20] The new order in commodity trade might begin with efforts to stabilize prices via buffer stocks, but it also required efforts to restructure the economies of the developing countries (diversification, increased domestic processing, a greater role in marketing and distribution), to improve market access to the developed countries (and even to intervene to control or "harmonize" the production of syn-

[19] UNCTAD, *Commodities* (TD/184), p. 3.
[20] UNCTAD, *An Integrated Program for Commodities* (TD/B/C.1/166), December 1974, p. 21. This reflected the judgment that previous commodity agreements had been too narrow in scope. Controlling production or prices, for example, was not sufficient for commodities facing a downward price trend—diversification would also be necessary. In addition, worldwide inflation and monetary instability were now critical factors that had not been previously taken into account in commodity agreements. They too needed to be dealt with though this was bound to be extraordinarily difficult without complementary and wide-ranging changes in the international economic system itself.

thetics that compete with natural products), to intervene to control the "unfettered operation of markets," and to create a mechanism of guidance and control for this process that reflected and incorporated the new bargaining power of the developing countries.[21] In addition, the *first* step envisaged was not to seek to fill in details or to clarify uncertainties: what was demanded was initial agreement in principle—a potential blank check—after which details could be negotiated.[22]

This was a program calculated to enrage free-marketeers—several of whom dominated economic decision making in key Western governments. Moreover, many other powerful forces that benefitted from prevailing patterns of behavior were bound to be in opposition: multinational corporations that dominated distribution and marketing, speculators who profited from fluctuations, and various groups that feared the potential inflationary impact of rising commodity prices. Finally, there were economists doubtful that commodity agreements could work or that UNCTAD's analyses were accurate, and there were political analysts who doubted that so far-reaching a program could be negotiated in existing circumstances. Why was this powerful and variegated opposition ignored? As was previously noted, the general factors that influenced the environment of decision clearly played a role. In essence, these factors generated a new sense of possibilities and, as time passed, of needs. The possibilities and the needs seemed to justify a major challenge

[21] These measures are discussed in many documents. The quoted phrase is from UNCTAD, *Measures for Individual Commodities* (TD/B/C.1/194), October 1975, p. 5. It is further noted in this document that "reliance on market forces does nothing to remove the imbalance in bargaining power . . ." (p. 5). The degree of intervention is quite broad, for the IPC also presumes "that governments are ready to give more consideration in their domestic policies to the interests of their external suppliers or customers" (p. 5). This is more aspiration than reality—for *either* importers or exporters. One demand made in this context is for the "harmonization" of production of substitutes and synthetics with the production of natural products.

[22] I note the rationale for this shortly. For a clear statement by a leading Third World intellectual of the necessity of resolving disagreements of principle first, see Mahbub ul Haq, *The Poverty Curtain—Choices for the Third World* (New York: Columbia University Press, 1976), p. 182. My criticisms of this argument appear in Chapter 5.

to the existing order—despite the opposition. But the form that the challenge took and the tactics that seemed appropriate were also influenced by a number of other judgments.

Changed conditions might have made a new commodity order necessary and—for the first time—much less improbable, but they might also have justified an effort to revive and enhance a series of individual commodity negotiations on a case-by-case basis. UNCTAD itself had advocated such a course in earlier years.[23] These negotiations had failed dismally, but it was at least arguable that they now had a better chance of success—better anyway than a much more elaborate effort to deal with many diverse commodities according to common principles, objectives, and techniques.[24]

There were several reasons why this argument was rejected. I have already emphasized the desire to give UNCTAD a larger role in commodity negotiations. But once the decision had been made to seek a radical restructuring of commodity trade, one characteristic of UNCTAD had a significant influence on form and substance in the IPC. The UNCTAD staff had a very small number of highly skilled econometricians who were quite capable of analyzing the general patterns of commodity trade and of devising the outlines of comprehensive solutions to existing problems. However, UNCTAD did not have technicians intimately familiar with the detailed operations of particular commodity markets—that knowledge was elsewhere, either in other institutions (for example, the FAO), in individual commodity organizations, or in various governments. In this sense, if

[23] Thus in 1968 the Committee on Commodities argued that "in dealing with these commodities a pragmatic commodity-by-commodity approach is preferable to an attempt to devise universal solutions for commodity problems." Quoted in J. Robert Vastine, "United States International Commodity Policy," *Law and Policy in International Business* 9, no. 2 (1977): 407.

[24] Perhaps one should also note that it was neither new knowledge nor new techniques that were responsible for reversing the previous emphasis. UNCTAD itself noted that the "breakdown of earlier commodity agreements . . . cannot be attributed to faults in the basic techniques adopted." Thus production or export quotas, buffer stocks, and multilateral sales contracts were still the primary means of control, although now supplemented by the other measures already mentioned. The quote is from UNCTAD, *Measures for Individual Commodities* (TD/B/C.1/194), p. 18.

UNCTAD were to be the primary setting for a major challenge to the existing commodity order, the form of the challenge almost had to be general and comprehensive because UNCTAD lacked the manpower to control or decisively influence individual negotiations (and, of course, it feared a loss of power if the negotiating focus were diffused).

The dangers of dissipating or fragmenting Third World bargaining power also encouraged an emphasis on comprehensive and principled solutions. Individual negotiations tended to leave a handful of weak producers exposed to a majority of powerful buyers. Providing an institutional setting in which developing country producers were in the majority and insisting that individual negotiations be conducted according to principles and techniques established by a central forum thus seemed critical. In addition, since the primary goal could only be achieved if the developing countries were to remain unified, only a very general program cast a wide enough net to encircle all of the necessary supporters. Potential defectors could also be more easily kept in line in a single forum, and trade-offs between different commodities (or issues) could be more easily arranged.

Other arguments pointed in the same direction. For example, the Secretary-General of UNCTAD persistently maintained that previous commodity negotiations had failed because of the absence of sufficient financing for buffer stocks. This was clearly an overstatement, and most experts felt that competition among producers was the decisive factor in failures.[25] Indeed, the argument might well have been turned around: governments or producers had not provided sufficient financing because they did not believe that an agreement could be made to work. Still, even if overstated, this was not an irrelevant argument. In one case—tin—the buffer stock authority was not provided with enough financing to defend the ceiling price, and in all cases the guarantee that sufficient financing would be available (which usually implied

[25] Thus Behrman notes that "successful agreements broke down most often due to competition among the members, with competition from non-members being the second most common cause." *International Commodity Agreements*, p. 33.

consumer contributions) might provide poor and weak governments with the stamina and the incentive to hold fast in a down market (that is, not to cheat).[26] Poor governments buttressed by an adequately financed buffer stock would no longer have to increase production to maintain income as prices fell (thus worsening the situation), for the buffer stock would (or might) be able to stabilize the market.

There is, of course, no reason why sufficient financing could not have been provided within the framework of individual agreements—but it had not been, for whatever reason, and consumers were still unwilling to make a commitment to ensure that each agreement had enough resources. As a result, the argument that *prior* creation of a central financing mechanism with contributions from both exporters and importers might serve as a catalyst for agreement and an inducement for good behavior made a good deal of sense. But it also fudged some issues (If the agreement were in everyone's interest, why wouldn't sufficient finance be provided?), it raised other issues (Who could control the funding mechanism and how much would it cost?), and it seemed to threaten (especially in its original version) a degree of market intervention by the central financing institution that was neither acceptable to the developed countries nor necessarily wise for all producers.

The threat of going it alone with OPEC was periodically raised during the negotiations, if only as a reluctant last resort. The threat was never taken too seriously, however, for both UNCTAD and the Group of 77 were well aware of the weak bargaining position of many commodity exports, especially those facing strong competition from substitutes. It was particularly true that none of the ten "core" commodities in the IPC (except perhaps tin) were very likely candidates for withholding supplies from the market.[27] In this sense, the IPC and commodity agreements in general were "secondbest" solutions, for clearly a cartel in which no agreement on price ceilings or consultations with consumers had to be granted would have been preferable. Since the desirable and

---

[26] See Fox, *Tin: The Working of a Commodity Agreement.*
[27] See Behrman, *International Commodity Agreements*, pp. 33f.

the possible were in conflict, particularly for the weak commodities, concessions had to be made. Thus another reason for seeking support for a comprehensive approach was apparent: the developed countries were not interested in commodity agreements for the weak commodities (for example, tea, jute, sisal), but they might be induced to accept such agreements in exchange for agreements in some of the stronger commodities (for example, copper, tin, rubber). This presupposed that the producers of the strong commodities were willing to be used in this fashion or that they received substantial benefits in return; as we shall see, this gradually created substantial tensions within the Group of 77.

Finally, it bears emphasis that UNCTAD and the Group of 77 wanted to use the IPC to accelerate development. This implied not merely a more efficient use of resources or a less flawed market but also a transfer of resources. Conversely, the developed countries wanted only improved efficiency in commodity trade. Insofar as this response reflected ideological predispositions or narrow self-interest, it could be dismissed as shortsighted or unfair. But a much more serious charge could be raised against UNCTAD's goals, for it is far from clear that it is sensible to attempt to transfer resources by commodity agreements,[28] as everyone's welfare may be reduced, and the few that benefit may already be well-off. Transferring resources directly may be more sensible, but are such direct transfers likely? If not, is an inferior method of transferring additional resources better than no additional transfer at all? We shall return to these questions later.

The combination of circumstances that produced the decision to seek an initial principled commitment from the developed countries to a fundamental transformation of

[28] The conventional arguments against resource transfers in this fashion are discussed in Raymond F. Mikesell, "Commodity Agreements and Aid to Developing Countries," *Law and Contemporary Problems* 28, no. 2 (Spring 1963): 294-312. The negative effects on equity within developing countries are stressed by P. T. Bauer and H. Myint, "The Hidden Costs of Commodity Price Stabilisation," *The Banker* 126, no. 610 (December 1976): 1423-1426.

commodity trade—to strike while the opportunity was there, to enhance bargaining power, to give UNCTAD new power, to ensure adequate financing, to provide benefits for many developing countries, and to provide an impetus for development—was very compelling and persuasive. This is especially so when one recalls the prevailing euphoria about the new "resource power" of the poor. But the inclination to look at all sides of the issues, to worry about the reactions of the developed countries, or to build slowly on a record of narrower successes was not strong.

What UNCTAD and the Group of 77 tried to do cannot be automatically rejected. To seek wider, developmental goals through a commodity program or to seek to restructure markets that frequently are badly flawed or work to benefit primarily only a few is not necessarily wrong, unwise, or unjust.[29] Neither the existing arrangements nor whatever succeeds them are sacrosanct, for they are man-made arrangements that can and should be altered when different ends seem appropriate, when better ways of achieving traditional ends become apparent—or when the configuration of power that underlays a market system shifts. Even with the passage of time, no one aware of all the factors can be certain that another decision—a better mixture of judgment, fact, intuition—would have been more productive or wiser. Still, within these constraints, what UNCTAD and the Group of 77 sought to do does raise questions about prudence, feasibility, and the nature of the international policy process. Was too

[29] Some would disagree. Note the comment by Harry G. Johnson in "Commodities: Less Developed Countries' Demands and Developed Countries' Responses," in Jagdish N. Bhagwati, *The New International Economic Order: The North-South Debate* (Cambridge: The MIT Press, 1977), p. 240. He describes the IPC as "an attempt to paper over with semantic ambiguity a variety of inconsistent policies and policy objectives, . . . policies whose presumed feasibility rests on the creation of a degree of comprehensive monopolistic organization of international trade in commodities that has never even remotely existed in the past and has no possibility of being achievable in the present." But I believe this is far too strong an indictment—that it is too concerned with what Johnson calls "elementary" economic principles and not enough concerned with the empirical world and the conditions that *may* invalidate some traditional judgments.

much being sought too quickly in the quest for a "global resource management?" Was the Common Fund so important that more than three years of constant and concerted pressure had to be devoted almost solely to extracting a commitment to it? If so much emphasis on the Common Fund reflected a case of misplaced priorities, why was so little effort made to alter priorities? Did the strategy pursued to extract agreement on the IPC oversimplify technical issues and misperceive the way in which democratic governments make decisions? And did the bargaining process within UNCTAD ensure stalemate, obscure mutual interests, and inflate expectations about what could be reasonably expected from changes in commodity trade?

A common theme unites these questions. The IPC reflected an effort by UNCTAD and the Group of 77 to establish an entirely new pattern of decision making in one very important part of the international economy. What was being sought, at least initially, was in some ways unprecedented: a new level and degree of international decision making and international management, the imposition of common principles and a central financing (and presumably supervising) institution, and joint support for a major redistribution of benefits and a new ordering principle for at least part of the trade and aid system.[30] This was extraordinarily ambitious, and criticisms on ideological, practical, or theoretical grounds are within easy reach—as we shall shortly see. But the criticisms are not all that need to be cited.

Common sense suggests the limitations of a quest for global

[30] These goals were considerably scaled down after the failures of the Common Fund negotiations in 1977, and they have become increasingly moderate and conventional. But I am concerned here with original intentions and their implications. Also, as I have noted in Chapter 1, although some of the rhetoric was very radical and threatening, a number of key developing countries would have been willing to accept relatively moderate changes (and a relatively moderate pace of change), and there were also many moderate or pragmatic actions or policies that were in both side's interests and that might have been undertaken—if both sides could have agreed to disagree about whether these were merely sensible measures of reform or the initial stages of a revolutionary new order. Why this did not happen will become clear in Chapter 4.

solutions. Decision making is bound to become increasingly costly and unstable as the number of participants and the range of values that have to be satisfied increases; even without the additional complications from uncertainty, the only prudent alternative seems to be incrementalism—if not "muddling through," at least not "charging through." Nevertheless, incrementalism is not in itself sufficient because of the danger of drift without some kind of central direction and because a large number of developing countries need more than marginal improvements in the policymaking process.

I know of no simple solution to this conflict between the desirable and the possible. In the last chapter I shall address the question of whether some improvements—a better balance—are possible, but even there my answer will be provisional and contingent. I note the issue here, however, because it serves to highlight two very general questions that are crucial to this study but that may be somewhat obscured by the detail. In the first place, what can we reasonably expect the international decision making system to do—or, alternatively, how can we moderate a process of demand formation that seems to generate excessive or unrealistic expectations about likely benefits? And in the second place, under the present circumstances, once goals are set, by what means can they be most effectively pursued? UNCTAD and the Group of 77 sought a very ambitious goal, but both need and opportunity seemed sufficient justification at the time; conversely, the means chosen—the "how" question—seemed much less justified, especially when tactics were not altered in response to persistent failure. Why this happened will be a major theme of Chapter 4.

In the next chapter we shall raise a separate but connected issue: What is the relationship between the technical and the political in the commodity debate and, inferentially, in much of the North-South arena?

Chapter 3

The Integrated Program
for Commodities

Neither the principles, the objectives, nor the techniques of the Integrated Program were really original. Even the idea of a central fund to finance a series of buffer stocks had been foreshadowed at UNCTAD-III in Santiago when staff papers had advocated a multicommodity approach that would require the "mobilization of international financial and technical assistance."[1] Indexation, the attempt to preserve the purchasing power of commodity exports, was also not new, for it had been employed in various domestic contracts and in some long-term commodity supply agreements (for example, between Japan and Australia). In effect, one might argue that there has been a kind of secular trend toward commodity agreements in the international system, with varying degrees of support from producers and consumers as prices fluctuated and a narrower secular trend to expand the idea of commodity agreements to encompass the full commodity cycle and even the relationship to external economic conditions (for example, worldwide inflation or monetary instability).

In this context, debate on the originality of the IPC is neither important nor interesting. Moreover, a focus on originality tends to obscure the critical role that the UNCTAD staff has played in the commodity negotiations. The staff certainly borrowed ideas and initiatives that had been loosely circulating for some time, but it also did much more. In the first place, it did not take ideas as given: the empirical work it did and the analyses of commodity trade that it undertook have added to the knowledge we have about commodities and to

[1] *Proceedings of the United Nations Conference on Trade and Development*, vol. 2, *Merchandise Trade* (New York: United Nations, 1973), pp. 65-66.

the awareness of commodity problems that now exist. (I note again, however, that most of this work was very general and that some of it—as we shall see—was sharply disputed by several outside experts, particularly a number of early studies.) In the second place (and more critically) the staff transformed a number of disparate proposals into a comprehensive and coherent program that became the framework for the commodity debate. The staff took advantage of the opportunity created by the external environment in 1974 to launch a major initiative in commodity trade, an initiative that set the terms of reference for a significant diplomatic struggle between North and South. Finally, this initiative also ensured that the staff itself would become a political actor in the struggle, because packaging the IPC necessarily involved a number of political judgments about substance and strategy and because the staff inevitably became a prime advocate of the program that it had produced and a critical judge for one side of what might and might not be an acceptable compromise. In this chapter we shall be primarily concerned with the first two roles; the third role will be treated in Chapter 4.

Noneconomists may find a few of the arguments that follow a bit difficult. I want strongly to emphasize, however, that my purpose is not to provide a detailed or technically sophisticated discussion of these complex issues but rather to provide sufficiently persuasive evidence that important technical disagreements existed (and persisted) among competent experts, that these disagreements were frequently obscured for various reasons, and that the failure to deal with these disagreements—however necessary in the short run—was costly in the long run. Accordingly, my focus will be on the political implications of the technical debate (or nondebate) and not on the technical issues themselves. The failure to understand what the stabilization debate was all about, or what buffer stocks had to do with stabilization, or why a central financing mechanism might save money is not crucial in this context—as long as one *does* understand that disagreements did exist and that they were not always ideologically induced. I should also note that a few political judgments about why certain actions were taken or not taken are treated briefly in this chapter; more detailed discussion of the "why" questions follows in Chapter 4.

Principles and Objectives

There was little overt conflict within the negotiating process over the principles and objectives of the IPC. On some issues this reflected widespread consensus on the wisdom or necessity of a number of proposals. On other issues conflict has merely been delayed or obscured, not avoided. Ambiguous phraseology of generalities simply shifted the date of conflict forward to the detailed negotiations on individual commodities (that is, to the period *after* the IPC had been accepted). Confrontation on these issues was not delayed or obscured because nothing useful could be said about them in general terms (the ostensible rationale) but rather because to do so would exacerbate conflict both within and between groups. We shall shortly see why. But a very important point about the politics of nondiscussion needs to be understood: the failure to attempt to clarify some critical issues, however difficult it would have been, permitted misperceptions of potential benefits and significant distrust of real intentions to play a key role in the attitudes and orientations of the two groups.

The essential principle underlying the IPC was producer-consumer cooperation. This did not imply that producer associations were proscribed from acting alone to strengthen prices or to improve their bargaining position.[2] But presumably it also did not imply cartellike actions that would have violated the principle of cooperation. As already noted in Chapter 2, the prospects of emulating OPEC were too dim to justify unilateral actions, and the theme was very muted at UNCTAD. For the most part, public assertions about going it alone were left to Third World meetings outside of UNCTAD, although care was taken to ensure that the developed countries were aware that the idea had not been totally

[2] UNCTAD, *An Over-all Integrated Programme for Commodities* (Geneva: TD/B/498), August 1974, pp. 5, 9.

rejected.[3] At any rate, the argument that producer-consumer cooperation was preferable to any of the alternatives was generally accepted by most of the participants. What cooperation meant, however, depended on agreement about the objectives of the IPC.

Many of these objectives were noncontroversial. Improved access to markets for exporters, expansion of the processing of commodities in developing countries, some restructuring of distribution and marketing, diversification into commodities with better long-term demand prospects, and increased research were all widely supported, although there were differences in degree and timing. For the developed countries many of these measures were noncontroversial for two reasons: they did not involve strong intervention in markets and they were not likely to have any significant rapid effect. The last point—the time it would take before these measures could be very helpful—also explains why they were not particularly central to the developing countries' demands. The latter wanted help quickly and they wanted a transfer of resources, but these aims could only be achieved by using the price mechanism. As we shall see, this was an illusion, for there were really no significant "quick fixes" for commodity problems, and the long-term measures were in fact the most important means of change. The UNCTAD staff came to recognize this somewhat belatedly, but not before playing an important role in raising expectations about short-run benefits.

The explanation for this misunderstanding requires some comment on one very controversial objective of the IPC, its pricing policy. But before discussing this, one other controversial objective ought to be noted. Guaranteed access to supply was an important issue to both developing and developed countries. For the developing countries, it was important in

[3] The Dakar meeting of the nonaligned countries in February 1975 particularly emphasized unilateral producer actions. The Dakar Declaration was circulated by UNCTAD (TD/B/C.1/L.45), but it was not the only pressure in this direction. UNCTAD itself had commissioned a study of the possibility of producer action by a Scandinavian social scientist, but decided not to publish the results—which, in comparison with other studies, were unusually optimistic. UNCTAD clearly felt publication might be unnecessarily provocative.

terms of their own food imports, but the food issue was left aside because the major exporters were developed countries.[4] Access to supply for the developed countries was a sensitive issue—as the various charters, declarations, and programs of action attest—but it remained more or less quiescent during the debate, deliberately ignored by the developing countries: according to informed opinion, access to supply was to be a last concession to the developed countries in exchange for agreement on the Common Fund. The developed countries rarely raised the issue because denial of access did not seem to be a practical possibility for UNCTAD's "core" commodities and because insufficient investment in future supplies seemed more critical than withholding supplies. This led to a controversial proposal by the United States at Nairobi for an international resource bank, a point we shall return to later.

The IPC has incorporated two price objectives. Price stabilization—the attempt to diminish the fluctuations that characterize trade in many commodities—is the most familiar and, in practical terms, probably the most important.[5] Price increases (presumably above the long-run trend) are a second objective. There is little economic support for this objective, but it is worth some discussion because it has been the most

[4] In any case, the developed country exporters would not have agreed to UNCTAD control. But the food issue was not irrelevant, since some large importers feared that an IPC that led to increased prices would lead also to higher food prices.

[5] The following table illustrates some of the problems with fluctuations:

Indices of Fluctuations in Commodity Prices
(1974 constant dollars)

| Commodity | Average Percentage Deviation from Moving Average | | |
	3-Year	5-Year	7-Year
Cocoa	10.13	16.54	19.91
Coffee	4.36	7.10	8.41
Tea	3.13	3.57	3.06
Sugar	8.30	9.90	11.46
Cotton	3.63	5.08	3.93
Jute	6.99	9.98	12.54
Sisal	9.95	15.48	18.11
Rubber	7.55	12.59	11.92
Copper	8.39	14.79	14.65
Tin	4.77	6.16	7.71

SOURCE: The World Bank, Report No. 814/76, Price Prospects for Major Primary Commodities, June 1976.

important sub rosa issue in the commodity debates. Underlying much of the resistance to the IPC in the developed countries, particularly among free market advocates, was the suspicion—or the assumption—that the essential objective of the IPC was a resource transfer via higher prices.[6] Given the developmental objectives of the IPC, this was not an irrational suspicion. Apart from the question of whether prices should be raised, the question of whether this could be accomplished by indexation also became very controversial.

On the surface, price stabilization appears to be a noncontroversial goal. Everyone supported it, albeit with varying degrees of enthusiasm. Beneath the surface, however, matters were considerably different. Indeed, the stabilization debate is something of a microcosm of the larger debate, for it illustrates the complex interrelationships between the political and the economic and between what was said and what could not be said (but was suspected) in the IPC negotiations.

Diminishing price fluctuations can have many advantages, especially if fluctuations in earnings are also diminished.[7] In-

[6] See especially David L. McNicol, *Commodity Agreements and the New International Economic Order*, California Institute of Technology Social Science Working Paper, no. 144 (Pasadena, 1976), p. 11.

While UNCTAD officials frequently denied any intention to transfer resources via higher prices (above the trend), even outside analysts who were sympathetic to developing country demands assumed this was the IPC's real objective. Thus J. N. Bhagwati notes that "commodities today have become a chief vehicle through which the developing countries want resources transferred via increased prices." See Jagdish N. Bhagwati, "Introduction," in *The New International Economic Order: The North-South Debate*, ed. Jagdish N. Bhagwati (Cambridge: The MIT Press, 1977), p. 8. And in a comment in the same symposium Paul Streeten noted that "when Third World practical men talk about 'stabilization' they mean a combined operation of stabilizing and jacking up prices" (p. 375). This is one reason why UNCTAD had to be ambiguous about pricing objectives, for insistence on stabilization alone would have antagonized those who wanted more.

[7] Instability can have a variety of causes: dependence on outside markets, new technologies, speculation, varying elasticities of supply and demand, wars and other disturbances, etc. Note that several of the causes have nothing to do with economic factors (for example, war, or nationalization) and are thus not amenable to control. But this ought not be used to justify the argument that attempts to control instability are useless, since seeking to control what can or might be controlled still makes sense. For a discussion of the various factors, see Alton D. Law, *International Commodity Agreements* (Lexington, Mass.: Lexington Books, 1975), pp. 2-17.

stability can be costly, for it increases uncertainty, it may lead
to a decline in investment, it may diminish competitiveness
with more stable substitutes, and it may redistribute income
arbitrarily between producers and consumers.[8] Consequently, stabilization can benefit producers by facilitating
more effective development planning and by providing more
bargaining leverage against competitors and against much
richer consumers who have the flexibility to diversify imports.
For the consumers, conversely, there may be a relatively small
transfer of resources to the producers, but compensation for
this may come in terms of a more assured supply of resources
in both the present and the future (from increased investment) and perhaps in terms of some reduction in inflationary
pressures. All interests thus *seem* to coincide—producers and
consumers, rich and poor, global and individual welfare (bar-
ring a few speculators). But the experts are less certain, not so
much about whether there might be benefits as about how
large these benefits would be, or about who would get them,
or by what means they could or should be sought.

The UNCTAD staff and the developing countries clearly
believed that price instability had very negative effects for
commodity exporters. But there were outside experts who
argued that the effect was minimal and that it was likely to be
limited to a small number of countries that exported particularly unstable commodities (for example, sugar and cocoa).
There were even some experts who argued that instability (of
both prices and earnings) had had a *positive* effect on growth
rates: the more instability, the higher the growth rate.[9] More
general agreement existed that earnings instability was likely
to be harmful, although again there were doubts about the
extent of the damage.[10] Perhaps most critically, doubts also

[8] See C. L. Gilbert, "Does it Pay to Stabilise Commodities?" *The Banker* 126,
no. 610 (December 1976): 1427.

[9] On the minimal effects of instability, see Alasdair McBean, *Export Instability and Economic Development* (Cambridge: Harvard University Press, 1966); on
the benefits of instability, see O. Knudsen and A. Parnes, *Trade Instability and
Economic Development* (Lexington: Lexington Books, 1975).

[10] See Constantine Glezakos, "Export Instability and Economic Growth: A
Statistical Verification," *Economic Development and Cultural Change* 21, no. 4
(July 1973): 670-678. McNicol, *Commodity Agreements and the New International*

existed about whether or under what circumstances price stabilization would lead to income stabilization.[11] We shall return to this issue momentarily.

Other uncertainties existed about who would benefit (both internally and externally) from price stabilization. For example, a paper by Karsten Laursen of the World Bank notes that

> consumers and producers taken together will gain; one group will gain, the other will normally lose, but the gain will always exceed the loss, if the cost of price stabilization is ignored so that the gainers can compensate the losers. But the extent of these gains and losses and whether they accrue to consumers or producers is crucially dependent upon a great number of factors such as the type of price expectations which under fluctuating prices underlies producers' output decisions, whether prices are wholly or partially stabilized, whether price fluctuations originate on the demand or the supply side, and the elasticities of demand and supply.[12]

Economic Order, pp. 44-45, contends that at best the effect is very small. Shamsher Singh, "The International Dialogue on Commodities," *Resources Policy*, June 1976, pp. 88-89, notes that fluctuations were not decisive for countries with high export growth rates, "but for countries experiencing low growth of exports, fluctuations proved to be a decisive handicap." And, as noted in the last chapter, most Third World commodity exports have had a slow growth rate.

[11] Price stabilization may not lead to income stabilization if, for example, it were to increase competition or if it were to generate higher prices that, in turn, were to generate substitutes or economizing in use. If instability were primarily on the demand side (for example, from the business cycle in industrial countries), price stabilization usually stabilizes producer earnings, although the average level of earnings may be reduced. If instability were from supply shifts (as it usually is with agricultural commodities), price stabilization may actually increase earnings instability if both supply and demand curves were elastic; if both curves were very inelastic, earnings stability would increase. There are obviously other variations possible if the supply and demand elasticities were to be mixed. In short, this is a very complex issue. Nevertheless, many economists seem to agree that UNCTAD's partial stabilization scheme (that is, between price ranges) and low price elasticities (especially of demand) for the core commodities imply that price stabilization will probably also be income stabilizing. See the comment by I.M.D. Little in Bhagwati, *The New International Economic Order: The North-South Debate*, p. 253.

[12] Karsten Laursen, "The Integrated Program for Commodities" (Washington, D.C.: The World Bank, 1977), p. 5.

After analyzing a number of studies, he concludes that "empirical evidence on the effects of commodity price stabilization is missing, for producers, consumers, and the world economy; although much opinion may be found in the literature, there is little basis for conclusions."[13]

These disagreements and uncertainties are very crucial because they strike at the heart of the IPC. If the major objective of the IPC does not seem likely to provide significant benefits to many developing countries and if many of the benefits seem likely to go to developed countries or if only some producers benefit while others lose, global welfare may be improved, but more than a few developing countries may lose or not benefit very much. In addition, if price stabilization does not necessarily lead to earnings stabilization—the key factor in terms of improved prospects for development planning and enhanced bargaining leverage—support for price stabilization could diminish, while support for compensatory financing of reductions in export earnings might increase.[14]

The final set of uncertainties about stabilization related more specifically to the IPC. A number of outside studies attempted to evaluate the benefits of stabilization for the ten "core" commodities in the IPC. Most of the studies appeared after the Nairobi Conference and thus had little effect on the period of conflict with which we are mainly concerned. But a study by Paul MacAvoy (a member of the Council of Economic Advisers in the Ford administration) is worth a brief comment not only because of MacAvoy's position and influence but also because it illustrates once again the wide range of disagreement among the technicians. MacAvoy's conclusions are summarized in Table 2. In sum, producers would gain $250 million per year (mostly to middle income develop-

[13] Ibid., p. 8. See also Law, *International Commodity Agreements*, who argues that "it is clear then that market instability in primary commodities is often overstated and overgeneralized" (p. 15).

[14] And it is, of course, compensatory finance that most of the developed countries have favored, primarily because it does not require market interventions or easily lend itself to price raising. See also the discussion in the next section.

TABLE 2

Expected Annual Net Benefits to Price Stabilization
(millions of 1974 dollars)

(a) *Commodity*	*(b)* *Benefit to* *Producers*	*(c)* *Benefit to* *Consumers*	*(d)* *Global* *Benefits* *(b)+(c)*	*(e)* *Interest* *Cost of* *Stock* *10%*	*(f)* *Storage* *Costs*	*(g)* *Net Global* *Benefit* *(d)−(e)−(f)*
Coffee	29	−9	20	20	5	−5
Cocoa	21	−7	14	10	2	2
Tea	8	−2	6	8	4	−6
Sugar	226	−67	159	72	61	26
Cotton	26	−6	20	72	9	−61
Rubber	−2	4	2	12	3	−13
Jute	0	0	0	0	0	0
Sisal	2	1	3*	0	0	3*
Copper	−50	132	82	500	55	−473
Tin	−10	29	19	80	2	−63
Total	250	75*	325*	774	141	−590*

NOTE: 0 = negligible.
SOURCE: Paul N. MacAvoy, "Economic Perspective on the Politics of International Commodity Agreements," mimeo, 1976; storage costs derived from UNCTAD TD/B/C.1/184, Table 5.
* Denotes corrections of the original source.

ing countries), and consumers would gain $75 million; but given storage and interest costs of $915 million, there is a predicted net global loss of $590 million.

MacAvoy's analysis has been sharply challenged by the UNCTAD staff. For example, a new study by J.D.A. Cuddy of the Commodities Division projects a net global benefit from price stabilization of over $1.2 billion per year (as against MacAvoy's net loss of $592 million).[15] In addition, this study (as well as other works in progress) argues that the effects of price instability have generally been underestimated and that the benefits of stabilization for both producers and consum-

[15] Personal Communication from Dr. J.D.A. Cuddy of UNCTAD. Cuddy's calculations are given in the following table:

ers could be substantial.[16] It is not my purpose to adjudicate these complex disputes, which is in any case probably impossible before the fact. But it needs to be emphasized that these UNCTAD studies are still in progress—more than a year and a half after the Nairobi Conference and more than three years after the IPC was launched.

Why is this so? The UNCTAD leadership can hardly plead ignorance, for controversy about the effects of price stabilization has been prevalent in the commodity debate for some time.[17] Nevertheless, in the period before Nairobi UNCTAD did not expend many resources on studies that might have diverted or diminished the controversy. One important result of the decision not to expend resources was to increase suspi-

Expected Annual Net Benefits to Price Stabilization
(millions of 1974 dollars)

(a) Commodity	(b) Benefit to Producers	(c) Benefit to Consumers	(d) Global Benefits (b)+(c)	(e) Interest Cost of Stock 10%	(f) Storage Costs	(g) Net Global Benefit (d)−(e)−(f)
Coffee	50	90	140	20	5	115
Cocoa	17	13	30	10	2	18
Tea	17	26	43	8	4	31
Sugar	311	428	739	72	61	606
Cotton	200	170	370	72	9	289
Rubber	56	21	77	12	3	62
Jute	10	6	16	0	0	16
Sisal	1	2	3	0	0	3
Copper	321	321	642	500	55	87
Tin	39	20	59	80	2	−23
Total	1022*	1097	2119	774	141	1204

SOURCE: Dr. J.D.A. Cuddy, *International Commodity Control* (forthcoming).
* Denotes correction of original source.

[16] Cuddy's *International Commodity Control* provides a study of stabilization that includes—as MacAvoy's analysis does not—microfactors (improvements in the investment climate, fuller use of capacity in slack periods, increased stability of supply, etc.), and these benefits added to the macroeffects on inflation suggest substantial benefits from price stabilization to both producers and consumers.

[17] There was much earlier debate about the study by Alasdair McBean, *Export Instability and Economic Development*, which was published in the mid-1960s.

cion of UNCTAD's intentions among many of the developed countries: If the benefits from stabilization were so uncertain and if the developing countries were unlikely to benefit massively even in the best of circumstances, what then were they really after? But the UNCTAD leadership seemed willing to incur the suspicion of the developed countries or felt that they had no choice but to do so. I believe that there were three factors responsible for this decision.

The first factor was institutional. As I have noted, the IPC was a staff creation. But it was not the creation of all the staff or even of all the Commodities Division: a strikingly small number of people did virtually all the work. UNCTAD is a small organization without much manpower to deploy (during the period under discussion, it consisted of about two hundred professionals, under thirty of whom worked on commodities). And even these numbers are deceptive, for many staff members lack technical competence and have been appointed to fill national "preserves" or as a result of personal ties, while others are competent but not trusted with sensitive work because of political affiliations. As a result, the few who did the work were extremely busy, especially at the outset when most of the effort concentrated on outlining the general nature of the elements of the IPC. Subsequently, when doubts began to appear, much more effort was devoted to illustrating the benefits of stabilization.

A second factor was political. The UNCTAD leadership clearly made a deliberate decision to de-emphasize questions of impact and effect (we shall see the significance of this again in a later discussion of potential losers from the IPC). As the Secretary-General once noted, such discussions could be "insidious" for a bargaining strategy that required unity from over one hundred very disparate, very poor countries. Discussion of "winners" and "losers" had best be left until momentum had developed and agreement on principles of a new commodity order had been established. But momentum did not develop, at least in part because of the demand to accept principles before it was very clear what they meant. And when questions of impact inevitably surfaced, the demands of the losers for compensation complicated the negotiating process at a moment when the possibility of a small compromise *might* have existed.

Finally, there was a perceptual factor. Doubts about the IPC were bound to arise among developing countries that felt they might lose from the IPC (for example, those who imported more of the core commodities than they exported). Much time and energy had to be expended on preventing defections and keeping the package of demands from coming unraveled. The political process thus tended to become encapsulated: the Secretary-General and the leadership of the Group of 77 were so involved in the internal politics of the Group of 77 that there was little time left to worry about how Group B (the Western industrial countries) would react or about how to frame proposals that seemed to reflect mutual interests (such proposals might have exacerbated tensions within the Group of 77 or diminished the ardor behind a commitment to the whole package of demands). Internal unity always took precedence over the creation of compromise proposals that might be relatively more attractive to the other side. In any event, beyond occasional outbursts of rhetoric the idea of framing proposals that took account of political realities and economic doubts in the leading Group B countries was never very prominent.

The failure to think seriously about likely Group B reactions to technical proposals (as with price stabilization) and the failure to worry sufficiently about what Group B could accept in political terms had an impact throughout the commodity discussions: the degree of unnecessary surprise rose and the belief in unnecessary illusions persisted. More farsighted and sophisticated leadership—a major deficiency for both sides—might have diminished the degree of encapsulation (the ships passing in the night syndrome). This can be illustrated within the context of the price stabilization issue itself, for more thought about what the other side would do and could accept might have led not only to an earlier response to criticism but also to a somewhat different emphasis within the range of arguments in defense of stabilization. Perhaps it also would have led the UNCTAD leadership to a somewhat different emphasis on what benefits could be expected in what time period.

A number of analysts argued that a "pure" stabilization scheme (that is, one without attempts to restrict supply and raise prices) would probably result in a reasonably large transfer of income to the producers. For example, Behrman foresaw a transfer of $5 billion per year (in 1975 dollars) to the producers; McNicol, in contrast, foresaw a transfer of only about $1 billion.[18] The developed countries were not likely to see this as an attractive or sensible way to transfer resources, especially since most of the more or less random beneficiaries (geographically, politically, economically) were relatively advanced developing countries. How might the developed countries have been made to look more favorably at this transfer? One answer might have been showing them studies that demonstrated much wider benefits from stabilization (to both developed countries and to the poorest developing countries), but such studies were unavailable. Another answer might have been an agreement on access to supply, but this was too explosive an issue for the rather fragile unity of the Group of 77. This left one other possible answer: a system-wide reduction in inflationary pressures.

A recent analysis has argued that a 14.5 percent increase in the price of nonfood, nonfuel raw materials in the developed countries results in a 1 percent increase in the consumer price index.[19] The effect is wider than the direct impact on commodity prices, for there is also a "ratchet" effect on the price of manufactured goods and on wages; even when commodity prices go down the outcome can be inflationary, since investment may decline and future supplies may be insufficient.[20] Behrman has suggested that stable prices might reduce in-

[18] Jere R. Behrman, *International Commodity Agreements* (Washington, D.C.: Overseas Development Council, 1977), p. 55; and McNicol, *Commodity Agreements and the New International Economic Order*, p. 18. It should be noted that Cuddy calculates much higher aggregate global benefits per year (between $5.8 and $19.4 billion). But Cuddy's figures were not available until well after Nairobi.

[19] The figures are from a Brookings paper by Joel Popkin, reported in Clyde H. Farnsworth, "Coordinating Commodity Prices," the *New York Times*, 12 June 1977.

[20] See the interesting discussion in N. Kaldor, "Inflation and Recession in the World Economy," *The Economic Journal* 86, no. 344 (December 1976): 703-714.

flationary pressures in the United States by 0.2 percent to 0.4 percent for a number of years in a decade, with gains of about $1.5 billion in those years. He notes that this "suggests the possibility that the really large gainers from international commodity stabilization may be the residents of the developed nations. . . ."[21] In addition, whatever the short-range effects, stabilization could be an important factor (not "the" factor, since political fears of expropriation are also crucial) in engendering sufficient investment so that long-run supply shortages are avoided. The key here is more psychological than economic: the confidence generated by more stable patterns of production and trade could make investments in the development of commodities more attractive.

I do not mean to suggest that these arguments are conclusive. Several economists, for example, have been very skeptical about the relationship between inflation and commodity price stabilization.[22] In addition, as we shall see, concern for inflation does not necessarily imply acceptance of the Common Fund, for buffer stocks (and not their means of financing) are the most important stabilization mechanism. Nevertheless, this was potentially a very critical argument, for its significance was recognized, it had the support of some very respected economists, and it responded directly to the most salient fears of the developed countries. Presumably the UNCTAD leadership was aware of these factors, but whether they were perceived correctly is unclear. What is clear is that UNCTAD made almost no substantive contribution to the analysis of the relationship between stabilization and inflation in the developed countries. Perhaps this reflected the need to keep open the possibility that prices would be raised (except for commodities facing competition from substitutes) and not merely stabilized. Conversely, the impact of inflation in the developed countries on the developing countries was, of course, an ever-present issue (as it should have been). Thus the stabilization debate tended to focus primarily on the

[21] Behrman, *International Commodity Agreements*, p. 66.

[22] See Gilbert, "Does It Pay to Stabilise Commodities?" See also Laursen, "The Integrated Program for Commodities," who stresses the difficulties of isolating the impact of commodity prices on inflation when so many other variables play a role.

range of benefits for the developing countries. The point is not simply that UNCTAD and the Group of 77 were wrapped up in their own concerns but that there was a lack of political sophistication implicit in the failure to emphasize the arguments that were most crucial to the other side and a lack of economic sophistication in not stressing sufficiently the interests that *both* developing and developed countries had in controlling inflation.

An earlier effort to deal with the stabilization issue might well have confirmed some of the critics' arguments (but not all of them, since UNCTAD's responses were not unpersuasive). Since questioning the benefits of stabilization seemed threatening to Group of 77 unity, the effort was only made rather late in the game and even then only when the issue finally became salient. Nevertheless, the risk may well have been worth taking, for UNCTAD could have balanced a more realistic statement of the short-run benefits of stabilization with an emphasis on the potentially larger long-term benefits from trade liberalization (especially for processed commodities).[23]

But UNCTAD chose not to do so, and trade liberalization remained a subsidiary theme within the debate. One reason for their decision was probably that this was a GATT, not an UNCTAD, issue. In institutional terms, it was simply not very attractive to argue that the main benefits were likely to come from a negotiating process lodged elsewhere. Perhaps also (especially in the early days of the IPC) there was a genuine if illusory hope that the greatest benefits would come from sharply higher prices. But beyond this, trade liberalization did not promise many immediate benefits (for substantial domestic restructuring was necessary to be able to grasp the opportunities that developed), it led only to a slow and not rapid restructuring of the commodity trading system, and it was not likely to be of much help to weak commodities facing a downward price trend. All of this was unfortunate, or perhaps ironic, for trade liberalization was also an issue that trapped the conservative opposition to the IPC in its own rhetoric; given the difficulties of liberalization for the devel-

[23] See especially the brief discussions in Singh, "The International Dialogue on Commodities," and Laursen, "The Integrated Program for Commodities."

oped countries, the latter might suddenly have been forced to discover some hidden virtues in the IPC's espousal of intervention in the market. None of this happened, however, for the UNCTAD leadership was itself trapped by the need to promise quick and widespread benefits to keep the Group of 77 together.

Economists are in general agreement that attempts to raise commodity prices above their long-run equilibrium trend are bound to fail. Such efforts will make substitutes more attractive, encourage economizing in use, and probably engender large increases in production.[24] Some short-term success might be possible for a few commodities for which demand is inelastic (for example, coffee, cocoa), but success could not be sustained. For the other commodities, prospects are even more doubtful.[25] Also, higher prices are obviously not beneficial to Third World importers of food products or raw materials for nascent industrialization programs. UNCTAD's technicians were well aware of these considerations, and they generally argued only for stabilization—in private. Publicly, however, UNCTAD documents were more ambiguous, and from time to time they contained statements that left open the question of what "strengthening" prices implied.[26]

[24] See Richard N. Cooper, "A New International Economic Order for Mutual Gain," *Foreign Policy*, no. 26 (Spring 1977), pp. 94-98; and Nathaniel H. Leff, "The New Economic Order—Bad Economics, Worse Politics," *Foreign Policy*, no. 24 (Fall 1976), p. 203. See also the previously cited works of Laursen, McNicol, and Behrman.

[25] Any degree of success would have to depend on the rich countries agreeing to police the agreement by not buying from outside suppliers and restraining the production of substitutes—very unlikely actions under the circumstances.

[26] References to "strengthening" prices appeared in many UNCTAD documents and in many Third World speeches at various UNCTAD meetings. Significantly, several countries within the Group of 77 were worried about the "adverse effects" of the IPC. But if the IPC were only to stabilize prices, these effects would be minimal; conversely, higher prices would hurt Third World importers substantially. For some of the fears, see UNCTAD, *Report of the Third Preparatory Meeting for the Negotiation of a Common Fund* (Geneva: TD/B/IPC/CF/8), March 1977, pp. 5-6.

This was a very important issue, arguably *the* most important issue in the commodity debate. A great many Western delegates and government officials as well as some outside analysts simply assumed that the real objective sought by UNCTAD and the Group of 77 was higher prices (above the trend). Indeed, the subject usually dominated corridor and private discussion. This suspicion, for example, may have been a more important factor than the technical issues in generating hostility to the Common Fund, for there were substantial fears that the Fund would seek to intrude in markets to raise prices illegitimately. Some of the suspicions were ideologically induced—anything the developing countries demanded was interpreted as a preface to or a disguise for more radical demands. Other suspicions, however, reflected the fact that an agreement limited to stabilization did not transfer many resources to the developing countries, certainly not enough to have a major effect on Third World development.[27] Conversely, higher prices could transfer very significant amounts of resources—Behrman for example, calculated that a 2 percent increase in prices could increase producer gains by a factor of twenty.[28] Thus McNicol's suspicion that "stable" prices were a euphemism for "higher" prices was widely shared.[29]

Given the suspicions and ambiguities generated by uncertainties about higher prices, an obvious question arises: Why was so little effort expended by either side in trying to clarify the issue? The response that the issue could not be clarified until actual negotiations began on individual commodities is not completely satisfactory; while clearly true in detail, it misses the degree of obscurity that could have been di-

[27] This is especially true because the gains would be spread among many countries, not all of whom will use them well. At any rate, gains of the order foreseen (*roughly* $1 to $5 billion) are not irrelevant, but they are also not likely to be of major significance.

[28] Behrman, *International Commodity Agreements*, p. 85. The gains for eight of the ten core commodities would go from about $4 billion to $87 billion. A transfer of this order of magnitude is not feasible either politically or economically—note the problems with adjustment to the new oil prices.

[29] McNicol, *Commodity Agreements and the New International Economic Order*, p. 27.

minished by an effort to confront the problem openly. After all, outside economists have not had much difficulty in establishing the general proposition that raising prices above the trend is not likely to be beneficial. For the developed countries (especially the conservative ones) the answer may be that they already knew (read: "assumed") that this was the objective and that it could not work. No further clarification was needed. But this is a position that misunderstands its own logic: if higher prices were the actual goal and if they could not be achieved, a careful effort to elucidate and educate might have been very useful. Above all, clarification of the issues might have diminished expectations that had already been raised dangerously high, and it might have facilitated a less ideological and more realistic bargaining environment. That is, it might have softened the bloc to bloc confrontation and enhanced the role of those who actually had a major interest in the outcome.

For the developing countries, the issue was more volatile. In the first place, keeping intact a coalition of over one hundred countries was inordinately difficult; it probably would have been impossible without some prospect of substantial and widespread gain. Close examination of who would get what was not encouraged. Ambiguities about the meaning of "strengthened" prices were not accidental.[30] In the second place, however, failure to clarify may simply have made a virtue of necessity, for the notion that past and present price relationships were exploitative and had to be quickly rectified had so much force and resonance within the Third World that it could only be finessed, not opposed. Hence questions of equity and justice were mixed with technical disagreements and practical uncertainties in a very confusing fashion.

UNCTAD and the Group of 77 have demanded price stabilization around a target level that is, in real terms,

> equitable to consumers and remunerative to producers, taking
> full account of the rate of world inflation, the need to provide

[30] This has been denied by the Secretary-General and a few other UNCTAD officials in interviews, but it has been affirmed privately by other officials—and some spokesmen for the Group of 77.

incentives for adequate investment in commodity production, the depletion of nonrenewable resources and the need to keep the prices of natural commodities competitive with those of their synthetic substitutes.[31]

But debates about what this might mean in practice have been very inconclusive. The problems begin with the terms themselves. There is no figure in the real world patiently waiting discovery by objective analysts that is obviously equitable to producers and fair to consumers. The figure shifts not only in response to economic trends but also in relation to the relative bargaining powers and skills of the negotiators. Each figure looks very different to producers or consumers and to different producers and different consumers. The uncertainties may be so substantial that none of the participants has great confidence in the stability of the outcome or in its intrinsic legitimacy and fairness.

The difficulties are compounded by ideological considerations. A "fair" price for developing country producers is not simply an economically viable price; compensation for a persisting secular decline in the terms of trade for commodities is also necessary. Many economists doubt that there has been a secular decline in the terms of trade for commodities, but what is believed or assumed—taken on faith—is more important here than analytical argument.[32] Another ideological

---

[31] UNCTAD, *Commodities* (Geneva: TD/184), March 1976, p. 5.

[32] There is an excellent treatment of the terms of trade debate in Paul Streeten, "World Trade in Agricultural Commodities and the Terms of Trade with Industrial Goods," in *Agricultural Policy in Developing Countries*, ed. Nurul Islam (London: Macmillan, 1974), pp. 207-223. Streeten suggests that poverty causes bad terms of trade, not vice versa, because the poor countries cannot move easily into better exports and have bad records with the quality of exports (doing worse than the rich countries even with the same exports). This implies that the terms of trade for *countries* (the LDCs) may decline, but not for commodities per se.

I should add that UNCTAD has a study in progress that—according to information given to me—examines the factorial terms of trade (and not the net barter terms of trade) and comes to the conclusion that there has been a secular decline over a long period of time. Whether or not this is true, in the period with which we are concerned the Streeten position was widely accepted by economists.

difficulty also complicates the argument. No one disputes the fact that many commodity markets operate very imperfectly. But there is disagreement about what this implies. Because UNCTAD is intent on establishing prices that are "consistent with developmental objectives" or that permanently rectify earlier patterns of exploitation, major interventions in the market to establish fair prices seem imperative. But for market enthusiasts, administered prices are anathema—unless set by Western corporations. Hypocrisy abounds in this discussion, for ideology also protects (or hopes to protect) real interests: it is the mixture of hypocrisy, felt beliefs, and important elements of truth on both sides of the issue that makes agreement so difficult.

There are also nonideological factors that exert a good deal of influence on the issue of higher prices. Perhaps the most important is how the objective is to be achieved. For example, the emphasis on stabilization in real terms—"taking full account of the rate of world inflation"—seems fair: price relationships in some cases have altered to the detriment of the developing countries who have also been victimized by inflationary trends for which *most* of them bear no responsibility and against which they have few acceptable defenses. But to seek to protect against adverse inflationary trends by automatic indexation is very problematic, for it may create more technical problems and more inequities than it solves. In any case, if current commodity prices were low or if demand for commodities were likely to rise sharply in the future, indexation may actually be harmful to the interests of many developing countries.[33] Nevertheless, the developing countries—but *not* the UNCTAD staff—have continued to press the issue because of technical misunderstandings, because some influential developing countries will benefit, and because anything opposed so violently by the industrial countries is bound to attract some Third World support.

[33] See Cooper, "A New International Economic Order for Mutual Gain." And note Bhagwati's comment: "As most sensible economists will agree, indexing is crude, simplistic, inefficient, inequitable (among developing countries, exactly like oil price increases), and virtually impracticable." Bhagwati, "Introduction," p. 14.

The question of methods was important in another way. An effort to strengthen commodity prices is not intrinsically wrong or illegitimate, and indexation is not the only means by which it can be achieved. Both sides have agreed that there is justification in raising prices to reflect cost increases or inflationary trends and that price rises that reflect increased demand are also acceptable. But the developed countries have been fearful that some of the mechanisms in the IPC will be used or misused to transfer income arbitrarily: via supply restrictions, denials of access, market interventions to set "political" prices, controls on research or the production of substitutes, and other such measures. There are ambiguities here because some of the objectionable tactics have been sanctioned in emergency cases—and they have been used by the developed countries themselves when national interests so decreed. But attempts to clarify this issue by establishing rules and procedures have been avoided, and suspicions about future intentions continue to dominate.

I noted in the beginning of this section that there was little overt conflict over the IPC's objectives within these negotiations. The burden of my argument is that there should have been, even in light of the strong qualification that much of the pricing issue could not be clarified until detailed negotiations began. For different reasons, each side decided that nothing useful could be achieved by clarifications—one side was already convinced that the benefits of stabilization would be small and that higher prices were the real goal, and the other decided that too much would be revealed if the benefits of stabilization were indeed small and if higher prices were not really possible.

Allusions to the virtues of ambiguity are a familiar theme in the discussion of negotiations. So, too, are the potential advantages of pushing conflict down the road in the hope that something useful will turn up along the way. But I have substantial doubts that the benefits outweighed the costs in this case—doubts that reflect the particular difficulties of negotiations in a context where sharp distrust and basic disagreement about principles and rules of the game prevail. UNCTAD, faced with the difficulties of devising an acceptable global package for a world in which rich and poor are both exporters and importers of commodities and in which gains and losses are distributed in very asymmetric patterns, was almost forced into excessive ambition and a degree of deliberate ambiguity by the need to promise or provide some benefit to nearly all of its constituency—and quickly. This led to an emphasis on general principles on which all of the Group of 77 could agree and to some overstatement, explicit or implied, about what could be expected from the IPC and its techniques. Conversely, the conservative Group B countries simply discounted UNCTAD assertions on faith, and they persisted in believing that the IPC was a (temporarily) disguised assault on their treasuries. Each side happily exchanged manifestoes, assured of its own rightness and the bad faith of the other side; the real issues in commodities and the real gains to both sides from agreement were incidental.

In these circumstances, I believe both sides would have benefitted from an effort to clarify contentious issues such as pricing policy, for it could have been potentially educational and it might have provided some shared ground on which to build. Clearly, there would have been costs involved, especially in the potential threat to unity within the Group of 77. But since there *were* significant though hardly revolutionary benefits to be gained, the consequences of a few defections would have been outweighed by the benefits of a more realistic negotiating strategy and a wider degree of cooperation from the industrial countries. I do not mean to suggest that the result would have been quick agreement, for there were some basic conflicts that could not be resolved by analysis and there were ideologues on both sides impervious to argument. But at least the area left open to exhortation might have been narrowed.

The tactics chosen guaranteed stalemate, but that may have been inevitable. The antipathy to commodity agreements (and, in some cases, to the developing countries) was so strong in a number of critical institutions and individuals that the prospects for an acceptable settlement were never high. What was particularly disabling, however, was that the prevailing tactics guaranteed stalemate *on the wrong issues*: the conflict revolved around divergent principles, different interpretations of the world, and mistrust of real objectives and intentions. These are extraordinarily difficult issues to resolve. They left the weaker side with only the hope of conversion or the arrival of new actors on the stage—a gamble that may seem to have payed off, except that the new actors are *now* asking the questions (or some of them) that should have been confronted earlier. In addition, there was also built into the prevailing pattern of confrontation a failure to seek to build for the future, that is, to remove or diminish issues that would hinder settlement once (or if) the ideologies were muted. Finally, since there were partial or even relatively strong supporters of the IPC even in the most hostile governments, an opportunity to forge some potentially useful transnational alliances was also lost.

That technical issues in the international system have become heavily politicized is by now a commonplace. But the politicization of technical issues does not mean that they are no longer technical. To treat all the issues in dispute as if they were "simply" political—a strong tendency at UNCTAD—is a mistake, for it fails to clarify what is really at stake and it encourages a particularly difficult kind of negotiating process, especially when the intellectual and ideological frame of reference is itself in conflict. One result is that everyone has his own "expert" and the area of disagreement is never narrowed as much as it might be. Another result is that the process of agreement is delayed and that whatever agreement results may be excessively ambiguous and thus unstable.

Techniques

The IPC sought to attain its objectives through the application of five or possibly six techniques. These were the creation of a series of international buffer stocks, a Common Fund for financing the stocks, multilateral long-term supply contracts, compensatory finance against fluctuations in export earnings, and the expansion of processing and increased diversification within the developing country producers.[34] Indexation was occasionally listed as a sixth technique.

The debate over buffer stocking and the Common Fund dominated the IPC's negotiating history. The controversy over these two techniques may seem excessive, for normally the choice of techniques is relatively less ideological and relatively more empirical than the choice of objectives. But while there were serious technical disputes about buffer stocking and the Fund, it needs also to be emphasized that a good deal of the conflict reflected underlying disagreements about price stabilization or underlying suspicions about real intentions. As in most social conflicts, a simple separation of means and ends is primarily a matter of analytical convenience. In what follows we shall discuss multilateral contracts and compensatory finance only in passing and as they intrude upon the general debate. Processing and diversification shall not be discussed at all because they were not contentious issues. They were, however, very important issues insofar as fundamental improvements in the commodity order were something more than a passing rhetorical fancy.[35] But the immediate pressures on poor countries trapped in a very difficult and complex environment made assertions of the need to concentrate on long-run tasks such as diversification seem irrelevant—or even cynical.

The manager of a buffer stock attempts to maintain a stable price that brings long-run demand into equilibrium with long-run supply. He does this by defending an agreed price range—by buying stocks when the price hits the floor and by selling the accumulated stocks when the price hits the ceiling.

---

[34] The techniques are discussed in many UNCTAD documents. See, for example, UNCTAD, *An Integrated Program for Commodities* (Geneva: TD/B/C.1/166), December 1974.

[35] Thus Laursen, "The Integrated Program for Commodities," notes that "the benefits to be derived from diversification and perhaps improved compensatory finance substantially exceed those to be expected from a Common Fund and price management" (p. iv). Increased trade liberalization to facilitate access for processed commodities should also be added to this list. But this was, as I have already noted, primarily a GATT, not an UNCTAD, area of concern. For some figures on the potential gains from trade liberalization, see Singh, "The International Dialogue on Commodities," p. 88.

In effect, variations in the size of the stock substitute—hopefully—for rising and falling prices. But buffer stocks are not the only means of stabilizing prices. Production cutbacks or export quotas could accomplish the same goal, but not without substantial costs. Restricting output diminishes economic activity, cuts employment in the commodity sector, and inhibits quick reaction to rising demand. Export quotas leave the burden of stocking with individual producers, are very difficult to negotiate, and tend to freeze the market and thus penalize the most efficient producers, keeping prices high, but at a loss in terms of consumer welfare. Moreover, from the consumer's point of view, restrictions or quotas may contribute to a decline in investment and, in any case, cannot defend a price ceiling as demand rises. Of course this is hardly surprising since restrictions and quotas are measures of supply control, not price stabilization. Finally, a buffer stock (which by itself can stabilize but not raise prices) may be used in conjunction with restrictions or quotas when oversupply forces the buffer stock to accumulate too many stocks (thus running out of money to buy more stocks) or when stabilization and higher prices are joint goals.

There are critics who concede the potential advantages of buffer stocks as mechanisms of stabilization, but doubt that they will be achieved in practice. Buffer stocks may involve less tampering with the market, they may not diminish economic activity or freeze trade into inefficient patterns, they may be able to act quickly and directly in response to market signals, they may reduce the need to negotiate difficult quota agreements, and—if jointly financed—they may spread the burden of adjustment more equitably between producers and consumers, but whether they will do so is unclear. Some of the doubts reflect earlier experiences with buffer stocks. Only the tin buffer stock functioned reasonably well—although primarily in defending the floor, not the ceiling price—but even in this case some analysts have attributed most of the success to an outside factor (the way in which the nationally controlled stocks of the United States were used).[36] More re-

---

[36] See G. W. Smith and G. R. Schink, "The International Tin Agreement: A Reassessment," *The Economic Journal* 86, no. 344 (December 1976): 715-

cently, the experience of the European Economic Community in accumulating "mountains" of butter and wine has also engendered a good deal of hostility to the idea of stockpiling.

Other analysts doubt that buffer stocks can actually reduce instability. Henderson and Lal, for example, argue that fluctuations are usually caused by underlying factors that cannot be affected by manipulating buffer stocks: the low short-run price elasticities of supply and demand for many commodities means that they do not respond significantly to price changes but rather that changes in supply and demand, conversely, can have substantial effects on prices. But shifts in supply and demand are constant and unpredictable. This means that a buffer stock can reduce instability only if its managers can foresee the future more accurately on the average than the market—for which superior foresight there is no persuasive evidence.[37] This suggests that export taxes or other local fiscal and monetary actions will be more effective either singly or in combination than buffer stocks, production restrictions, and quotas.[38] McNicol argues that "there is no real doubt that a *properly managed* buffer stock could produce a high degree of price stability," but "properly managed" means no resistance to permanent changes in the market, nonpolitical operations, and sharp restraints on how large an accumulation of stocks will be permitted.[39] These are difficult limitations for an organization dominated by developing countries. Moreover, es-

728. Both tin and coffee were better at defending the floor than the ceiling price, which at least suggests consumer interest in participation to ensure that enough financing is available to defend both ends of the price range.

[37] P. D. Henderson and Deepak Lal, "UNCTAD-IV, the Commodities Problem and International Economic Reform," *ODI Review*, no. 2 (1976), pp. 22-23. The point here is that if the long-term equilibrium price were predicted incorrectly, the buffer stock will either run out of stock as prices rise or run out of money to buy stock as prices fall. As a result, reliance on the stock might actually increase instability.

[38] This is also a theme in P. T. Bauer and H. Myint, "The Hidden Costs of Commodity Stabilisation," *The Banker* 126, no. 610 (December 1976): 1424. But the viability of export tax schemes has been questioned in an interesting article by M. J. Westlake, "Export Taxation and International Commodity Agreements," *ODI Review*, no. 2 (1977), pp. 57-70.

[39] McNicol, *Commodity Agreements and the New International Economic Order*, p. 68 (italics in original).

tablishing a price range that reflects the long-run equilibrium trend seems nearly impossible unless technical and structural factors change very slowly. Similarly, the difficulties are not diminished by underlying disagreements about "just" prices.

These are very critical issues for they go to the heart of what the commodity debate *should* have been about: whether commodity agreements based on buffer stocks could function effectively, how one could make judgments about this before the fact, and what might be done to help the manager of the stock to perform as well as possible. But workability and implementation were not very salient values during this debate. UNCTAD documents, for example, simply *assumed* that the buffer stock manager would have accurate information about future price movements and that he would be able to resist political pressures to maintain unjustified prices. I do not mean to imply that there were magic solutions to these problems but rather that there were some ways in which the stock manager's difficulties might have been allayed and that, in any event, it was surely important to discuss the difficulties openly and at length.[40] That no one else appeared to agree once again implicitly suggests a debate in which short-run rhetorical triumphs—or avoidance of the appearance of defeat—were more important than whether an agreement could be made to work.

Other questions about the effects of buffer stocks were also raised. The fear that publicly held stocks would lead to overproduction, since the producers would have a guaranteed buyer at a guaranteed price, was especially prominent—although in theory it could be met by lowering the floor price or by insisting on restrictions or export quotas (or by limiting the amount that the buffer stock manager had to spend). There was also some fear (reflecting the experience in American agricultural markets) that stocks might "overhang" the market, allowing floor and ceiling prices to be maintained but relatively closer to the floor.

[40] One interesting proposal to diminish some of the manager's difficulties (as well as his discretionary powers) can be found in John E. Tilton, *The Future of Nonfuel Minerals* (Washington, D.C.: The Brookings Institution, 1977), p. 100.

While the uncertainties about the utility of buffer stocks were surely justified—for the political, economic, and financial conditions that have to be present to make a buffer stock an effective mechanism for price stabilization are difficult to realize—they were not necessarily decisive. The possibility of consumer cooperation in policing an agreement, in contributing to financing, and in establishing and maintaining a sensible price range tended to create (or, minimally, to suggest the existence of) a new commodity environment in which simple extrapolations from earlier patterns of behavior were no longer decisive. Cooperation by consumers would not only provide the benefits of stabilization but also increase access to supply and establish some consumer voice in the operation and control of the buffer stock.[41] The critics of stocking also tended to suggest alternatives that thrust the burden of adjustment on the producers themselves (for example, export taxes), which might have made sense for developed country producers but was not realistic for poor and administratively inexperienced developing countries. In addition, although some early UNCTAD documents were ambiguous on the point, UNCTAD was not arguing that buffer stocks alone were sufficient to stabilize the market. Supply management, multilateral commitments, compensatory finance, diversification, and other measures might be necessary—with or without buffer stocks—depending upon the circumstances.

Whatever the doubts about the future performance of buffer stocks, there was fairly widespread agreement among the governments in Geneva that buffer stocks were preferable to restrictions or quotas and that they might be the best available means of stabilization.[42] They were hardly a panacea either

[41] Ibid., pp. 96-99. Tilton discusses some of the objections to buffer stocks and concludes: "Upon careful examination, many of the reservations regarding economic stockpiles are simply not valid. A few do raise legitimate concerns, but even in these cases there appear to be promising avenues for circumventing the problems" (p. 99). I quote Tilton primarily to indicate that not all outside experts were opposed to stocks and not all felt the record of the past was necessarily decisive.

[42] Secretary of State Kissinger specifically noted that buffer stocks were the preferred stabilization technique at his speech to the Seventh Special Session of the General Assembly in September 1975. Within the American government, however, there was not complete agreement on this.

alone or in combination with other measures, but the alternatives did not seem more promising and the new resource environment might generate the kind of cooperation that would permit stocks to perform more effectively than they had in the past. Even the most doubtful agreed that there were some commodities for which stocking made sense. This left two issues unsettled: Which commodities could be stockpiled at an acceptable cost? How should the stocks be financed? These issues were central elements in the debate about the Common Fund.

The commodity coverage of the IPC was bound to affect the degree of commitment the developing countries were likely to manifest: the fewer the commodities, the less profound and widespread the support. Certain technical characteristics of the individual commodities clearly played an important role in the decision on which commodities to include, but the decision was also influenced by and had an influence on bargaining strategies. As such, I will defer discussion of most aspects of the commodity coverage issue until the next chapter. But one aspect of the issue—which commodities were reasonable candidates for stocking—intersects so saliently with the Common Fund issue that some discussion is necessary.

Almost anything can be stockpiled, but whether it makes sense to do so in financial terms depends on a very complex mixture of factors. Storage costs, interest costs, the drift of prices, the agreed price margins, the nature of the business cycle, and the effectiveness of supply control can exert some influence on the financial viability of a stock.[43] Many of these variables can only be very loosely estimated on the basis of recent experience, and for one important variable—storage costs—experience was limited and the uncertainties (for example, where the stocks were to be kept) were difficult to

[43] There is a good discussion of these issues in UNCTAD, *A Common Fund for the Financing of Commodity Stocks: Amounts, Terms and Prospective Sources of Finance* (Geneva: TD/B/C.1/184), June 1975, pp. 9-15. World Bank studies suggest a rate of return on stocks of about 7-8 percent a year, probably too low to attract outside investors. But the economic rate of return may be higher than the financial rate. See Singh, "The International Dialogue on Commodities," p. 80.

eliminate. Nevertheless, UNCTAD arrived at a list of ten "core" commodities (from wider lists that variously included seventeen or more commodities) that met all of its conditions.[44] Initially (in December 1974) UNCTAD seemed to argue that all the commodities on its list (not just the core commodities) were going to be stocked: "The proposed programme embraces the establishment of international stocking arrangements for most commodities of significance to developing countries."[45] Under pressure and as a result of further research the list was cut to ten (coffee, cocoa, tea, sugar, copper, tin, rubber, cotton, jute, sisal), and UNCTAD documents gradually began to emphasize that stocking was only one element of the IPC. For these ten, however, stocking was clearly envisaged as the primary mechanism by which prices were to be stabilized and strengthened.

A number of developed countries as well as several independent analysts were very doubtful that all of the core commodities could or should be stocked. Most of the governments kept their doubts private, preferring to settle the issue when individual commodity negotiations began. But some examination of their positions has been made possible by inference from public comments and particular actions (for example, participation in existing agreements such as the tin and sugar agreements that included buffer stocks) or from private discussions and official papers that "somehow" got into general circulation.

An internal World Bank paper suggested that five commodities were suitable for stocking (coffee, cocoa, copper, tin, rubber) and five others were possible candidates (sugar, tea, cotton, jute, sisal)—in effect the UNCTAD list with some qualifications added. OECD experts were in general agreement with the World Bank. The EEC Commission was doubtful about jute, hard fibres, tea, and rubber.[46] The United States shared these doubts and had additional doubts about cotton.

---

[44] The political aspects of this list will be discussed in the next chapter.

[45] UNCTAD, *An Integrated Program for Commodities* (TD/B/C.1/166), p. 9.

[46] See Michael Sakellaropoulo, *The Controversy on Commodities: The Present and Prospects for the Future* (Geneva: Center for Research on International Institutions, 1976), pp. 19-20.

Conversely, two World Bank economists suggested that storage costs would be too high to justify stocks in coffee, cocoa, tea, and sugar.[47] McNicol, however, believed stocks might be viable for cotton, sugar, jute, sisal, and rubber but not for metals like copper and tin.[48] In sum, there were serious disagreements among the outside experts, disagreements that reflected different judgments about costs, about the necessary size of various stocks, about the effects of stocks on the market, and about the availability of other measures of stabilization. None of these differences could be resolved before the fact, but they are worth noting for they had an important effect on judgments about the potential benefits and the potential dangers of the Common Fund.

However many buffer stocks were finally established, financing was bound to be a problem, especially if the full burden were left to fall on developing country producers. Indeed, UNCTAD officials argued strenuously that only a *prior* guarantee that sufficient financing would be available—a guarantee that necessarily implied consumer contributions—would avoid the haggling and cheating and uncertainties that had undermined previous efforts to construct effective buffer stock facilities. As I have already noted, while there is no conclusive way to verify or refute this proposition, there is little doubt that the confidence generated by the assurance of financing could be a very valuable asset. In any case, whether financing was *the* key question or only *a* key question, the issue of how it was to be provided was very critical.

Consumers had only rarely agreed to contribute to buffer stock financing in the past, since only producer interests seemed to be at stake. If consumers were now to agree that stocking could contribute to stabilization and that stabilization reflected *mutual* interests, a commitment to shared financing

---

[47] Ernest Stern and Wouter Tims, "The Relative Bargaining Strengths of the Developing Countries," in *Changing Resource Problems of the Fourth World*, ed. Ronald G. Ridker (Washington, D.C.: Resources for the Future, 1976), pp. 28-30. The Bank report noted earlier in the paragraph is by different authors.

[48] McNicol, *Commodity Agreements and the New International Economic Order*, p. 112f.

might have seemed equitable and wise. For example, a consumer guarantee that no buffer stock that producers and consumers had jointly agreed to establish would fail because of insufficient finance might have deflected the Common Fund debate into less conflictive channels: the key question would (or might) have become whether sufficient financing would be available, not whether it could only be provided by a particular mechanism, the Common Fund. The more conservative developed countries (the United States, Japan, West Germany, the United Kingdom) were unwilling, however, to go even this far. It needs to be emphasized, nevertheless, that UNCTAD and the Group of 77 might have rejected even this offer (although there were numerous countries in both groups who favored it) because of an insistence that financing had to be provided through the creation of the Common Fund. Moreover, commitment to the Common Fund had to precede both the individual commodity negotiations that would determine whether or not to establish a buffer stock and the detailed negotiations that would determine what the form, the financing, and the powers of the Common Fund would be. That is, the commitment had to precede proof that creation of the Fund was necessary or wise.

The major objective of the IPC was price stabilization, and buffer stocks were presumed to provide the primary mechanism of stabilization. The Common Fund itself, however, has little to do with stabilization beyond assuring sufficient financing for the stocks. The point is that the effectiveness of buffer stocks was really the key issue, but that a specific means of financing them became virtually the *only* issue in the commodity negotiations. This is not to argue that the Common Fund was irrelevant or an inferior means of financing, for it *might* well be an effective and influential part of a new commodity order; but it is to suggest that the strategies pursued by both sides were questionable, a point addressed in detail in Chapter 4. Here I want to analyze some of the technical and quasi-technical issues that arose during the discussions of the Common Fund.

The Common Fund was to be financed by contributions

from governments (according to a formula to be devised) and by borrowing from other lending institutions or governments (that is, the OPEC countries).[49] The Fund was envisaged as a source of finance for the individual commodity organizations, not merely as a pool of the resources collected by those organizations. The ownership of the actual stocks and the decision on whether and when to buy or sell would remain with each commodity organization.[50] The Fund was thus not perceived as an operational organization but primarily as a lending and a facilitating organization.

As the UNCTAD staff argued, the Common Fund seemed likely to generate a number of financial savings. In comparison to the cost of financing each buffer stock separately, there could be offset savings, since the purchase of stocks that needed to be supported could be financed by the sale of other stocks whose prices were at the ceiling.[51] Better borrowing terms might also be available to the Fund and, insofar as the stocks could be operated to show an acceptable rate of return,

---

[49] The Fund is discussed in many documents. An early effort that laid out many of the issues is UNCTAD's *A Common Fund for the Financing of Commodity Stocks: Amounts, Terms and Prospective Sources of Finance* (TD/BC.1/184). After Nairobi the staff's version of the Common Fund became somewhat more restrictive, a point to which we shall return in Chapter 4.

[50] Ibid. See also UNCTAD, *A Common Fund for the Financing of Commodity Stocks* (Geneva: TD/B/C.1/196), October 1975.

[51] Except for the years 1973-1975 stocks had moved in an offsetting manner, thus supporting UNCTAD's argument. In the latter period there would have been no unused funds available to buy the depressed commodities: that is, all were moving in the same direction. *If* this were the new pattern and stocks were to move in a common cycle (and not in an offsetting cycle), what would happen? The answer is that the IPC would be in severe difficulty, probably collapsing if prices were to move upward in common. If they were to move downward in common, supply controls can and must be instituted by individual commodity organizations. In any case, one cannot sensibly provide insurance against all possible disasters, and some judgments of probability are necessary. Still, if interlocking business cycles and other aspects of rising interdependence were to mean consistently symmetrical price movements, the whole commodity package might have to be rethought, especially in relation to judgments about necessary amounts of finance. There are only opinions on this matter, but UNCTAD may be excessively optimistic in its contention that the 1973-1975 pattern is not likely to be sustained.

new sources of financing might see the Fund as an attractive investment vehicle. The availability of sufficient financing might also discourage speculators.

The potential for savings was surely there, but there was some disagreement about whether the savings would be as large as foreseen or even realized at all. For example, the fewer the number of commodities stocked, the less likely that offset savings from divergent price movements would be achieved, and there were sharp disagreements between UNCTAD and many developed countries on the number of stockable commodities. There were also substantial doubts that all of the commodities that could be stocked would join the Common Fund, since commodities doing well without the Fund might not see the need or the advantage of joint efforts with weaker commodities. There were also a number of independent estimates of the costs of the stocks that were considerably higher than UNCTAD's, in part because of different judgments about the level of stocks that could be conceived as an adequate safeguard.[52] Since higher costs meant smaller profits, the attractiveness of the Fund as an investment vehicle might be compromised. These and similar uncertainties were irresolvable before the fact, and the debate was inevitably inconclusive. This was not especially debilitating since no one disputed that the potential for savings was there—that UNCTAD might be right. But there were very few in Group B who thought that this was the real reason UNCTAD and the Group of 77 were so intent on establishing a Common Fund.

UNCTAD also argued that the Common Fund would have a very important catalytic function in stimulating other commodity agreements. With financing assured, poor and weak governments would presumably be willing to make the necessary commitments to a commodity agreement that otherwise seemed imprudent or problematic. If the catalytic function were limited to the core commodities for which buffer stocks (arguably) seemed to make sense, no problem arose. But if the Fund were to be a catalyst for agreements on *other* com-

---

[52] See Laursen, "The Integrated Program for Commodities," p. 13.

modities—as it seemed to be argued in various documents—
and if the purpose of the Fund were to finance stocks, the
catalytic function was bound to be controversial. There were
simply not that many other commodities of interest to the
Third World for which buffer stocking could be justified. As a
result, the developed countries feared that the prior availability of financing (before it had been determined in individual
negotiations that a buffer stock should be established) would
generate unnecessary or uneconomic buffer stocks.[53]

Suspicions about exactly what would be catalyzed also
exacerbated another disagreement. UNCTAD's documents
were ambiguous about the purposes for which the financial
resources of the Fund could be employed. The primary purpose was buffer stock funding, but whether available resources or some part of them could also be used for other
activities was a question—so UNCTAD said—that the governments themselves would have to decide. The answer was
clear, however, to many members of the Group of 77, in particular those with commodities that could not be stocked: they
wanted the Fund to finance a whole range of "other measures," including diversification, research, national stocks, and
price support.

The possibility that the Fund would finance these activities
became increasingly controversial after Nairobi (it was less
controversial before because it was not clear that there would
be a Fund to finance anything). The developed countries did
not want to turn the Fund into another aid mechanism, especially since most of the suggested other measures were already being financed elsewhere. Moreover, a lack of clarity
about how the Fund's resources would be used might
threaten its financial integrity and diminish its attractiveness

[53] See J. Robert Vastine, "United States International Commodity Policy,"
Law and Policy in International Business 9, no. 2 (1977): 462. The fear seems
somewhat excessive in view of the fact that the consumers would also have to
agree to the stocks (unless the producers dominated the Common Fund's decision making, an unlikely outcome since each group would presumably have
a veto). Still, the Treasury and other conservative opponents of the Common
Fund were worried about both the "salami" tactics of the developing
countries and the lack of will to resist such tactics here and elsewhere—
especially if less "tough" administrations were to fail to keep the faith.

as an investment vehicle, a point with which a number of developing countries agreed (but not, of course, those who would receive help). Another question about how the Fund's resources would be used reflected uncertainties about the willingness of governments to see their own contributions to the Fund expended in efforts to support one or two stocks that might be falling sharply. If the commodity that needed support were especially costly (for example, copper), the Common Fund might run out of money—*everyone's* money—and the other commodities whose contributions had now been spent could not be supported if their prices were also to begin falling. Limiting the amount that could be spent in support of any single commodity was an obvious solution, but UNCTAD was reluctant to set limits to the extent of intervention for individual commodities for fear that it would encourage speculative activity as the limits were approached.[54] There was also the danger that producer discipline would be reduced by awareness of the large sums available to buy stocks—in effect, that production for the stock, not the market, would be encouraged.

The other important benefit of the Common Fund was more explicitly one-sided: improvement of the bargaining power of the developing countries in commodity trade. A few producers in an individual commodity agreement had very little leverage against powerful consumers, especially when the latter tended to control processing, distribution, and marketing. By gaining an important share of the responsibility for operating the Common Fund, however, the developing countries would not only be guaranteed a substantial new

[54] In effect, it was necessary to balance the threat to the Fund's liquidity (from not setting limits) against the threat of speculative activity. Dropping the buying price for a commodity that was using up too much of the Fund's resources might reduce the problem—*if* agreement to do so could be gained from the producers. Limiting the amount the Fund could spend on a single commodity would also mean that the Fund would only pool individual finances and not serve as a general source of finance. This would considerably reduce both the savings of the Fund and its potential power to act—which may explain why the pooling versus the central source financing issue became so prominent after the Carter administration accepted the idea of "a" common fund. I shall discuss this in the next chapter.

source of financing but would be able to group together all of the producers in an effort to establish new principles and procedures. How important a greater voice for the developing countries in the operation of the Common Fund would be depended, of course, on the voting and decision-making structure of the Fund and on what role the Fund was allowed to play. The voting and decision-making structure could not be settled before detailed negotiations, which is one reason why the developed countries were reluctant to make a commitment before they knew what it meant. What role the Fund would play could also be settled only in negotiations, but some judgments about what was intended could be extracted from documents and statements or inferred from estimates of what role the Fund would have to play for it to create major benefits for the developing countries. In an environment of distrust, ideological hostility, and genuine intellectual uncertainties the result was a mutual exchange of "worst-case" hypotheses.

The conservative developed countries were inevitably very suspicious about how the Common Fund would be operated. In part, these suspicions reflected significant doubts that the developing countries would be so obsessed with establishing a Common Fund if it were really to be limited to funding buffer stocks designed to stabilize commodity prices. The suspicions also reflected ambiguities in some UNCTAD documents, for other objectives occasionally received a good deal of emphasis: for example, supporting prices in weak markets, direct intervention by the Fund in markets where no commodity agreement existed, and financing various kinds of "other measures."[55] Moreover, since the relationship between individual commodity organizations and the Common Fund was unclear, the developed countries feared that the manager of the Fund would seek to influence the buffer stock manager to raise prices as a disguised resource transfer mechanism. There were also fears that the Common Fund would somehow be used to encourage the creation of commodity

[55] See UNCTAD, *Commodities* (TD/184), p. 9; and UNCTAD, *A Common Fund for the Financing of Commodity Stocks: Amounts, Terms and Prospective Sources of Finance* (TD/B/C.1/184), pp. 24-25.

agreements for commodities of little interest to the developed countries (that is, those for which they wanted the market to take its course) or for commodities with the wrong kind of technical characteristics. UNCTAD and the developing countries responded as if these suspicions, fears, and doubts were irrational or a disguise for narrow self-interest, but they never seemed to devise a strategy that took into account the reality of these attitudes, whatever their justification.

The arguments for and against the Common Fund were a complex mixture of hypothetical advantages and hypothetical disadvantages. Legitimate technical doubts that were widely shared by experts in the developed countries about the benefits from or the necessity of the Fund led Laursen to conclude that

> the Common Fund is more a political than an economic issue. For economic reasons it is relatively unimportant whether stocks are financed individually or in common.... The Common Fund has become a symbol of the Integrated Commodity Program, but economically it is neither a sufficient nor a necessary condition for its implementation.[56]

And political and ideological doubts led McNicol and others to assume that the real aim was the creation of an "International Department of Agriculture and Mines" to transfer resources to the developing countries.[57] Suspicion and distrust thus dominated the debate, and what should have been (and

[56] Laursen, "The Integrated Program for Commodities," p. 14. I should add that I believe Laursen may have understated the potential economic benefits from the Common Fund, for the confidence generated by the availability of sufficient finance may be more important than narrower issues of storage and interest costs, etc. In any case, there are also important political benefits implicit in the Common Fund debate not only in terms of commodity trade but also in reference to the Fund's symbolic importance in the North-South "dialogue." (See Chapter 4.) My primary interest here, however, has been in indicating the range of disagreement between UNCTAD and the various developed country governments and experts.

[57] McNicol, *Commodity Agreements and the New International Economic Order*, p. 7.

what could have been) a reasonably pragmatic and limited discussion of the potential utility of a new financing mechanism became a protracted ideological—and at times virtually metaphysical—confrontation over an institution invested with powers and effects it was never likely to develop or manifest. Why this happened will be discussed in Chapter 4. But the discussion thus far suggests some questions that will be worth keeping in mind. When doubts about the Common Fund were expressed, the UNCTAD directorate either dismissed them as ideologically inspired or insisted that details could only be spelled out in negotiations *after* the principles of the Common Fund were accepted. Neither answer was completely satisfactory. Not everyone who expressed doubts or reservations was a free market ideologue, and not all the issues raised (especially those dealing with goals and powers) were beyond useful clarification *before* a commitment was granted. We shall be concerned not only with why clarification was considered either unnecessary or dangerous but also with the influence that political and institutional constraints had on these decisions.

Another issue ought to be kept in mind throughout the discussion of bargaining strategies. The UNCTAD staff had written that the Common Fund proposals were not a blueprint but a "set of concepts for discussion and judgment."[58] Secretary-General Corea had himself declared that "it is difficult to define exactly the contribution the Common Fund can make, but intuitively I feel that if it is set up it will be pivotal."[59] But how did the entire North-South dialogue come to be dominated for nearly three years by the Secretary-General's intuition about a "set of concepts" that might or might not yield significant benefits to the developing countries? How did it come about that the fate of the IPC came to rest upon the fate of one of its components? And what kind of political process is it that rests upon the need to compel democratic governments to make hard commitments, financial,

[58] UNCTAD, *Report of the Committee on Commodities on the Third Part of the Eighth Session* (Geneva: TD/B/C.1 [viii]/Misc. 9), December 1975, p. 11.
[59] Quoted in *African Development*, May 1976, p. 487.

economic, and political, to an entity whose costs, powers, and potential benefits were matters only of surmise?[60]

Finally, an important theme runs through the discussion of technical issues. The critics pointed to difficulties, to uncertainties, to past failures. They were surely correct in doing so. But UNCTAD was gambling that one very critical change—active consumer support for commodity agreements—would overcome the deficiencies that had undermined earlier efforts to reorder or stabilize commodity trade. This was not an unreasonable gamble, for the alternatives to commodity agreements for *both* sides did not seem any less costly or difficult. The likelihood of eliciting strong consumer support—and thus the likelihood of a successful outcome—would have increased if both sides had interpreted the need for change (and the amount of change) in the same manner. But judgments and intuitions differed. Since UNCTAD and the Group of 77 could not compel the industrial countries to accept their views, a strategy of persuasion was necessary. And here, as we shall see, the imperatives of maintaining unity and operating the bargaining system within UNCTAD tended to conflict with the imperatives implicit in a strategy of persuasion. Rigidity at one level inhibited compromise at the other; or compromise on one level threatened disunity at the other.

Before turning to the bargaining process, I want to comment briefly on three other techniques of the IPC. All are complex and potentially important, but I am interested here only in the perspective they provide on the central conflict over the Common Fund.

Multilateral long-term commitments involving an agreed amount of trade at a target price were meant to be another

---

[60] As an illustration, more than three years after the discussions had begun a spokesman for the Group of 77 noted that "the entire international community now agrees that a Common Fund should be established and we can *now* set about negotiating its objectives and purposes as well as its other constituent elements" (italics added). In other words, no one knew what they had agreed to negotiate. For the statement, see UNCTAD *Press Release* (Geneva: Information Service, TAD/INF/895), 7 November 1977.

element of stability. The exporter would be guaranteed access to markets, and the importer would be guaranteed an agreed supply of the commodity. Buffer stocks would still be necessary (where feasible) to ensure that contractual obligations would be met (the importer buying from the stock when the exporter could not deliver, the stock manager buying from the exporter when the importer reneged) and in cases where excessive instability or a declining price trend made long-term contracts problematic. Nevertheless, multilateral commitments never became a major issue in the debate. Some developed countries such as the United States and West Germany argued that they could not compel their importers to accept such commitments, although it should be noted that the economic and legal difficulties had been surmounted in a few cases (for example, the U.S.-Soviet grain agreement and the new sugar agreement). In any event, from UNCTAD's point of view multilateral contracts were bound to be a subsidiary element of the IPC: such contracts are primarily only stabilization devices, and they cannot easily be used to strengthen prices.[61]

Compensatory finance is designed to provide automatic compensation when earnings from exports fall below an agreed level. Even with buffer stocks, shortfalls in earnings are still possible because of natural disasters or other non-economic factors (such as wars). Shortfalls are also possible for commodities not included in the IPC or for commodities facing a persistent decline in prices. The potential benefits of compensatory finance are widely accepted, although there are disagreements in detail over access to the funding facility and the requisite funding level. What was especially interesting in the IPC debates was the extent to which attitudes toward compensatory finance reflected fundamental differences in perspective toward changes in commodity trade. Both the United States and the EEC Commission were in favor of compensatory finance, and they viewed it as a substitute for the creation of large numbers of buffer stocks and a

---

[61] There are also some doubts about the likely stabilization benefits, as the contracts may force increased speculative activity in the part of the market not controlled by specific commitments.

Common Fund.[62] Ex post facto payments for shortfalls did not involve any prior market intervention and did not threaten to raise price trends significantly. Compensatory finance was thus the kind of short-term reform measure acceptable to countries that did not want (or could not see how to accomplish) a major restructuring of commodity trade. Conversely, for the developing countries compensatory finance could never be more than a supplementary measure—albeit an important one in many cases—for it did very little to help countries with weak commodities to diversify or to increase earnings. Moreover, it left the existing power relationship between producers and consumers intact.

As I have already noted, indexation seeks to preserve the purchasing power of developing country exports by linking ("indexing") them to the prices of their imports. The runaway inflation of the 1970s has created pressures to protect countries that have been most grievously injured by the decline in what their exports can buy. The desire to maintain real prices in the face of inflation is understandable, but there are extraordinary technical and political anomalies in seeking to do so by indexation. The difficulties of devising an acceptable index (of what exports by what countries to weigh against what imports by what countries) are widely recognized, and even the principle that export purchasing power must be automatically preserved is not everywhere accepted.[63] Beyond this, the wisdom of indexing commodity prices now, when

[62] The EEC was particularly attached to the idea of extending the compensatory finance scheme (called "Stabex") that it had devised for its former colonial possessions to the rest of the developing world. See Sakellaropoulo, *The Controversy on Commodities*, p. 18. Although Stabex had a number of shortcomings (especially in amounts of financing), it was a considerable improvement on the IMF's compensatory financing facility in several ways. For a discussion of the elements of Stabex, see Bishnodat Persaud, "Export Earnings from Commodities: Export Stabilisation in the Lomé Convention," in *The Lomé Convention and a New International Economic Order*, ed. F.A.M. Alting von Geusau (Leyden: A. W. Sijthoff, 1977), pp. 81-90.

[63] For an excellent study of all the technical problems, see UNCTAD, *Preservation of the Purchasing Power of Developing Countries' Exports* (Geneva: TD/184/Supp. 2), May 1976. See J.D.A. Cuddy, *International Price Indexation* (Farborough, Hants: D.C. Heath, LTD., 1976) for a detailed analysis.

such prices may be on the rise, has been questioned by a number of observers—including several from the developing countries.[64]

The developed countries have been virtually unanimous in rejecting indexation. They have argued that it will be inflationary (true only if the real terms of trade for commodities decline in the future), that it will encourage the search for substitutes for indexed commodities, that it will be inequitable to many developing countries (the resource-rich benefitting at the expense of the resource-poor), and that it might freeze the market in particular commodities and hinder diversification. Since indexation at current price ratios might begin to benefit *importers* of commodities, another factor behind the opposition of the developed countries should be noted: the strongest support for indexation came from the oil countries, and many of the developed countries (at this time) still hoped to see oil prices decline. As a surrogate measure, the developed countries have offered periodic review of previously negotiated price ranges, and this kind of nondirective measure may be a viable compromise. The UNCTAD staff was never very enthusiastic about indexation, fearing it would distract attention from more manageable or important issues, but they could never simply drop the issue because of pressures from the Group of 77 (especially from OPEC countries who assumed they would benefit, even if many other LDCs were to lose). This was not, as we shall see, the only time when the staff (or some part of the staff) and the developed coun-

[64] See Mahbub ul Haq, *The Poverty Curtain—Choices for the Third World* (New York: Columbia University Press, 1976), pp. 197-198; and Singh, "The International Dialogue on Commodities," p. 94. Haq makes the additional point that freezing present price relationships is illogical because the developing countries should be seeking to move out of exporting unprocessed raw materials into exporting processed goods. Indexation consequently could decrease incentives to industrialize. Thus, by freezing a price relationship that is still unfavorable to the developing countries (except for OPEC), indexation would diminish the likelihood of achieving the gains implicit in changing patterns of comparative advantage. In effect, indexation should be used to protect gains that have *already* been made by raising prices. One should also note that the gains would be eroded if the higher prices were to induce excess production.

tries were in tacit agreement, although lagging perceptions of changes in each other's views inhibited tacit—let alone open—alliances.

Some of the technical disputes that we have discussed could not have been resolved within the context of this negotiating process. Others might have been resolved or clarified, but the effort was not made either because of institutional constraints or because of political fears about the consequences. As a result, the political bargaining over the IPC (which shall be discussed in the next chapter) did not rest on widespread agreement about the expected range of probable benefits, about the workability of various proposals, or about the real goals of the negotiating process. On the contrary, each side felt that it had "won" the technical debate and that the other side disguised its "defeat" by appeal to ostensibly higher political or moral principles.

Two questions emerge from this discussion. The first concerns the effects of technical indeterminancy on a debate that focuses on questions of principle.[65] Since agreement would require some compromise of sharply conflicting principles—obviously an inordinately difficult task—would a more serious effort to confront technical disputes in the negotiating process have provided some common ground on which to build a compromise? For those who did not want a compromise agreement and for whom stalemate was the preferred outcome, the question is irrelevant; for those who did want an agreement, the question is very relevant. The second question concerns power and influence. Even if we can understand why the decision to focus on principles was made, the question still remains of who made the decision and why it could not be altered. The discussion in the next chapter will not provide definitive answers to these questions, but it will seek to provide at least provisional answers.

---

[65] There are analysts on both sides who believe that there was really no indeterminacy—that their technical arguments were superior. But I reemphasize that, while this may or may not be true in analytical terms, it is very clear that neither side had convinced the other, which was the key political fact.

Chapter 4

Commodity Bargaining

Background and Context

There have been five factors that significantly influenced the bargaining process over the IPC,[1] and in a narrow sense, the success or failure of a particular negotiation has usually been attributed to two of these factors.[2] The first is the skill of the bargainers. How competent are they, how dedicated and tireless, how persuasive in defending their own positions and undermining the position of their adversaries, how skilled in knowing just when and what to concede? Care has to be taken not to place too much emphasis on this factor because there are many additional factors that can affect the outcome of negotiations and because identifying the "winner" as skillful and the "loser" as bumbling may only create a tautology. In any case, the negotiators in Geneva were seldom free agents. Critical decisions were generally made at home and within each group; consequently, many of the group versus group confrontations were exercises in ritual and rhetoric, for each side, tightly bound by instructions, could only exchange manifestoes. This was particularly true as the date of the Nairobi Conference approached, for many of the developed countries did not want to make any concessions before then.

---

[1] There are many definitions of bargaining and negotiation. Here I shall use the terms more or less interchangeably to refer to a process the objective of which is to find a mutually acceptable compromise. This obviously implies the presence of both common and conflicting interests. For a similar definition, see Otomar J. Bartos, *Process and Outcome of Negotiations* (New York: Columbia University Press, 1974), p. 16.

[2] The two are briefly discussed in Edith Penrose, "Ownership and Control: Multinational Firms in Less Developed Countries," in *A World Divided: The Less Developed Countries in the International Economy*, ed. G. K. Helleiner (Cambridge: Cambridge University Press, 1976), pp. 147-174. The influence of bargaining skills is also discussed in a different North-South context in David N. Smith and Louis T. Wells, Jr., *Negotiating Third-World Mineral Agreements* (Cambridge: Ballinger, 1975).

Differences in the technical and analytical resources of the developed and developing countries were not, of course, completely irrelevant, but they were less decisive than they might have been, even in a negotiation with so many technical complexities. There were several reasons for this. In the first place, the Group of 77 could call upon the resources of the UNCTAD staff. Indeed, many of the papers of the Group were merely restatements of UNCTAD papers (and frequently virtually written by a staff member). In the second place, several of the developing countries (for example, India and Brazil) had very talented economists fully capable of analyzing the issues at stake, although they were not always present in Geneva (another factor that somewhat reinforced the tendency toward ritualistic confrontations). On the other hand, many developing countries lacked sufficient analytical resources, which frequently left definition of national interests in the hands of the staff—with some danger that as individual interests became clearer over time a backlash might develop against the staff's carefully created package. In the third place, since technical conflicts tended to be put off to the future and since the contentious issues tended to be political and ideological disputes over principles, analytical deficiencies were not critical. As a result of these factors, technical and political skills were actually most important in the bargaining process within the Group of 77 itself: here an unusual individual with some technical competence and a willingness to do his homework could exert a great deal of influence. This was particularly true if the individual were to also represent one of the "key" countries within the Group (for example, Brazil, India, Iran), but the road to influence was also open to delegates from the less powerful countries (for example, Jamaica or Tanzania).

A second factor that had a substantial impact on the bargaining process reflected the ratio between desire and need: How much does one side want what is at stake, and how willing is the other side to concede it? In a broad sense, what is at issue here is setting the boundaries wherein an agreement is likely to fall. The prevailing conventional wisdom is that this is a period in which mutual vulnerabilities rather than mutual strengths dominate calculations of relative power. In this sense, new perceptions of resource vulnerabilities presumably imply a better bargaining position for the possessors of resources—the bargaining terms of trade appear to have shifted. This calculation surely animated many of the decisions of UNCTAD and the Group of 77, and they clearly had some effect on even the most devoted defenders of the old order.

But this argument must not be carried too far. Thresholds of deprivation vary considerably: the fears of the industrial countries refer primarily to *future* shortages (except for oil), whereas the needs of the developing countries are immediate. Thus the need for quick agreement and for continuing transfers of resources tends to diminish the leverage provided by potential future increases in power. This is especially true because perceptions of whether resource vulnerabilities would exist or how significant they would be varied considerably in the developed countries. For conservative analysts and officials who believed that repetition of the oil "shock" was improbable, that the crisis was cyclical and not revolutionary, and that the price system would prevent supply shortages, arguments about the need to make concessions now to avert disasters in the future were regarded as "sentimental" or "soft."

As I have already noted, the OPEC threat might have swung the balance sharply toward the developing countries. But OPEC's position was never clear, and there was widespread skepticism among the developed countries (and many of the developing countries) that OPEC would actually provide funds to support an overt challenge (via producer cartels) to an international order from which it benefitted massively. Still, however improbable, the dangers and costs of such a challenge were so fundamental that they could never be completely discounted. And although no precise judgment about the strength of these conflicting perceptions and expectations is possible, the fact remains that many developing countries believed and virtually all acted as if they possessed a new weapon capable of compelling a new order, and the uncertainties and confusions of the developed countries did nothing to invalidate this judgment. Thus there is little doubt that the power of the developing countries to extract more favorable terms had surely risen.

A third factor with considerable influence on both the process and outcome of negotiations has been the intellectual and psychological climate. This has affected the set of assumptions and perceptions that influence notions of what "stands to reason" or what can be "taken for granted"; these, in turn, strongly influence the demands that are made or not made and the actions that seem wise and necessary or imprudent and excessive. This factor cannot always be directly extrapolated from words or actions, but must be inferred from judgments about what words or actions "really" mean or from close familiarity with the climate in which the negotiations took place. But despite the difficulties of precise documentation, the importance of this factor—perhaps even its preeminence—ought not to be underestimated.

I have already noted the significance of the OPEC phenomenon in altering perceptions to include a wider range of possibilities and in generating more willingness to bear some risks that were once seen as too high. More specifically, perceptions of a new resource universe and a shift in bargaining power also directly influenced strategic and tactical judgments. Thus the decision by UNCTAD and the Group of 77 to demand general commitment to a comprehensive program lacking in details would have been unlikely without the assumption that a revolutionary upheaval was in train. The perception of a new resource universe also led, however, to an inflation of expectations about how quickly changes could be instituted and how great the presumptive benefits would be, and it made it difficult to compromise initial demands. Too much had been promised and too much was expected for easy acceptance of lesser bargains.

The prevailing climate was also significant in another way: it was unstable. The initial decision to seek a major restructuring of commodity trade for the benefit of the developing countries was made in an environment of decision when much seemed possible; but the actual negotiations took place in a very different environment. Recession in the industrial countries, the limited benevolence of OPEC, and the increasingly desperate condition of many developing countries suffering from both the recession and the rise in oil (and food and fertilizer) prices sharply altered the calculus of bargaining strengths. The euphoria of the October 1973 war began to dissipate, and aspirations and expectations had to be adjusted. What is quite striking under these circumstances is not how difficult it was for UNCTAD to unite the Group of 77 but how well (and by what means) unity was maintained. The key here, however, is the effect of these developments on the major industrial countries: they were more confident that the new resource environment was transitory, and they were less able or less willing to make concessions that did not promise mutual benefits. In effect, the different interpretations of how much had been changed by recent events became increasingly disabling.

Another element in the intellectual climate was a rather general uncertainty about the validity of prevailing ideas. In a broad sense, the Keynesian conventional wisdom seemed to be producing too many unforeseen consequences or at least not enough foreseen consequences. More narrowly, there were also doubts about the wisdom of the IPC—not only technical doubts about price objectives and cost estimates but also doubts about a program that *might* freeze some countries into patterns of development that were unsatisfactory, or that paid insufficient attention to questions of domestic or international equity, or that concentrated too many of the Third World's energies and resources too exclusively on a single goal. The assumption that only enemies of the Third World questioned the UNCTAD strategy—a very comforting illusion for some of the UNCTAD hierarchy—was in fact dangerously simplistic. In any case, the various uncertainties tended to engender hesitation, delay, and a desire to reaffirm traditional pieties, all of which seriously threatened an effort to restructure the whole commodity order quickly and massively.

A fourth factor of significance has been—or ought to have been—the tacit learning process that goes on within any set of negotiations. Three years of constant discussion of the IPC should have presumably clarified and diminished some of the disagreements and made each side more aware of the other's concerns and of the true issues at stake. But the mystery at UNCTAD is why so little learning seemed to take place. Indeed, the same points that were unclear in the summer of 1974 were still unclear in the summer of 1977. Of course it is possible that learning may take place in a more subterranean fashion: new ideas may germinate slowly, and old ideas may be increasingly questioned in private, while the conventional wisdom is still defended publicly. Consequently, even immediate failures may be ascribed as successes in a long-term perspective. But in the negotiations evidence of such "invisible" progress was difficult to detect. Still, apart from the intrinsic difficulty of detection in any relatively short period of time, one needs also to remember that the commodity negotiations are an ongoing process—thus the shape of the "learning curve" may be very flat in the first year or so. This is especially so because tactical considerations (for example, the desire to avoid admitting an early decision was in error) might have encouraged either or both sides to obscure what they had learned until a more propitious moment.

This hypothesis should not be permitted to generate excessive optimism about future prospects, however. I note this because it is my own judgment that little of this learning has actually taken place, perhaps because ideological commitments encourage rigidity or perhaps because each side is so concerned with its own problems that little attention has been paid to what the other side is saying or to the need to educate the other side. In addition, whatever learning has occurred may well be in respect to the wrong things: the lessons are likely to relate to tactics or to details but not to the need to build for the future or to question where the bargaining process is going and how it might be improved. But of course these are personal and unverifiable judgments—at least for the next few years—and they do not have great significance for the period that is to concern us here.

The UNCTAD Setting

The institutions wherein negotiations occur do not always exert either an independent or a significant effect on what transpires. The tendency to ignore or de-emphasize the role of the setting is particularly strong with respect to the UN system: the record of impotence and inefficiency seems to justify the image of the United Nations as a "theatre of the absurd" or a minor bit player in a larger drama. This image needs to be adjusted for North-South issues, however, for form, substance, and outcome all reflect to some important degree the locus of confrontation. This is not to say that the UN is less affected by inefficiency or by meaningless (and oftentimes cynical) rhetoric on North-South issues; rather, it is to argue that the charge of impotence is no longer completely true. Also, this clearly implies that while this is primarily a book about North-South bargaining, it is additionally a book about the institutions that provide the setting for bargaining.

At this point I want briefly to note several reasons why the UNCTAD setting has been significant, some of which have already been mentioned. Although I shall discuss institutional issues at greater length in Chapters 5 and 6, it does not seem premature to emphasize the need to be alert to this dimension of the conflict. Unhappiness with the performance of the UN system on North-South issues has led to a number of efforts to seek alternate institutional processes and settings—and even a "proliferation" of institutions—and to devise a more effective institutional strategy for the developed countries. The material that follows ought to be considered in these efforts.

The primary reason why the UNCTAD setting was important is that the IPC was an UNCTAD staff creation. The Secretary-General and the staff became independent actors in the negotiating process with a central role in defending the IPC and keeping waverers in line. Moreover, the particular characteristics and abilities of the staff also affected the form and content of the IPC. A limited number of qualified staff as well as the absence of staff intimately familiar with specific commodity markets tended to strain the capacity of the staff to prepare for all likely responses and to generate an approach based on very broad and general principles. UNCTAD also had institutional interests of its own to defend and promote not only because the failures of UNCTAD-II and UNCTAD-III generated a need for a success but also because the IPC itself—if accepted—would give UNCTAD a central role in commodity negotiations and perhaps ultimately in other negotiations. But as we shall see, it should not be supposed that the staff's dominant role is either risk-free or without costs of its own. The inevitable adversary relationship with the developed countries from whom concessions must be extracted is bound to be exacerbated, charges of bias and incompetence are likely to be raised, and the failure to produce all that is promised and expected may gradually antagonize the staff's natural constituency in the Group of 77. In sum, the staff is powerful and influential, but it is a derivative power and influence.[3]

The UNCTAD setting was also important because of the way in which the process of decision is structured within the organization. The group system (about which much more will be said) seems the only alternative to chaos in an organization with over one hundred and fifty members. But the groups themselves each contained so many countries at different levels of development and with divergent or even conflicting interests that group positions tended to be shopping lists that merely lumped everyone's demands together.[4] Negotiations between the groups are extraordinarily difficult, for compromise usually seems to threaten to unravel one or the other side's package. Symbolic and rhetorical exchanges and demands for the acceptance of new principles and new rules are substituted for hard bargaining over narrower and more soluble issues. The costs and dangers of this decision-making system—or nondecision-making system—will be addressed later, but the critical question is not whether the system can be eliminated (for it cannot and probably should not be) but whether it can be improved and adapted and whether reforms of UNCTAD itself can facilitate more productive and timely decisions.

---

[3] I will discuss the staff role in detail in the next chapter. Here I mean only to emphasize that the staff had a strong political role as well as its usual technical role, but that it was less capable in the former than the latter.

[4] I refer here primarily to the Group of 77. Obviously China or the socialist countries did not have the same problems in putting together a list of common demands.

The five factors that we previously discussed came together to form a very unique kind of bargaining environment. I shall illustrate this by examining the three most important bargaining relationships: the relationship between the UNCTAD staff and the Group of 77; the relationships within Group B; and the relationship between Group B and the Group of 77.[5] In the section that discusses the latter relationship an attempt will be made to put some of the pieces together, particularly from the point of view of the developed countries. An ensuing section will discuss the strategy and tactics of UNCTAD and the Group of 77 and offer some comments on the difficulties of bargaining between unequal partners in an unsettled environment. Throughout I shall be concerned not only with analyzing the position each side adopted but also with why they did so and with what effect it had on the other side. A final section will briefly compare the IPC negotiations with a number of other North-South negotiations.

UNCTAD and the Group of 77

The commodity coverage of the IPC had been designed "so that the special interest of countries in some commodities could be an incentive to them to reach agreement on others."[6] The Secretary-General and the staff were well aware of the need to incorporate into the program enough commodities to provide a strong incentive toward widespread and continuing support. Indeed, trading-off different interests was imperative, since there was no possibility of devising a program in which all developing countries benefitted and none lost. In addition, the intention of creating a package that included

[5] There are a number of bargaining relationships at UNCTAD that I shall not examine. China and the socialist countries did not play an important role in these negotiations, and it would be useful to analyze why this is so. But limitations of space and knowledge preclude an effective treatment. I also shall not examine bargaining within the UNCTAD bureaucracy, an interesting topic since many divisions resented the prominence given to the commodity issue. This did not, however, greatly affect the process itself, for there was little the other divisions could do about it.

[6] UNCTAD, *An Integrated Program for Commodities* (Geneva: TD/B/C.1/166), December 1974, p. 3.

both strong and weak commodities was clear, presumably in the hope that the developed countries' interest in agreements on the strong commodities would induce them to accept agreements of less interest in the weak commodities. Finally, the commodities included had to be those of primary interest to the developing countries, a complex problem since many commodities exported by the developing countries were also exported by the developed countries.[7]

There was no great mystery in discovering who the potential dissenters might be, but what to do about them was another matter.[8] Since the developing countries exported about 75 percent of the total exports of the ten core commodities, the critical problem initially was what to do about developing countries that were also substantial importers of these commodities.[9] In general, the developing countries imported only about 12 percent of the core commodities, and the imports were not too highly concentrated, so the problem did not seem insuperable. Moreover, eighty of one hundred developing countries in one UNCTAD study were net exporters of the relevant commodities, and for sixty of the eighty countries the value of their exports of these commodities was three times the value of their imports of the

[7] This meant that some developed countries were also going to be major beneficiaries of the IPC and that some commodities of great importance to particular developing countries could not be included because the largest exporters were developed countries (for example, Argentina with beef and wheat).

[8] One thing to do was not to tell them if they did not already know. Statements on impact were thus de-emphasized. One impact analysis prepared by the staff was inadvertently published in an UNCTAD document written for the information bureau. The analysis created substantial problems because it revealed over forty developing countries with negative balances in the key commodities. See the Annex in Helen O'Neill, *A Common Interest in a Common Fund* (New York: United Nations, 1977). I have not reproduced the chart summarizing the analysis because it was an early and not very good piece of work. It does indicate, however, the level at which the Information Office functioned.

[9] Coffee, cocoa, tea, rubber, jute, and hard fibres were exported only by developing countries. It should be noted that if the core list were extended, more of the benefits went to the developed countries. Thus the wider the commodity coverage, the more that gains and losses tended to cross bloc lines.

same commodities.[10] But there were still problems, for twenty countries were obviously net importers of these commodities, and other countries that were net exporters had other fears that needed to be allayed.

Most of the twenty net importers were compensated by other commodity exports (oil for Saudi Arabia, Iran, Iraq, Algeria, Libya, and Kuwait and phosphates for Morocco and Jordan), or were major exporters of manufactures (South Korea, Singapore, Yugoslavia), or relied on earnings from invisibles (Lebanon and the Bahamas). The remaining seven were very small and underdeveloped and would have to be compensated by differential measures in their favor (for example, special prices or compensatory payments).[11] Still, two points ought to be emphasized. First, of the thirteen net importers who were compensated by other exports, six were members of OPEC and three others were Arab countries (as was one of the remaining seven). Doing well with other exports was surely a form of compensation, even if UNCTAD had nothing to do with it, but the compensation would be even higher if they did not have to pay more for imports of the core commodities. This was another factor that cast some doubt on the likelihood of strong OPEC support for the IPC. At any rate, altruism would have to triumph over short-run calculations of interest, or potential future benefits would have to be valued very highly. Second, most of the net import deficits came from food imports. Sharp price increases for wheat, maize, and rice would be very costly not only to the net import losers but also to other countries that were net export gainers but particularly dependent on food imports (India, Bangladesh, Sri Lanka, Senegal, Upper Volta). These countries feared that higher prices for the core commodities would be quickly followed by higher food prices, wiping out

[10] These and earlier figures come from UNCTAD, *An Integrated Programme for Commodities: The Impact on Imports, Particularly of Developing Countries* (Geneva: TD/B/C.1/189), June 1975, pp. 9-12. The trade figures used were from the years 1970-1972. This study covers seventeen commodities of interest to the developing countries, not merely the ten core commodities. The seventeen included several food commodities, which is why there is a brief discussion of food import deficits in the next paragraph.

[11] See the table in Ibid., p. 12.

whatever gains might have resulted on the export side. Fears were exacerbated by some public discussions in the United States and elsewhere of using food exports as a "weapon" and by the absence of the key food commodities (except for sugar) from the core list because they were under the control of the United States, Canada, and Australia.

Import deficits in key commodities and potentially higher food prices were not the only reasons to fear defections. Countries with a growing manufacturing export sector that rested on imports of cheap raw materials (for example, India, South Korea, Singapore, Yugoslavia, Taiwan) could find themselves in severe difficulties. In any case, many developing countries are likely to become increasingly important importers of minerals (and perhaps some agricultural raw materials) in the years ahead, and the gains from stable or higher mineral prices will be limited to a handful of (mostly high income) developing countries.[12] Whereas these are exceedingly complex questions concerning who benefits now and who benefits later as the developing countries increasingly process more of their own commodities and develop a more sophisticated manufacturing sector, in this discussion it is my intention only to highlight an area of uncertainty that was rarely discussed seriously.[13]

There were also other potential defectors. For example, countries that already had preferential access to specific developed country markets were not happy to see the IPC's emphasis on generalized conditions of access: persistent conflicts between the Latin Americans and the Africans on this issue were always threatening to erupt into open warfare. Some countries that were already in commodity agreements or in a very strong position in a particular market were also worried

[12] Ernest Stern and Wouter Tims, "The Relative Bargaining Strengths of the Developing Countries," in *Changing Resource Problems of the Fourth World*, ed. Ronald G. Ridker (Washington, D.C.: Resources for the Future, 1976), pp. 35-38. Stern and Tims note that there are only ten LDCs for whom the major mineral exports (copper, bauxite, tin, manganese) are important, and most are high income LDCs.

[13] There were difficult technical problems implicit in clarifying this issue, but political fears about the divisive effects of clarification were probably more important.

about the effects of the IPC. These countries feared that stable or rising prices would lead to overproduction, conflicts over quotas, and depressed long-run prices, especially for agricultural commodities in which new producers could easily enter the market. In effect, those who were already doing well without the IPC were reluctant to create conditions that might generate new competitors or to see their contributions to the Common Fund used to support weaker commodities: they needed to be guaranteed that conditions after the IPC would be better than before, an issue not likely to trouble producers of weak commodities. Colombia's reservations to the commodity resolution at Nairobi illustrate the problem. According to the report of the Nairobi Conference that summarized the Colombian statement:

> any integrated program for commodities should specifically and unambiguously exclude commodities that were already governed by an existing agreement or one that was in the process of being ratified. . . . [Colombia] moreover, was not entirely convinced of the appropriateness of the common fund for financing commodities historically characterized by structural overproduction. . . . Colombia had not opposed the resolution, on the understanding that [at a later time] . . . it would be possible to argue the case for excluding coffee from the list.[14]

Colombia, no doubt, would be more enthusiastic if coffee prices were lower and if the notion of accepting a ceiling price were not—momentarily—so unappealing. Nevertheless, fears about new producers (or about being frozen out of a market by old producers) were not entirely specious.[15]

One last group of potential defectors needs to be noted. These were not countries that lost from the IPC but rather those that did not gain enough to guarantee a unified stance against a reasonably forthcoming compromise proposal. India, fearful of higher prices for food and raw material im-

---

[14] UNCTAD, *Report of the United Nations Conference on Trade and Development on its Fourth Session* (Geneva: TD/217), July 1976, pp. 98-99.

[15] The entrance of a number of African countries into coffee and tea markets was illustrative. Brazil illustrates both cases, being fearful of new producers in its current exports but also fearing exclusion from a number of markets (for example, the iron ore market) that it hoped to enter in strength.

ports, was at the top of this list: the Indians, along with a number of other large countries (Pakistan, Mexico, Colombia, Argentina), had less than one third of their exports in the core commodities.[16] In addition, a large group of very poor developing countries were also likely to be affected in only a marginal fashion. Thus one unpublished study by a European government noted that

> with respect to raw materials, a mechanism controlling raw materials will benefit the least developed countries and the most severely affected countries [by the rise in prices] only in a limited manner; few among them produce and export raw materials in significant amounts.[17]

No international program provides equitable benefits to all the developing countries, and some, like the General System of Preferences, tend to benefit a relatively limited number of countries. The IPC was not an exception. In one sense this is not an important criticism, for it only suggests the need for a range of programs to help as many countries as possible, not rejection of programs that inevitably have a limited effect. In another sense, however, an important question of choice is implicit in this issue: If all or most programs were to have asymmetric patterns of benefits, which programs ought to have first priority? This makes the question of distribution—who gains what—more salient than it has usually been, for in a universe of scarce resources some care ought to be taken to insure that the gainers are countries that need help or deserve help or are the countries that the donors desire to help. But the distribution issue was virtually ignored at UNCTAD by *both* sides.

The major share of the benefits of the IPC seemed likely to go to a number of higher income developing countries that had the "correct" export-import profile and the ability to diversify and move into more "downstream" activities. Sub-Sahara Africa, India, and parts of Southeast Asia might lose

---

[16] See Jere R. Behrman, *International Commodity Agreements* (Washington, D.C.: Overseas Development Council, 1977), pp. 74f.

[17] This is my translation from the original, which appeared in a privately circulated document by a European government. Other studies, also unpublished, reached similar conclusions.

or not gain very much. In addition, if supply restrictions were also necessary, a number of the poorest countries might be hurt by prohibitions on entering the market; within each country, the poorest producers were also likely to be first injured and last recompensed. Higher prices, especially for food commodities, also hurt the poor who spend a larger share of their income on basic commodities. Moreover, the benefits were likely to go from individual (and relatively poor) consumers in the developed countries to individual (and relatively rich) producers in the developing countries. In effect, a reasonably good argument could be made that the international distribution of income would be worsened to the detriment of the poorer developing countries, favoring instead the richer developing countries, the well-off producers and workers within the developing countries, and the well-off consumers within the developed countries.[18]

None of this necessarily meant that the IPC should be rejected or that it was deliberately biased against the poor. The problems were in the nature of the commodity order, not in the IPC, and governments genuinely committed to development and equity could take measures to offset the less palatable distributional effects. But not paying any attention to these effects meant that some producers were likely to benefit unfairly, that some governments were not going to be encouraged to think about considerations of equity, and that the choice of programs on the international agenda would not reflect sufficient concern with an increasingly important issue. The conservative developed countries occasionally raised the issue, usually as part of the increasingly frequent charge that the whole trade and aid package benefitted the rich in the poor countries at the expense of the poor in the rich coun-

---

[18] There are many studies that have stressed the equity effects, but none are by UNCTAD staff. For one comment, see Thomas Balogh, "Failures in the Strategy against Poverty," *World Development* 6, no. 1 (January 1978): 14-15. Michael Lipton, *Why Poor People Stay Poor—Urban Bias in World Development* (Cambridge: Harvard University Press, 1977), argues that in agriculture, price stabilization usually leads to a decline in average farm prices and that only the big, rich farmers are likely to be compensated by increased sales volume. For the poor farmer, price stability may thus be bought at the price of a drop in earnings. See especially pp. 319-321.

tries. They did not really press the issue, however, perhaps for fear that increasing concern for distribution would lead to demands for more aid to diminish poverty (this was obviously before the Carter administration's brief and apparently ceremonial flirtation with a basic needs strategy). The developing countries did not raise the issue, perhaps in part because they did not understand it, or because even the losers had been promised benefits, or because the elites who dealt with these issues were not unhappy with prevailing patterns of distribution.

There were so many countries that might defect from full support for the IPC and there were so many signs that a few key countries (for example, India, Brazil, Colombia) would begin to seek private compromises that would be cumulatively disastrous that the unity of the Group of 77 was obviously fragile. India's tenuous support for the IPC had been made publicly clear as early as February 1975, and bitter fights between the Latin Americans and the Africans had been barely compromised at the Manila meeting of the Group of 77 in early 1976.[19] As was previously noted, what is surprising in these circumstances is how well the Group of 77 held together. No single explanation is adequate, but a number of critical factors undoubtedly played a role.

One ought not avoid the obvious. There were far more potential gainers than losers from the IPC, so the support of a solid majority was always assured. The potential losers were also promised compensation against losses, although how these remedial or differential measures would be implemented was never made clear. A deliberate decision by the UNCTAD directorate not to stress the differential effects of the program—that is, not to publish studies estimating possi-

[19] For the Indian statement, see UNCTAD, *Trade and Development Board, Committee on Commodities* (Geneva: TD/B/C.1/SR. 117-129), October 1975, pp. 72-73. The disagreements at Manila continued a prolonged conflict between the Latin Americans (accused of "Latinizing" Third World problems in the Prebisch and Perez-Guerrero eras at UNCTAD) and the less developed Afro-Asians.

ble gains and losses for individual countries—also may have been influential, for some small, technically unsophisticated countries simply took it on faith that they would benefit.[20] Conversely, some *very* sophisticated countries continued to support the program, despite strong reasons for opposition, because they felt that the developed countries would never accept it. Why, then, lose face by breaking ranks for something never destined to be implemented?[21]

The symbol of group unity was also used very effectively by the majority, for defectors would have to violate one of the Third World's most powerful norms. The developed countries persistently misunderstood the force behind the idea of unity. For example, American officials were frequently bitter about the fact that developing country diplomats sometimes said one thing in private and another in public. (There were even occasional discussions about how to force an end to this nefarious practice, which appeared to be acceptable only when the United States indulged. In any case, complete transparency in political relationships is an improbable and perhaps even a dangerous goal.) But this tactic, properly understood, was merely an illustration of vice paying homage to virtue: unity was so powerful a symbol that even countries fearful of the consequences were very reluctant to risk ostracism.

It needs to be emphasized, of course, that unity was sustained by more than symbolic pressures. Increased institutionalization of the Group of 77 was also very important. Constant meetings in Geneva and elsewhere were very effective in maintaining interest in an issue, in shaping a common position, in developing expertise—and in checking on potential defectors. Efforts were also made to harmonize policy positions with other groups such as the Nonaligned Movement (or the Group of 77 in New York), or even with influential private groups such as the Third World Forum. Coordination and cooperation were never perfect, but they were steadily

[20] This is one reason why the report quoted in footnote 9 of this chapter put further pressures on the unity of the Group of 77.

[21] I discovered this judgment in private discussions with a number of representatives from these countries.

improving, perhaps enough to justify a comment frequently made by the UNCTAD directorate: "You (the developed countries) can no longer hide from us by switching from arena to arena." Finally, another factor that facilitated the maintenance of unity (one to which I have already alluded) should be noted. Many developing countries lacked the technical capacity to deal with the issues or were simply indifferent to whatever transpired in Geneva. For these countries, it was always the course of least resistance to support whatever the Group supported.

There is also another side to this argument. The potential gains from the IPC might have seemed less attractive and unity might have been less compelling *if* the developed countries had countered with proposals that promised real benefits to the developing countries and seemed to reflect a commitment to make some necessary changes in commodity trade—not "the" or even "a" new international economic order but recognition that there were some aspects of the existing system that were unfair to the developing countries and other aspects that seemed unfair to all. But the conservative countries responded with hypocritical lectures about the market and reiteration of the need to try a case-by-case approach that had patently failed in the past. These lectures and speeches (whatever their rationale) were not a threat to developing country unity.

The potential for disintegration of unity was so high that it had a number of critical effects on the negotiating process. The most obvious, as I have already noted, was the stubborn insistence that agreement on general principles had to precede negotiation on the details that made clear what the principles meant: this was the only level of discourse at which all doubts could be easily suppressed. It was also the only level of discourse at which vague promises of compensation for all losses and inflated expectations of real benefits could be made without fear of refutation and disillusionment. Perhaps, too, the constant need for reassurance and re-emphasis with the Group of 77 was so preoccupying that neither the UNCTAD directorate nor the leadership of the Group had much time or inclination to worry about Group B and its interests.[22] Finally, many of the developed countries saw only the potential for defections and listened only to the private expressions of disagreement; as a result, they felt little need (never having the inclination) to offer more than cosmetic concessions. What one side saw as essential prevented it from compromising; what the other side saw as counterfeit prevented it from compromising.

In the beginning, the position of the UNCTAD staff and the Group of 77 was nearly identical. In public meetings the Group of 77 demanded acceptance of the whole IPC, and they insisted that doubts and reservations or requests for clarifications were ill-conceived efforts to maintain the old order. The spokesmen for the Group of 77 were only marginally more extreme than the UNCTAD staff itself, primarily because staff papers were still somewhat loose and had not been exposed to criticism. There was, of course, good reason for the Group of 77 to appear relatively more radical and demanding than the staff. The Group of 77, after all, had to carry on the formal negotiations with Group B. Consequently, some demands had to be made to be surrendered in the bargaining process—the "bargaining chip" argument again. A carrot also had to be kept dangling, and the most likely candidate was an agreement that guaranteed some kind of access to supply and an improved climate for long-term investment in resources. There was no discussion of these issues in the Manila Declaration, in part because of internal disagreements, but primarily because they were the concessions to be offered in exchange for acceptance of the IPC. The public stance that ensued and was maintained throughout the negotiations was thus very "hard": demands were made for

[22] I have already noted in the previous chapter the failure to stress issues like inflation and access to supply that were of prime importance to the developed countries. The theme of interdependence was also used in terms of the negative impact of external events on the developing countries, but only rarely in terms of the negative effect on developed countries of the loss of increasingly important Third World markets and the decline in investment in natural resources.

complete acceptance of the IPC, including indexation and an independent and powerful Common Fund, a refusal to debate specifics, and only implicit areas of concession. If the developed countries were to adopt a "soft" position in response, gains to the Group of 77 could be substantial; however, if they were to adopt a "hard" position, both would lose.[23]

The relationship between the staff and the Group of 77 did change over time. On the one hand, the staff position (or the position of *some* key staff members) became relatively more moderate, although more so in private than in public. This reflected two factors: a response to some justified criticisms of early work and a desire to see something salvaged from all the effort expended to put together a viable commodity program. The change was not limited to diminished support for controversial proposals like indexation; there was also willingness to accept a more limited Common Fund, more explicit emphasis on price stability and less on raising prices, and more concern with long-run issues such as diversification. These were the kinds of changes in detail that might have made acceptance of general principles more palatable—if they could have been openly discussed along the way.

Many countries in the Group of 77, especially the more radical, did not respond well to these changes. In fact, the Group of 77 remained more or less locked into its original position—a position that only benefitted the radicals in the Group of 77 and the reactionaries in Group B—for compromises seemed dangerous to unity. This began to create some tensions between the staff and its major constituency, but they were always a minor theme within a relationship that was generally close and supportive.[24] An open confrontation

[23] The distinction between "hard" and "soft" negotiating stances is stressed in a number of works. See, for example, Richard E. Walton and Robert B. McKersie, *A Behavioral Theory of Labor Negotiations* (New York: McGraw-Hill Book Company, 1965), pp. 6f.

[24] There was sharp disagreement within the UNCTAD bureaucracy about what seemed to many to be an excessive preoccupation with commodities and especially the Common Fund. There was even some dissent within the Commodities Division on the latter point, but it was silenced. The key point is that internal dissent was effectively contained by a number of factors: the salience of the commodity issue at the time, the Secretary-General's great personal in-

was unlikely because the staff changes could be analytically (and perhaps politically) justified and because Group B did not respond perceptively and continued to treat the staff as its prime enemy.

Bargaining Among the Rich
(and not so Rich)

There was a good deal of disagreement within Group B about the IPC, but the lines of disagreement did not exactly parallel the breakdown between potential winners and losers. For example, an UNCTAD study predicted that eight developed countries (the United States, Australia, Canada, South Africa, New Zealand, Sweden, Greece, and the Soviet Union) would have a favorable trade balance in the core commodities. But of these countries only Sweden was a strong supporter of the IPC, the United States was sharply opposed, Australia and Canada were ambivalent, the Soviet Union was hardly enthusiastic, and the rest kept a low profile. In general, the stockable commodities constituted less than 15 percent of total imports for the developed countries (except for Japan where the figure was 26 percent), and in most cases they were under 10 percent of the import bill. This suggested that the effects of the IPC probably could be absorbed relatively easily.[25] In any case, except for the Japanese, the effects were not likely to be heavily concentrated, and neither the costs nor the benefits in relation to the importance of commodity trade were likely to be profound for the great majority of developed countries. But that, of course, presumed that only price stabilization and not sharply higher prices was the end in view.

UNCTAD and the Group of 77 were constantly preoccupied with the range of disagreement in Group B and with the potential significance of public defections by a few countries. The spectrum of views within Group B was well-known: the United States, West Germany, Japan, and the United

---

volvement in the various decisions on commodities, and the fear of losing support and influence if internal disagreements led to open fighting.

[25] See UNCTAD, *An Integrated Programme for Commodities: The Impact on Imports, Particularly of Developing Countries* (TD/B/C.1/189), pp. 9-10.

Kingdom on the right; the Nordics and the Dutch on the left; and the rest scattered about, mute, or willing to accept whatever consensus emerged. These disagreements were less significant than they appeared to be, and the failure to understand why this was so undoubtedly contributed to the decision of UNCTAD and the Group of 77 to stand firm—always hoping, naively, that a defection would engender a cumulative process of commitment to the IPC, thus rendering unnecessary a dangerous process of concession and compromise.

The most important reason why internal Group B disagreements were not very important was that the economic weight of the United States and its allies was so overwhelming that what the dissidents chose to do or not do was hardly ever likely to be decisive. This self-evident fact also tended to generate a good deal of feeling within Group B that the Nordics and the Dutch (and the French, with a somewhat different practical position) were essentially "free riders," ingratiating themselves with the developing countries and pledging their support to the IPC only because they knew the pledge would never have to be redeemed.

Another reason why internal disagreements were not too critical is that they were not actually very widespread. Phrased another way, the economists in Group B shared a wide measure of agreement on many issues, and what disagreement there was tended to be political and ideological. For example, there was widely shared agreement among the technical people that indexation was unworkable, that only price stabilization made sense, that buffer stocks were not appropriate for all of UNCTAD's commodities, and that diversification and compensatory finance were probably the most important long-run measures.[26] Disagreement, however, centered on principles, on ideologies, on interpretations of intentions and of the future. These could not be resolved easily or perhaps at all. As a result, a defection or a disagreement could be dismissed as shortsighted, misguided, or naive; a cumulative effect on the rest of the group was always unlikely.

---

[26] I do not mean to suggest that there were no technical disagreements (for there were certainly some), but they were never significant at this stage of the conflict.

The disagreements within Group B were not decisive for another reason. The battle within and between the groups seemed to be taking place in Geneva, but the real decisions were not made there. Most of the delegates within Group B were tightly bound by instructions from their home governments. For the home governments, however, the issues at stake in Geneva were only one among many issues; they were not always or even usually priority issues—as they were for the developing countries. But the home governments were unwilling to risk a major fight with the very powerful conservative countries over what might be a transitory or minor issue, especially if they themselves were not likely to benefit from the IPC or a new commodity order. This meant that even some of the most enthusiastic supporters of the IPC such as the Dutch and the Swedes were more enthusiastic in Geneva than at home—the treasuries and the economic ministries in the capitals were frequently more cautious than the diplomats in Geneva. All of this sometimes lent an element of shadowboxing to the disagreements in Geneva.

A split among the conservative countries might have changed the complexion of the game considerably. A switch by either Japan or West Germany—potentially the two biggest losers—would have been especially significant. The Germans seemed immovable, however, and were the strongest defenders of the virtues of the market (despite the dominance of a Social Democratic government). The Japanese were properly inscrutable and seemed content to hide behind the American Treasury. Still, throughout the negotiations they were exposed to the heaviest pressures from the Group of 77, particularly to threats of isolation in the Far East. In any event, while they bent, they did not break.[27] As a result, the position of the United States dominated Group B discussions and was the major obstacle in the path of UNCTAD and the Group of 77.

[27] The Japanese did complain severely about the lack of consultation with the United States, especially in Nairobi. They were under the most severe pressure from the developing countries—who saw them as the weakest link among the hardliners—but were not receiving much support (or information about U.S. policies) from their allies. And in both a short- and a long-range perspective, the issue was far more critical for the Japanese.

Some part of the United States' position was ideologically inspired. But how much was ideology and how much was not is difficult to disentangle, and it varied with individuals, with different bureaucracies, with the play of events, and with the change in administrations. The UNCTAD leadership was not very sophisticated about these matters: by seeing primarily the ideological component of resistance, some opportunities to construct potentially useful alliances and to influence the tone and substance of the domestic debate during the Republican administrations were lost. In addition, too much change was foreseen from the election of a new Democratic administration.

The United States' position emphasized improving the market, compensatory finance, trade liberalization for Third World exports, and a case-by-case approach to negotiations. There was also concern for improving the conditions for private investment, and there was some desire to seek an agreement on supply access.[28] But what the United States did not want or what it feared was probably as important as what it wanted: there was a fear that advanced funding of the Common Fund would induce unwise buffer stocks and that the Fund would seek to intervene in markets to raise prices above the trend.[29] There was also a strong desire to avoid turning the IPC into a resource transfer mechanism—to avoid mixing together an effort to improve commodity trade with a disguised aid program.

There were great difficulties in finding a meeting point between this position and the position of UNCTAD and the

[28] For a discussion of the American position by a former Treasury official, see J. Robert Vastine, "United States International Commodity Policy," *Law and Policy in International Business* 9, no. 2 (1977): 422-443. The United States seemed to lose interest in the access to supply issue over time, perhaps because none of the core commodities were likely candidates for withholding supplies. Still, I think this was a mistake, for the issue had wider long-term implications (for example, in keeping the problem of sufficient investment in resources high on the *joint* agenda). Also, it was a useful "bargaining chip" in the sense that having something to ask for (as distinct from merely reducing Third World demands) may be useful in slowing down the demand-response-new-demand process. For further comment, see Chapter 5.

[29] Ibid., p. 462.

Group of 77. As I have already noted, disagreements about whether the crises were cyclical or part of a world order transformation complicated matters, as did a general distrust (and dislike) that pervaded the atmosphere. The fact that the United States was in the midst of an election campaign, that the President and the leadership of Treasury and the Council of Economic Advisers were simplistic free-market ideologues, and that the recession made it even more difficult to get measures through Congress that favored the Third World did not improve the prospects for agreement. Similarly disruptive was the belief that the end of the recession would engender a recovery that pulled the developing countries along in its wake, diminishing demands for a new order and a comprehensive commodity program.

The negotiating atmosphere changed markedly with the arrival of the Carter administration. The desire of the leadership of the new administration to be more forthcoming with the Third World was apparent. Although I shall discuss this change in the next section, here I want to emphasize that the technical and political issues still had to be resolved and that too little effort had been expended to do so in the previous years. The problems of creating a new commodity order were not eliminated by the departure of the Ford administration (that is, by the election of an administration with that magical property "will"): some of the ideological and psychological obstacles had been considerably diminished, but the technical and political barriers were as strong as ever. Moreover, many of the strongest advocates of a "tough" line in the previous administration were still in influential positions in the new administration and were still content to argue that concessions were unwise and that the Group of 77 would soon fall apart.[30]

The European Economic Community had great difficulty

---

[30] This was a persistent theme in private discussions: the LDCs would "blink first," and OPEC would not offer much but soothing words. The tendency of some of the developing countries to talk differently in private bilateral contacts than in public sessions had some effect here in decreasing fears that the Group of 77 would or could do much more than make nasty speeches.

in establishing a common position, hardly surprising in view of the very divergent views of the Dutch and the Germans. The EEC Commission was very doubtful about the possibility of commodity agreements. Its experts argued that a number of conditions had to be met before a commodity agreement could operate successfully: the commodity had to have an independent price range (without substitutes affecting it); it had to be relatively homogeneous (without great variety in quality); price data had to reflect the market (unlikely where vertically integrated multinationals controlled production, distribution, and marketing); and all the major producers and consumers had to join. Jute, hard fibres, and rubber were thus eliminated by competition from substitutes, and various minerals were part of a captive supply chain. Tin, coffee, and cocoa were already in commodity agreements, and negotiations were underway on sugar. That left tea, a very weak commodity, cotton, with too many producers for easy agreement, and copper—the one good candidate left.[31]

Consequently, the IPC's emphasis on buffer stocks and a Common Fund did not seem very sensible. Instead, the commission argued for increased emphasis on an improved compensatory finance facility (perhaps by expanding the EEC's recently negotiated "Stabex" scheme), more concern with diversification, and a long-term effort to correct domestic structural weaknesses. Of course, the fear that stocks might be used or misused to drive up prices was not without influence on the position of countries heavily dependent on imports. Even within its own terms, however, the commission's argument suggested that new or improved agreements were possible for copper, tin, coffee, cocoa, sugar, and cotton. Moreover, the UNCTAD staff was very aware of the problems confronting the remaining commodities. They had been deliberately included in order to facilitate an important trade-off: agreement on the strong commodities in exchange for developed country support for measures (that might include some transfer of resources) to help the weak commodities. At

[31] For a discussion of the commission's position, see Michael Sakellaropoulo, *The Controversy on Commodities: The Present and Prospects for the Future* (Geneva: Center for Research on International Institutions, 1976), pp. 19-20.

any rate, the prospects for the weak commodities looked dismal if negotiations were limited to a traditional case-by-case appraisal. This raised one very critical issue for UNCTAD: Would the producers of the strong commodities (Brazil, Malaysia, Chile, Zaire) be willing (or able) to make some sacrifices or maintain solidarity with the producers of the weak commodities (Sri Lanka, India, Tanzania)? Rhetorically, the answer was always yes; practically, the answer was never better than maybe.

The major challenge to the hardline position of the United States came from the Nordic countries and the Dutch. These countries, however, did not have a very considered policy. They simply advocated accepting the IPC more or less intact, a position that never had the slightest chance of influencing events. This was all the more so because the "like-minded" countries never made a serious effort to deal with the technical and political issues that had created doubts not only among the ideologues but also among a good many competent and disinterested analysts. The charge that they were merely seeking to ingratiate themselves with the developing countries may have been unfair, but the evidence that the Nordics and the Dutch were really concerned with reaching a viable compromise is sparse.

The conflict between the "radicals" and the "conservatives" was, I believe, very important. But it was very important because of what did *not* happen. By simply accepting the position of the Group of 77 and UNCTAD, the Dutch and the Nordics lost the ability to play a key role as "honest brokers." Within Group B their partiality was taken for granted and their opposition discounted; no one listened because they only repeated a familiar tune.[32] Their influence may have

---

[32] In addition, they were "leaking" Group B positions immediately to the UNCTAD staff and the Group of 77. I believe that this was a counterproductive action on their part: there was nothing very mysterious to be leaked, and—since the United States and other countries were well aware of what was going on—it impeded open Group B discussions. This was one factor that slowed the consultation process and hindered the creation of a common group position, for concessions or probes or even "thinking aloud" had to be kept private or they would be immediately used or manipulated by the Group of 77.

been even more counterproductive on the Group of 77 and UNCTAD. The leadership of the latter was always far too optimistic about the effects that the dissidents could produce: at virtually every meeting, for example, rumors about a "big" breakaway speech by someone like the Dutch Minister Jan Pronk engendered extraordinary—and illusory—expectations among the developing countries. What the Dutch and the Nordics did not do was to moderate expectations, to seek common ground, or to suggest new strategies or tactics of negotiation. Since the leadership of UNCTAD and the Group of 77 were equally deficient, an important opportunity was lost. The Dutch and the Nordics were obviously heavily influenced by their own domestic constituencies who were generally more liberal toward Third World demands, but they could not translate this into new Group B policies without a more sophisticated diplomatic policy.[33]

Group B spent many agonizing hours attempting to construct a common position toward the IPC. It is far from clear that the effort was worthwhile, since whatever emerged was bound to reflect the lowest common denominator of agreement. Still, the effort was necessary, if only because UNCTAD could only function on the basis of a Group B response to a Group of 77 demand. At any rate, the Group B position paper that emerged a month before the Nairobi meeting clearly indicated one thing: almost two years after the IPC had been launched, there was no agreement on a single controversial issue. The Group B paper did not even mention the Common Fund or any form of shared financing for buffer stocks; it did not accept the need to stabilize prices or earnings in real terms; it did not discuss differential or special measures for the least developed countries or for potential net import losers; and it refused to accept "the" Integrated Program

---

[33] One should also note that when an issue was of great practical significance for these countries a less forthcoming position was the usual result—a factor in increasing the cynicism with which some Group B delegates greeted the initiatives of the Dutch and the Nordics. Thus the Norwegians, for example, refused to sign the Code on Liner Conferences, which might have been costly to their shipping industry or to join one of the textile agreements, which might have been injurious to another domestic industry.

for Commodities as the only basis for discussion in Nairobi.[34] To some extent, the range of disagreement was probably exaggerated, for the conservative Group B countries clearly did not intend to give away beforehand the few concessions they might be willing or compelled to make at Nairobi, but the concessions they were withholding were essentially cosmetic.

On the eve of Nairobi, then, the "hard" position of the Group of 77 confronted the equally "hard" position of Group B.

The Road to Nairobi and Beyond

A chronology of the bargaining process over the IPC need not take much time. Once initial positions were established, they were maintained. Intimations of progress were generally sleight of hand; they were necessary to keep the game going. Whether opportunities along the way were missed is unclear, since the combination of rigidity and self-righteousness that characterized *both* sides might have made anything short of unconditional surrender unacceptable. At any rate, what is clear is that no one was making much of an effort to create or discover opportunities for movement.

The stalemate that persisted for over two years illustrates the limitations of the proposition that a "linear concession rate" tends to prevail in many bargaining encounters.[35] The interaction between the skills of the negotiators and the value each side attached to the issue at stake yielded very little of consequence: as already noted, individual skills had little effect and values were not substantially altered because there was so little exploration of potential areas of compromise. Indeed, the process was more decisively affected by exogenous events (judgments about OPEC's behavior, the intellectual climate, a change in administration in the United States) than by anything that happened at UNCTAD. This might be said

---

[34] The Group B paper that I have summarized here was not an official, published paper, although various versions of it were in circulation in Geneva.

[35] There is a critique of this proposition in I. William Zartman, "The Political Analysis of Negotiation: How Who Gets What and When," *World Politics* 26, no. 3 (April 1974): 385-399.

of most North-South encounters, since the bargaining power of the participants in a particular negotiation tends to be so heavily skewed. Nevertheless, within these sharp constraints there are possibilities for movement, for building for the future, for increasing the capacity for grasping opportunities, and for providing some protection against adverse external developments that were lost—or simply not sought.

If the primary characteristic of the bargaining process in the two years before the Nairobi Conference was the absence of bargaining, presumably the Nairobi Conference itself was bound to change matters. Either serious agreements would be negotiated or there would be a major crisis with the continuation of the game at stake. Or, optimistically, perhaps the developed countries had held back in order to compromise—to accept the principles they had rejected—at the most prominent and noteworthy of the settings for the North-South "dialogue." There are elements of truth in each of these views, for all the participants felt that the stalemate could not persist past Nairobi and that some kind of turning point might be at hand. But this underestimated the unwillingness of either side to sacrifice principles (or perhaps for some of the leaders to admit that they had made a mistake) and it also underestimated the ability of skilled draftsmen to produce a resolution that resolved nothing—but avoided a breakdown. That is, the conference was only a heightened and more dramatic (more compressed, more newsworthy, more high-level) version of the bargaining process that preceded it.

The first three and one-half weeks at Nairobi merely repeated familiar arguments. The Group of 77 demanded a commitment to the Common Fund, after which negotiations on individual commodities would commence; these negotiations, however, would be carried on within the framework set by the principles, objectives, and techniques of the IPC. Group B (or most of it) insisted that the order be reversed: individual negotiations would determine the measures appropriate for particular commodities, and if buffer stocks were the preferred technique for a number of commodities, the case for "a" (not "the") common fund or another form of joint financing would be examined on its merits. The Group of 77 was adamant in its rejection of this position. Group B, during the first few weeks in Nairobi, had made some slow but important progress toward accepting a commitment that no buffer stock to which both producers and consumers agreed would fail because of insufficient financing. For the first time this accepted the notion of joint financing of stocks, but it clearly fell well short of a prior commitment to the joint financing of ten buffer stocks. Although it might have had some effect much earlier in the negotiations, this position was insufficient at Nairobi. The developing countries wanted more, and the conservative developed countries (in this case, especially Japan and West Germany) wanted to give even less.

Two days before the end of the Nairobi Conference the contentious issues had not been resolved, and a major crisis was imminent. Formal meetings were then suspended, and a small group of delegates—the "Mount Kenya" group—disappeared into the top floors of the Nairobi Hilton to attempt a salvage operation (on debt as well as commodities). Something of a compromise emerged from this "summit," but a major ambiguity remained: the resolution referred to negotiations on "a" common fund, not "the" Common Fund. The Secretary-General was requested to convene a negotiating conference on a fund "open to all members" not later than March 1977. This conference was to be preceded by preparatory meetings to discuss the objectives, financing, mode of operations, and decision-making and management structure of the fund. Presumably these meetings would fill in or clarify the details so that the negotiators would know, more or less, what they were negotiating.

The uncertainties about what had been agreed were exacerbated by the UNCTAD practice of passing resolutions by assent, without opposition, and by letting dissenters withdraw or qualify their approval in separate statements to the conference.[36] Thus the United States subsequently noted that

[36] How one feels about this procedural device tends to depend on the value attached to the process itself in relation to the value attached to clarity and substantive agreement. There is no simple policy to resolve this dilemma, for there are costs implicit in increasing the degree of ambiguity and uncertainty

the "preparatory meetings were consultations prior to a decision on *whether* to embark on negotiations" and that consequently they would participate in the preparatory meetings "without any commitment" to participate in the March negotiating conference. [37] A spokesman for the Group of 77, however, declared that it was not the purpose of the preparatory meetings "to engage in a repetition of discussions . . . on the merits of a common fund," and that "nothing other than *the* common fund" as a means of finance was to be discussed.[38] This was a very diplomatic compromise, for each side assumed that it had protected its initial position, and no one knew exactly what had been decided.

A similar "compromise" emerged on the question of real prices. The final resolution declared that the price levels aimed at would "take account of world inflation and changes in the world economic and monetary situations" and that the objective was "to improve and sustain the real income of individual developing countries." But how this was to be done was left unclear: indexation was not mentioned, and it was agreed only that price ranges would be "periodically reviewed and appropriately revised" ("taking into account" a number of factors, including inflation and price movements in imported manufactured goods).[39] What this means, if anything, is that the issue was left unresolved.[40]

---

and there are costs in saying no definitively. If a rule of thumb were to be devised, it probably should reflect a judgment about how important the disputed issue is and how deeply one feels about it. For the Republican administrations this probably would have led to an earlier crisis on the Common Fund, but they were reluctant to see this happen because of uncertainties about OPEC and the resource environment.

[37] UNCTAD, *Report of the United Nations Conference on Trade and Development on its Fourth Session* (TD/217), p. 102 (italics mine).

[38] Ibid., p. 97 (italics mine). [39] Ibid., pp. 4-5.

[40] At Nairobi the United States also proposed the creation of an International Resource Bank to facilitate investment in raw materials. This was voted down at the end of the conference in one of the few such instances of direct voting. The idea of the bank or another mechanism to encourage investment in resources was surely sensible, for investment costs are rising and so are the fears of expropriation by increasingly nationalistic governments. Nevertheless, the United States' initiative on the bank was tactically inept, for the decision to drop a new proposal on the table at the last moment, especially a pro-

The Secretary-General of UNCTAD called the commodity negotiations in Nairobi a "watershed in the evolution of international policy."[41] This was a very debatable judgment, since American officials insisted that they had made no new commitments at all. Thus Robert Vastine, a former Treasury official, noted that the United States' policy toward the IPC and the Common Fund after Nairobi was pretty much what it had been before: "passive opposition."[42] Still, some positions *had* changed, for the United States now conceded that individual commodity negotiations need not precede negotiations on a common fund, and both sets of negotiations could go on simultaneously. This was not much of a concession if "passive opposition" to a common fund were successful or if the common fund that emerged were sharply circumscribed in its powers and its financing (for example, only pooling resources of individual agreements instead of serving as a central source for financing), but it was perceived as important by the developing countries.

There is an even more important aspect to the discussion of what had or had not been conceded at Nairobi that should also be noted. The potential for inconsistency or, perhaps more critically, the potential for misleading the other side and raising expectations illegitimately was considerably enhanced by agreeing to join a negotiating process the ends of which—a common fund, many buffer stocks—had been persistently opposed by the United States government and to which "passive opposition" was still the ruling policy. This may well carry hypocrisy too far, for any good that is likely to come from merely seeking to keep the game going—especially when the game itself begins to take priority over the objectives it purports to seek or even over the need to clarify where the

posal for which the United States had not worked out the details or consulted widely beforehand, was bound to look like a Machiavellian trick to deflect attention from the IPC. This was particularly true because the bank seemed to reflect concern only with developed country problems (insufficient supply) in the commodity area, and it might indeed drive commodity prices down if enough new supplies were generated.

[41] UNCTAD *Press Release* (Geneva: Information Service, TAD/INF/869), 18 April 1977.

[42] Vastine, "United States International Commodity Policy," p. 467.

boundaries between the negotiable and the nonnegotiable lie. The result is likely to be the avoidance of a moderately costly short-range crisis at the expense of inducing a very costly long-range crisis, an outcome that I believe was very likely if the Ford administration were to have remained in power. It may also be a likely outcome for the Carter administration if its changes are only stylistic and not substantive.

It is a separate question whether it was inevitable for the Ford administration to have been caught in inconsistency by its desire to keep the game going and its desire to reject the stakes of the game. The United States agreed at Nairobi that "there might be advantages in linking the financial resources of individual buffer stocks."[43] In addition, while there was some internal disagreement, there was a good deal of support within the United States government for commodity agreements and for the use of buffer stocks as an instrument of stabilization in some of those agreements.[44] In effect, there was at least some support *in terms of perceptions of American interests* for treating commodity agreements, buffer stocks, and shared financing pragmatically and without excessive ideological posturing. And once the United States moved toward the position that commodity agreements could be useful to consumers, it made sense to accept the obligation to guarantee sufficient financing for a mechanism from which consumers also stood to benefit. Similarly, if the United States believed that a common financing facility might save money, why not make clear that the United States had nothing in principle against such financing, provided that enough individual commodity agreements were willing to participate and provided that the powers, the financing, and the operational responsibilities were adequately defined? That is, why not make clear that U.S. opposition was not merely ideological or a selfish defense of very narrow, very short-range interests but rather was practical and political: that it was, in effect, the re-

---

[43] UNCTAD, *Report of the United Nations Conference on Trade and Development on its Fourth Session* (TD/217), p. 102.

[44] Vastine, "United States International Commodity Policy," p. 448; and Harold B. Malmgren, *The Raw Material and Commodity Controversy* (Washington, D.C.: International Economic Studies Institute, 1975).

sult of fears of the consequences of signing a blank check in an environment where there were some common interests, but also some conflicting interests, and much distrust and uncertainty?

A compromise such as this might not have been acceptable to the Group of 77 and the UNCTAD leadership. There was little persuasive evidence of flexibility or a willingness to compromise on their part, short of prior acceptance of all of the IPC's demands. Even after Nairobi in the three preparatory meetings before the Common Fund conference the developing countries were obdurate: they refused to discuss details and continued to insist that they would be settled during the March conference (that is, after the commitment to negotiate "the" Common Fund was accepted). The developing countries themselves had not yet agreed on terms beyond a general commitment to the UNCTAD conception of the Fund, which may explain some part of their stance. But it is also likely that they were unwilling to discuss practicalities until they were more certain of a forthcoming response from the developed countries; in their view, agreement on specifics before an agreement on principles might have led to a common fund that was only nominally the Common Fund they sought.

Earlier movement on the part of the developed countries to an acceptance of shared responsibility for financing and to greater clarity about the kind of common fund that they were willing to contemplate would not have satisfied all of the Group of 77, but it would have moved the debate to a more practical and less ideological level, it would have indicated that the developed countries were genuinely interested in viable commodity agreements and in ending a stalemate that benefitted no one, and it would have attracted some important support among the moderates in the Group of 77.[45] Moreover, a guarantee that no agreed buffer stock would fail because of the absence of sufficient finance might have provided a sensible interim compromise between the developed countries' contention that a Common Fund could not be created before individual negotiations clarified the number of

---

[45] The last point is a personal judgment based on extensive interviewing.

buffer stocks to be established and the developing countries' contention that no buffer stocks would be established unless sufficient finance were available from the beginning. This would have been a position that sought some common ground between the two groups, and it would have done so not by rejecting principles but by seeking to clarify them before a decision had to be taken. Indeed, it might well have been a more sensible policy than the apparently larger concession implied by an acceptance "in principle" of a common fund, for "agreement in principle" in the North-South arena may only disguise sharp disagreement about the meaning of the principle. The injunction, "accept this principle, yes or no," may make sense in a settled universe of shared values, and it might even make sense in an unsettled universe if the principle were of transcendent importance and both sides understand it as so, but here agreement in principle may only be another way of obscuring substantive disagreement.

The IPC needs to be kept in perspective. Rhetoric apart, it is not a revolutionary program for either the developed or the developing countries. For the developed countries, losses are likely to be manageable (and compensated by gains from stability and security of supply), and a good many countries will benefit directly. Even the damage to the principles of the free market should not be disabling: ostensible commitment to the market has not inhibited recourse to a regulated market when sufficiently powerful groups see it as in their interest, and the costs have been bearable (if unfairly distributed). This suggests that the risks of compromise for the developed countries were not overwhelming and that the potential benefits were reasonably attractive. Moreover, even if the compromise offer were rejected (as initially it probably would have been), there was some utility in indicating that the rich were not stonewalling for their own sake or cynically disguising a defense of the status quo behind fervent avowal of at least partially irrelevant principles. Why, instead of moving in this direction, did the United States permit the issue to build to a crisis—an unnecessary crisis over an institution that might be useful but was not ever likely to be a decisive factor in commodity trade?

There are a number of answers to this question. Most refer to the interaction between bureaucratic conflicts, personal predispositions, and perceptions of the national interest within the American government.[46] The difficulties of extracting a common position, particularly a new one, from the several bureaucracies concerned with the commodity issue is a familiar theme. But the difficulty was compounded in this case by the dominance of an unsophisticated and frequently hypocritical ideology at the top levels of the administration. This tended to turn discussions of the IPC into metaphysical confrontations between competing faiths. In some cases, ideology masked (or buttressed) personal hostility toward the developing countries (and especially their leaders), a hostility exacerbated by the resentments generated by the oil crisis (for example, the feeling that we should suddenly be dependent on a handful of "backward" countries) and by the inflammatory and frequently absurd rhetoric dominant in the UN system.

The influence of ideology on the economic leadership of the Nixon and Ford administrations has been noted several times, but this should not be read as a blanket condemnation of "liberal" economics and free-market principles. What has been at issue throughout is the apparent use of these principles to mask the protection of narrow interests (frequently against the interest of American consumers) and the tendency to treat the choice between the market and central regulation in an either/or fashion. The nature of the choice was in fact far more complex and required a sophisticated evaluation of the actual behavior of commodity markets, the means of redressing some obvious inequities implicit in the existing structure of power and influence, and the proper trade-off between short- and long-range benefits. A more forthright recognition of the fact that many markets (perhaps most

[46] Since the focus of this book is on the confrontation in Geneva and Nairobi, I have said little about these domestic considerations, except in passing. But there are obvious points at which more extended comment is necessary. I should add that although I was not on the scene in Washington, my comments reflect interviews with many of the key participants in both Washington and Geneva.

markets in the commodity arena) were not only imperfect but also regulated by rules created and manipulated by a handful of large corporations would also have been helpful. So too would recognition of the fact that challenges to these rules were not always solely in the interests of the developing countries.

A more pragmatic approach would have recognized that UNCTAD's quest for "global resource management" was as much beyond the current state of the art as the developed countries' reliance on unfettered markets fell short of acceptable standards of either efficiency or equity. In the search for a viable compromise between these two extremes, efficiency (which, as Ragnar Nurkse once said, the world is too poor to despise) and equity (without which the developing countries may be forced into irrational actions and the developed countries left only with increasingly costly and inefficient options) need to be carefully balanced. A more equitable order that sacrifices too much efficiency will be as explosive and unfair as a more efficient order that sacrifices too much equity. In this sense, commodity agreements might provide the setting for interim settlements of some of these complex issues, and the quest for a new order in commodity trade might have provided a more general setting to establish the procedures, if not the principles, to guide these efforts. But such matters were ignored by both sides.

Distrust of the Third World's true intentions was also a significant influence on American attitudes, for it increased the suspicion that concessions would only lead to more extreme demands. Being "tough" and delaying concessions until the last possible moment thus seemed necessary.[47] Some officials were also opposed to commodity agreements not for ideological reasons but because they believed that they could not work or that they would be harmful to the interests of the United States. This is an arguable position, but its proponents

---

[47] The U.S. delegates sent to Geneva were very effective in presenting and maintaining the "tough" line, but they were not making policy in Washington. Some in the Group of 77 did not always understand this too well, perhaps because many LDC delegates had greater freedom in relation to home governments.

generally failed to consider whether new conditions justified a new look at the whole program of commodity trade or what the likely alternatives might be if the existing conflict continued. Finally, even officials who were more favorable to the IPC frequently argued that nothing could be done because of congressional hostility to the Third World and to higher commodity prices. This may well be true, but certainly lying supine before congressional biases is not the answer: *if* commodity agreements were perceived as in the American interest, an educational campaign with Congress might have produced some results.

A word also needs to be added about the significance of bureaucratic conflicts within the Ford administration. I have implied that the negative position of the Treasury and the Council of Economic Advisors dominated American policy, but others have argued that the more forthcoming posture of Kissinger and the State Department (with the Economics and Business Bureau dragged along reluctantly) actually dominated policy in most of this period.[48] This may well be true, but it was not perceived in this way in Geneva and no effort was made (and none perhaps could be made, given the constraints) to capitalize on internal conflicts within the Washington bureaucracy. The negative views of Treasury were simply taken as American policy. There were three reasons for this. First, the relatively more forthcoming statements of Kissinger (for example, in his speech to the Seventh Special Session in September 1975) were almost invariably followed by Treasury statements that nothing had changed. Second, Kissinger's proposals still fell far short of what the Group of 77 wanted and thought it could get. And finally, neither the UNCTAD leadership nor the Group of 77 had a very sophisticated understanding of how the policymaking machine in Washington operated.

These constraints were considerably diluted by the arrival

---

[48] Personal communication from Professor Henry R. Nau, who was working in the State Department at the time. See also his paper, "The Evolution of U.S. Foreign Policy in Energy: From Alliance Politics to Politics-as-Usual" (prepared for the International Studies Association Convention, February 1978).

of the Carter administration. The first negotiating conference on a Common Fund in March 1977 ended in complete stalemate because the new administration had not yet established its own position. Shortly thereafter, however, at the final session of the Conference on International Economic Cooperation (CIEC) a commitment "in principle" to "a" common fund was made. This was clearly intended as a signal to the Third World that attitudes and options had altered in Washington. Certainly the complex of factors that might inhibit agreement were considerably different, since the degree of ideological posturing was sharply diminished and the concern for evaluating real benefits and costs was somewhat enhanced. I do not intend to examine the new administration's policy toward the IPC in detail because it is still so much in train at the time of writing, but several brief comments seem warranted for the light they shed on earlier (and perhaps future) developments.

The new administration's economic analysis of commodity trade did not differ significantly from early analyses. But the new administration was far more sophisticated about the potential gains from developing a more productive dialogue with the Third World and far more willing to try to make an objective assessment of some of the benefits to the United States of a reformed commodity order.[49] What is striking, however, is how difficult it seems to be to transform new attitudes and new perceptions into policy agreements. One reason is that the Third World still demands commitment to broad and ambiguous statements of principle. In fact, since frustrations have grown as a result of three years of futility and since expectations and hopes were suddenly revived by the election of President Carter, the willingness to compromise (or feelings about the need to do so) may have declined. But even where agreement in principle has been established, negotiations on details have been extraordinarily difficult: much useful empirical work was not done during the preceding years (which still leaves great areas of darkness and

[49] One should note that the Third World is becoming an increasingly important market for American exports. See the comments at the end of Chapter 1.

uncertainty), and deepening fissures appear within each group as individual commodity negotiations proceed and as more of the details of the IPC are discussed. Also, some persisting disagreements about where the international system is going and about the range of politically feasible change have not disappeared. The point I particularly want to emphasize is that these difficulties clearly illustrate the naiveté of the proposition, so dear to the UNCTAD leadership, that only the absence of "will" prevents the developed countries from accepting the IPC. The will now exists, but none of the practical problems have disappeared—nor were they of sufficient concern when UNCTAD was content to blame all failures on ideology and will. No one has gained from the tendency on both sides to view these negotiations too simply.

There is another reason why there has been great difficulty in translating agreement in principle into agreement on specific policies. The leadership of the new administration obviously desires to establish a new image of American behavior in the eyes of the Third World and to move the North-South dialogue out of the cycle of futility that has dominated it in recent years. But it confronts significant domestic constraints not only in Congress and public opinion but also in the prevailing economic circumstances. There are also, however, important bureaucratic constraints on movement. The problem is that the working-level people who prepare position papers and lay out alternatives are the same people who prepared the last administration's policy proposals. I do not mean to suggest that the earlier policies were always wrong or unwise—only that it is both psychologically and practically difficult for many of these people to reorient their own thinking. ing. A kind of rear-guard action against new initiatives is one result. This helps to explain why agreement in principle is not always meaningful and why there may be less substantive change between administrations than meets the eye.

This was well illustrated in the outcome of the second negotiating conference on a Common Fund in November 1977. The position of the conservative Group B countries sharply diverged from the position of the Group of 77 on two critical issues. The first was financing, where the Group B proposal left the Common Fund without any financial resources of its own: the Fund was merely to pool the finances collected by individual commodity organizations. Among other things, this diminished the Fund's attractiveness to the producers of "strong" commodities, it diminished the Fund's potential as a catalyst for other commodity agreements, and—in both psychic and practical terms—it seemed likely to create only an empty shell. This was perfectly acceptable to the drafters of the Group B proposal (a number of whom objected to the "in principle" commitment at CIEC), for they were intent on establishing a common fund that could do almost none of the things the Common Fund was meant to do. In practical terms, this is probably not very important, since (as I have emphasized) the significance of the Common Fund has been excessively exaggerated by UNCTAD; in symbolic terms, however, it was a major blow to the effort to create a less hostile North-South dialogue.

The other issue that sharply divided the two sides concerned "other measures." The developing countries that produced commodities that could not be stocked wanted the Common Fund to finance other measures such as diversification, research, export promotion, and perhaps even price support. Without such help, these countries (mostly very poor African countries) felt that they would gain little or nothing from the Common Fund. The conservative Group B countries argued that all of these measures were already being adequately financed by other international institutions and that they would not establish a new aid mechanism. I should note that as of the summer of 1978 there were signs that the U.S. position was shifting toward acceptance of a *voluntary* fund to finance "other measures" in exchange for concessions from the Group of 77 on the financing and powers of the Common Fund itself. Whether this is true and whether, if true, it would be acceptable to the Group of 77, I cannot say—the answer is likely to come only at a reconvened negotiating conference or at UNCTAD-V in May 1979.

Still, even if agreement were finally reached, the resulting common fund is not likely to bear close resemblance to the

Common Fund originally demanded by the Group of 77 and UNCTAD. UNCTAD-IV mandated that individual commodity negotiations for eighteen commodities of interest to the developing countries were to go on simultaneously with the Common Fund negotiations. Both the individual negotiations and the Fund negotiations were to be concluded within two years. However, the individual negotiations have fallen even further behind schedule than the Fund negotiations: of the eighteen commodities, four had already established commodity agreements (before UNCTAD-IV), and only one of the remaining fourteen commodities was even close to agreement at the end of the two-year period. And the lack of a prior guarantee of adequate financing has not been the major factor in the conflicts that have delayed agreement: all the traditional conflicts between producers and consumers—as well as within each group—were sharply revived as the negotiations began to touch on practicalities.

In any case, delay and conflict in the individual negotiations is also very crucial for the Common Fund. If the Fund contains fewer than the ten core commodities, either because the producers or consumers could not reach agreement on a specific commodity or because the members of a successfully negotiated agreement do not wish to affiliate with the IPC (because of a reluctance to commit funds to the Common Fund), many of the Fund's presumed advantages would dissipate. For example, the potential offset savings would be much smaller and the attractiveness of the Fund to outside investors would probably decline. In effect, one might be creating a superstructure (the Fund) on a very weak base (four or five commodity agreements). In these circumstances the Fund would hardly be very powerful or influential, which might diminish some of the opposition to it—thus inducing cosmetic concessions—but whether it makes sense to create an institution in search of a role is another question.

The details of the conflict over "other measures" need not be described, but there is one aspect of it that is very significant.[50] I believe that one of the most important things to un-

---

[50] By November UNCTAD officials, most of whom were intent on trying to

derstand about the commodity negotiations is that the issue of implementation was virtually *never* discussed. The conservative developed countries seemed to take it for granted that commodity agreements would fail, and UNCTAD and the Group of 77 seemed to feel that a commitment to the Common Fund would somehow eliminate or diminish all the problems that had undermined previous commodity agreements. Thus both sides sought ceremonial confirmation of divergent statements of faith, and no one seemed very concerned with establishing the pattern of incentives and disincentives that might enable the agreements to survive. One needs to recall that commodity agreements do not succeed or fail in response to abstract principles or theories but rather in response to changes in the empirical world that can usually be moved in a relatively more benign or less malign direction; attempts to think about how this might be done would have diminished some of the playacting in Geneva. I note this here because it provides a different perspective on other measures: if the American government had been thinking ahead, a compromise agreement on other measures might have been perceived as a useful incentive to induce some of the poorest countries in various commodity agreements to maintain the commitment even in difficult periods. But no one was thinking very far ahead.

The difficulty with the American position could be usefully summarized in terms of the questions asked. The primary question for the United States and many other Group B countries was, what was the most efficient solution? Willingness to temper efficiency in the light of domestic political realities in the developed countries, however, did little to con-

---

salvage something from the wreckage (their tactics, after all, had produced nothing for three years), were blaming West Germany for African intransigence on other measures because the Germans had shown the Africans various analyses of how little they would gain. But the UNCTAD argument is specious, for other analyses with the same results had been produced by the ECA, and UNCTAD itself (as noted in Chapter 2) had suppressed its own studies—one of which was inadvertently published. The latter incident illustrates the staff's loss of influence over time, as it could not control the Africans once doubts began to surface, and it raises questions about the wisdom of trying to suppress an issue that would inevitably surface—at a bad time.

vince the developing countries that the efficiency criterion
would yield fair outcomes. A secondary question was, would
Congress accept whatever agreements might be negotiated?
These were legitimate practical questions, but they were also
insufficient. In an arena where mutual interests mixed with
conflicting interests, other questions also needed to be asked.
Were there compromises that might have moved the negotiations away from rhetorical stalemate? What were the costs in
prolonging the stalemate? These questions were not ignored,
but they also did not receive their due. Ideology and narrow
calculations of self-interest were very critical inhibiting factors
since some of the leadership was unwilling to move beyond
the efficiency criterion or was convinced that to do so was
against American interests (more precisely, against *some* powerful American interests in the short run). But failure to understand how to deal with the Group of 77 was also a very
significant inhibiting factor.

The Group of 77 walked out of the November negotiating
conference. Three and one half years after the IPC and the
Common Fund were placed on the international agenda,
there was still no agreement, progress had been made "in
principle" but not in reality, and there was uncertainty as to
whether there would even be another negotiating conference
or whether the Common Fund would ever be established and
what form it would take if it were established. The number of
people who cared about the IPC and the Common Fund
seemed to be declining and the number of people on both
sides who were pleased with the November failure seemed to
be growing. In the meantime, an important opportunity to
improve the conditions of commodity trade—to improve the
general welfare—may have been lost or delayed for too long.

I do not mean to leave the impression that American policy
was solely responsible for the stalemate that developed over
the IPC and the Common Fund. There is plenty of blame to
go around. One reason why the hardline opposition in the
United States (and elsewhere) could persist for so long is that
the tactics of the Group of 77 and the UNCTAD leadership
played right into its hands. These were enemies that deserved
each other, for each seemed intent on confirming the other's

worst fears. In the next section, I shall turn to the other side of the issue and examine the strategy and tactics of UNCTAD and the Group of 77. But I want to add a new dimension to the analysis, for it seems necessary to ask a number of general questions about the problems of bargaining between unequal partners, especially when the weaker side seeks to change the rules of the game.

Bargaining from Weakness: Theory and Practice

The bargaining process that we have examined was not the result—on either side—of a series of calculated decisions about strategy and tactics or about long-range and short-range goals. Loose notions of proper strategies undoubtedly played a role in decisions, particularly about the need to maintain unity at all costs, but tactical issues tended to dominate and were, in turn, frequently dominated by ad hoc responses to deadlines or targets of opportunity. Nevertheless, there is some utility in discussing several of the principles ("rules of thumb" is less elegant but probably more accurate) that bargaining theorists have suggested *ought* to apply in negotiations. The contrast with the principles and practices that were actually applied may be instructive.

The initial principle is defined by common sense: each side presumably agrees to negotiate only when the expected outcome is better than the expected outcome of refusing to negotiate.[51] In fact, several of the more conservative developed countries would have preferred to avoid any serious negotiations at all within the UNCTAD arena. A large public forum like UNCTAD, heavily ideological and extremely politicized, hardly seemed the appropriate setting for complex negotiations of commodity agreements with very asymmetric patterns of gainers and losers. But the developed countries had little choice since UNCTAD was seized with the commodity issue and there was no way to avoid discussion—

[51] See Jack Sawyer and Harold Guetzkow, "Bargaining and Negotiation in International Relations," in *International Behavior*, ed. Herbert C. Kelman (New York: Holt, Rinehart and Winston, 1965), p. 473.

especially if the refusal to participate actively angered OPEC or enabled it to use "stonewalling" as a rationalization for raising prices.[52] Two consequences ensued. First, as reluctant bargainers the developed countries failed to get into the game early enough and were left only with the option of debating a program devised by the staff. Preferring to be elsewhere, they were not especially skillful in dealing with the current circumstances. And second, a subsurface conflict between the conservative developed countries and UNCTAD persisted throughout the negotiations, the one seeking outcomes that diminished UNCTAD's role, the other seeking outcomes that enhanced UNCTAD's role as a central negotiating forum for international economic issues.

According to the theorists, successful negotiations would be more likely if the negotiators were to act on their expectations of how the other side will respond, if they were to seek solutions that are consistent with the other side's principles and that respect the other side's central power position, and if they were to avoid ideological conflict.[53] Negotiators are also advised to build on shared interests, to avoid excessive initial demands, and to "fractionate" or divide problems so that one can build momentum behind a series of small or partial agreements.[54] These seem eminently sensible injunctions, but

[52] There were also, of course, some positive gains foreseen from commodity agreements, if not from the IPC. But, again, this raises the question about the value of playing to keep playing. When is it more costly to do this than to say no and risk a crisis? Would the quality of the dialogue improve with more willingness to be forthright about disagreements, especially as the United States usually ends by conceding some part of what it is resisting? Are early crises better than late—or can the late crises be avoided? I have already commented on this issue (see note 37 of this chapter), but here I want to add that if the United States places the dominant value on keeping the game going, it ought to begin playing it better by presenting its own views earlier and by improving the domestic process of decision and the process of consultation with allies. For more detailed comment, see Chapter 5.

[53] On the first point, see Alan Coddington, *Theories of the Bargaining Process* (London: George Allen and Unwin, Ltd., 1968), pp. 12f; on the second and third points, see Paul Diesing, "Bargaining Strategy and Union-Management Relationships," in *Human Behavior and International Politics*, J. David Singer, ed. (Chicago: Rand McNally and Company, 1965), pp. 405-415.

[54] Large initial demands provide "room for bargaining" and the exchange

they were all violated or ignored in the IPC negotiations. But what is especially striking is that it is not clear that the decision to act on other principles or precepts was either avoidable or necessarily wrong, at least from the point of view of the developing countries.

As I have already noted, the bargaining process at UNCTAD was very encapsulated: the imperatives of intra-group unity dominated the imperatives of intergroup agreement. Group unity, particularly for the Group of 77, seemed necessary for major gains, and maintaining it seemed more important than the minor gains to be expected from a normal pattern of conflict and compromise. Concern for shared principles and the avoidance of ideological conflict with the developed countries was inevitably minimal. Massive initial demands—"blue sky" proposals—were necessary to maintain unity, and "fractionating" problems and settling what could be settled seemed likely to split the coalition and to facilitate the typical "divide and conquer" tactics of the rich.

Care has to be taken not to dismiss these contrary tactics as reflections of the incompetence or irrationality of UNCTAD and Group of 77 leadership. Severe criticism is surely possible, but only within the context set by the objectives sought and the structural obstacles confronted. The common-sense propositions of the theorists presume a relatively settled or stable universe in which basic values are not at stake, in which the rules of the game are not at issue, and in which bargaining over shares is central.[55] The bargaining process at UNCTAD

---

of information, but they also make it difficult to avoid the appearance of defeat in any compromise outcome. See Carl M. Stevens, *Strategy and Collective Bargaining Negotiation* (New York: McGraw Hill, 1963), pp. 33, 84-85; on "fractionating" problems, see Roger Fisher, *International Conflict for Beginners* (New York: Harper & Row, 1969), p. 92.

[55] There is more at issue here than a typical conflict between efficiency (the value sought by the developed countries, although it also masked a commitment to the existing distribution of gains or something close to it) and equity (the value sought by the developing countries), for equity in the North-South context has also implied new rules and a new game, not merely a bigger share in the old game. Of course, the two versions of equity were frequently mixed together in confused and even contradictory ways (that is, a better deal in the old system might inhibit the creation of a new system).

was *not* completely antithetical, for poor and weak states can rarely ignore the need for better terms in the existing game. But UNCTAD and the Group of 77 were never seeking only a better bargain: although they were playing for enhanced power, higher status, and a more important role in decisions in the existing system, it was always with the hope of using these advances to create a new order and new rules. Thus the answer to the question of whether they were seeking a new order or a reformed order is that they were actually seeking both.

The unique aspect of this bargaining process, then, is that in contrast to earlier attempts to reorder the structure of the system the challenge comes from notably weak states. This imparts to the process a number of unusual characteristics. First, there is the previously noted ambivalence of weak countries that cannot afford to ignore the needs of the present. This creates enormous problems in maintaining unity—a weakness that the rich and powerful can exploit by offering slightly better terms in the existing system in exchange for abandoning challenges to the system itself. Second, since the developed countries are playing a different game (or at least resisting the one the developing countries are trying to play), stalemate and rising tension are the most likely outcome. The two sides cannot agree on what is a fair outcome because the intellectual framework of beliefs, values, and perceptions is itself in dispute; that is, the idea of what is fair and legitimate cannot be resolved when the two sides disagree about what game they are really playing. In these circumstances, the developing countries' demands for acceptance of new principles do indeed delay and inhibit short-term agreements, but since the distributive bargains they have been offered provide only marginally improved outcomes and since whatever chance there is to get much more rests (or appears to rest) on the manipulation of the leverage provided by Group unity, the tactics followed may be dangerous or misconceived—but they are not ridiculous or irrational.[56]

[56] One might presume that the developed countries would have perceived this and offered much better terms in the existing game, but they did not do so. Again, ideology, perceptions of weakness, and self-interest played a role

The stance of the developing countries also implicitly rested on a relatively high tolerance for risk. The developed countries, with much to protect in the existing order, tended to want very strong proof that a new approach would bring clear benefits to both sides or at least not threaten the benefits the developed countries already enjoyed. Under the circumstances, they were not prone to take many risks, since evidence of future benefits was obviously hypothetical and uncertain—and in some cases virtually ruled out on ideological grounds. In contrast, the developing countries gained much less from the status quo and were much more willing to risk a new approach, provided at least some evidence existed that they themselves would gain. But even *if* the extreme case were granted—that tinkering with the status quo was insufficient and that "global resource management" was both necessary and feasible—the question of how to convince the rich and conservative countries of the need to take the risk still remained.

Criticism of what UNCTAD and the Group of 77 sought to do thus reflects judgments of feasibility and practicality. The developing countries have tended consistently to exaggerate the potential gains from any range of external change.[57] Nonetheless, even if a radical restructuring of the system were perceived as indispensable, is standing fast behind a demand for new principles also necessary? In the context of the times (the environment of the oil crisis) it may well have seemed a sensible tactic. But the developing countries lacked either the power to compel the developed countries to accept this kind of change or the persuasiveness to induce more than cosmetic changes from the prevailing regimes in the conser-

in this decision to offer minimal terms. But it needs also to be emphasized that even those well-disposed toward the developing countries would find it very difficult to offer very great benefits in commodity trade, for the nature of the trading system made much higher prices unlikely or even counterproductive. There was thus much uncertainty about how to provide much more than marginal short-range support (by stabilization) and genuine fears that so much stress on short-range changes in commodity trade were not justified.

[57] Why and how this is so is a major theme in Robert L. Rothstein, *The Weak in the World of the Strong: The Developing Countries in the International System* (New York: Columbia University Press, 1977).

vative countries. The absence of an effective political strategy to build a sufficiently wide coalition or an effective educational strategy to enlighten and convert the opposition meant movement was likely only if another external "shock" of some sort were to occur or if the developed countries were to ultimately yield more than they intended by "salami slice" concessions. These developments may or may not occur and they may or may not produce the desired results if they do, but waiting upon events in this fashion is probably not a sensible strategy for poor countries that need help quickly. In effect, UNCTAD and the Group of 77 badly overestimated their power, misperceiving the possibilities of change by the fiat of the week and taking delay, stalemate, and the failure to establish building blocks or to diminish misunderstandings as the necessary costs of creating a new order. The key question, then, is not really why the developing countries perceived (or misperceived) the opportunity to seek major change in 1974 (for there were many other advocates of the need for radical change at the time) but rather why they did not alter course in response to new developments and continued failure?

The initial decision to seek major changes quickly resulted in a bargaining process that for two years or more verged on "pure intransigence," with one side seeing bargaining as only a necessary evil, the other side refusing (or unable) to move from very large initial demands, neither side trusting the other or worrying very much about what the other might find acceptable.[58] Something like an armed truce ensued with each side hoping that something useful might turn up to break the impasse—at its most extreme points in the months before Nairobi, the resemblance to the bargaining process between hijackers and governments struck a number of participants.[59] In these circumstances, principles cannot easily be

[58] The model of "pure intransigence" is discussed in John G. Cross, *The Economics of Bargaining* (New York: Basic Books, Inc., 1969), p. 42.

[59] Stevens, *Strategy and Collective Bargaining Negotiation*, p. 5, discusses the notion of an "armed truce." The terrorists' invasion of OPEC's Vienna headquarters during the midst of the commodity discussions set off some of these speculations, especially about the power of a handful of determined individuals to threaten the stability of the entire system. But it is difficult to maintain that the terrorists gained more than notoriety as a result of their efforts.

compromised and each side is afraid to make a concession for fear that it will merely engender new demands. In addition, the concessions that are made are greeted with suspicion and analyzed for their "real" meanings.

Buy why did the leaders of UNCTAD and the Group of 77 remain trapped in a situation in which intransigence seemed preferable to limited gains? The answer, I believe, resides in the interaction between a number of structural, institutional, and personal factors. Before discussing these factors, I want to emphasize again that I believe the initial decision to seek a major restructuring of commodity trade was understandable and perhaps even justified given the circumstances of the times and the pressing needs of the developing countries. But in the light of subsequent events, two questions must be raised: Was the Common Fund so important that it was worth risking all other progress in the IPC negotiations in order to establish it, and once it became clear that the Common Fund was not acceptable to the major developed countries, was a change in strategy (beyond praying for a new administration in the United States) possible?

One needs to begin with the deeply felt belief that unity was the most powerful weapon that the developing countries had. Whether this is or is not valid or whether the kind of unity that over one hundred very different countries can establish will ever be a very credible weapon are separate questions. Here we need only note that the maintenance of unity had very severe costs. Expectations of benefits had to be raised well beyond anything that could be accomplished by buffer stock stabilization, and promises of compensation had to be made that tended to increase the aid (not trade) elements of the IPC. Anything that might split the Group (such as statements of impact or clarity about pricing objectives) had to be avoided; there was no choice but to seek commitment to the broadest principles, in the hope that progress at this level would provide sufficient momentum to maintain unity when conflicts over specifics actually began. But there was no progress.

The UNCTAD leadership maintained that the Common Fund was so important that a change in tactics was not justified.[60] I do not believe that this is a tenable position. The Fund might well play a useful role in commodity trade, but for it to do more would require that it have powers and resources that would never be granted by the developed countries (or by some resource-rich developing countries). Nevertheless, acceptance of the Common Fund was invested with a degree of symbolic significance in the North-South conflict that made it far more important than any objective examination of its possible benefits would justify. But an obdurate demand that democratic governments make an open-ended commitment to an institution that may or may not be necessary and that may or may not be given a proper role, resources, or powers does not make sense. Rather, it is my belief that the decision to demand this commitment and to measure success or failure in the commodity negotiations in terms of its acceptance was not only costly but also unwise. It was costly because too many resources were expended on the quest for a mechanism that was never likely to be as important as its advocates contended, and it was unwise because the goal was pursued in the wrong way and because it lost valuable time and distracted attention from other goals that were no less and perhaps much more important.

The explanation for the initial decision to establish a particular course and the explanation for the later decision not to change this course need not be identical. For the latter, I believe that the costs of altering course always seemed higher to the leaders of UNCTAD and the Group of 77 than the costs of persistence, of pushing forward in the hope that something might turn up. After so much effort had been expended on the creation and management of a unified position, to convince the Group of 77 that expectations had to be scaled down, that benefits had to be delayed, and that there were no "quick fixes" to reduce the gap between rich and

[60] Insofar as this argument is true, it raises a number of questions about the proper strategies for change in this international system, about the best means to achieve viable settlements, and about how we can begin to understand and explain this universe of interaction more effectively. Some tentative and provisional judgments about these matters will be offered in Chapter 7.

poor—in effect, to admit that the program was oversold, even if for honorable reasons and because of honest (and widely shared) misjudgments—was probably too much to ask of leaders whose reputation and future roles rested on meeting the expectations they had raised.[61] Moreover, even if they had wanted to compromise, they were trapped by the fear that a concession would unravel the whole package, and they were held hostage by the threat of defection. This was not a bargaining environment that generated or rewarded flexibility or suppleness.[62] But it was a bargaining process in which both sides felt the need to assert and defend different sets of principles. As I noted in Chapter 1, while I do not believe either set of principles was wholly adequate, the quest to establish ordering principles in a very unstable environment was neither surprising nor irrational. And although personal factors—background, ambition, skills—surely played some role in the negotiating process, if we were to seek to ascribe responsibility for the unsatisfactory results, the intermixing of intellectual factors with structural and institutional factors seems the most crucial. In effect, an arguably mistaken judgment about what goals should be sought was joined to a less arguably mistaken judgment about how to go about attaining these goals. The developed countries preferred stalemate to movement toward the Group of 77's principles; the Group of 77, committed to unity and convinced that gambling on large future gains was preferable to taking the best available offer, was trapped both by its principles and by the characteristics of the bargaining system that it had created. Thus reforms of both principles and practices were necessary: responsibility for the outcome must be shared not only between all the participants but also between the realms of thinking and doing.

[61] They were being asked, after all, to achieve an impossible goal: "to eliminate the economic imbalance between developed and developing countries." See UNCTAD, the *Manila Declaration and Programme of Action* (Geneva: TD/195), February 1976, p. 9.

[62] Insofar as there is validity to this argument, it raises crucial questions about the power of the handful of men who make or heavily influence the decisions to set the international agenda and to determine how it will be negotiated, about the institutional context of their decisions, and about the idea of unity itself. We shall look more closely at these questions in Chapters 4 and 5.

In short, at each stage of this bargaining process a similar set of factors influenced the outcome, but the relative weight of each factor varied in different periods. From this perspective, one might argue that the original decisions to seek a radical restructuring of commodity trade were most influenced by environmental and intellectual factors; that the decision to seek commitment to new principles before detailed negotiations commenced was most influenced by perceptions of the need to use the leverage provided by unity and by the particular capabilities of UNCTAD; and that the decision (or nondecision) to reject a compromise strategy was most influenced by the nature of the bargaining process and, to a lesser extent, by personal factors. But I emphasize that these are very relative judgments and that all the factors played some role in each period. For the United States, ideological factors and the "OPEC effect" dominated the early stages, technical issues became progressively important (especially after Nairobi), and domestic political factors (particularly the likely reaction of Congress) were important throughout but apparently dominant in the calculations of the Carter administration.

One final question needs to be examined in this chapter. Does this negotiation have parallels in other North-South negotiations, or does it have too many unique features to be valid as a basis for generalization? We treat these issues briefly in the next section.

Bargaining on Other Issues and in Other Areas

The structure of interests on most North-South issues is so complex and variegated that the tendency to divide the bargaining terrain into two opposed positions virtually always oversimplifies. In commodities, the developing countries are both exporters and importers; in the area of technology transfer, most are importers, but a number are becoming or may become exporters (note Brazil's arms exports); on debt, there are sharp divergences between higher income countries that fear debt relief will reduce future commercial loans and lower income countries that want government loans canceled; and in the Law of the Sea Conferences there have been bitter conflicts between landlocked and coastal states and between land-based mineral producers and mineral importers. The split between the least developed and the higher income developing countries appears in one form or another on most issues, but even here there are notable exceptions for geological, geographical, or ideological reasons. In this sense, the analysis of commodities has one important parallel with the analysis of other issues: despite sharp internal Group of 77 disagreements, the developing countries have managed to establish and maintain—at great cost in flexibility and time—an effective degree of unity.[63]

The explanation for this ability to transcend objective conflicts of interest with other Group of 77 members is far from simple. Clearly there is more to it than "an overlapping coalition of interests" in which support on one issue is bartered for support on other issues.[64] Extrapolations from pluralist and incremental systems tend to miss important dimensions of the process of consensus formation within the Group of 77, such as the commitment to a particular set of principles, a widely shared resentment against the existing order and a widely shared desire for more influence on international decision making, the impact of the idea of unity and of the institutionalization of the Group system, and the important role of the international bureaucracy and a few key delegates in setting Group priorities and negotiating strategies. These factors create a negotiating environment that generates some important parallels between apparently dissimilar issues. But I do *not* mean to argue that any of the parallels are exact—only suggestive.

The Law of the Sea negotiations seem to present the most striking parallels with the commodity negotiations. The Group of 77's commitment to a particular principle or set of principles and its inability to compromise are especially noteworthy. Thus two analysts note that the Group's "disin-

---

[63] But of course the internal splits are different in each case, and this at least implies the possibility of cross-issue trade-offs—of which there have been few.

[64] This is the explanation for unity in Douglas C. Smyth, "The Global Economy and the Third World: Coalition or Cleavage?" *World Politics* 29, no. 4 (July 1977): 602.

terest in incremental bargaining would be consistent with their insistence that the [seabed authority] is not a matter for compromise with the North, but a matter of principle."[65] And as Edward Miles notes, for most of the developing countries "the question of principle is the crucial one and concessions amount to capitulation."[66] Moreover, suspicion of the other side's motives, disagreement over some technical issues, and conflicts over distribution and redistribution have also diminished the possibility of compromise. Trade-offs were especially difficult not only because principles could not be compromised but also because the issues were very complex and not easily resolved even by technical analyses.

There were also other reasons why the Group of 77 found it difficult to compromise its principles. For example, Barry Buzan, in discussing the Group of 77's inability to respond to requests for clarifications, notes:

> The Group of 77 had great difficulty coping with this tactic for two reasons. First, the Group contained no delegations with the technical expertise necessary to handle a debate on that level. Second, the text represented a delicate compromise within the Group of 77 itself, and this made it almost impossible for the Group to bargain over the text without destroying its internal consensus.[67]

In the commodity discussions, the UNCTAD staff could provide the necessary technical expertise, but it should be noted that in both cases the Group of 77 was dependent on outside technicians. And the danger of compromise to Group unity was a familiar theme in the commodity negotiations.

A few other similarities in the two negotiation processes ought to be noted. Buzan emphasizes the influence of the original seabed proposals in shaping future negotiations. The original IPC proposals were also crucial in setting the bound-

---

[65] Robert L. Friedheim and William J. Durch, "The International Seabed Resources Agency Negotiations and the New International Economic Order," *International Organization* 31, no. 2 (Spring 1977): 379.

[66] Edward Miles, "The Structure and Effects of the Decision Process in the Seabed Committee and the Third United Nations Conference on the Law of the Sea," *International Organization* 31, no. 2 (Spring 1977): 226.

[67] Barry Buzan, *Seabed Politics* (New York: Praeger Publishers, 1976), p. 226.

aries and the terms of the commodity discussions. He also notes the costs implicit in the delay engendered by negotiating all of the Law of the Sea in a large, public forum, particularly the growing influence of external developments and the loss of support behind the original initiative. And just as in UNCTAD, each side was willing to pay the costs of delay, for each felt the other would have to yield first.[68] In sum, the recipe for stalemate was remarkably similar.

UNCTAD has also been the setting for controversial negotiations on debt relief and a code of conduct for the transfer of technology. Although these issues received less publicity than the commodity issue, they are likely to become increasingly prominent in the next few years, and the lack of salience in the current period has not meant that the negotiating process has had markedly different characteristics than it did with the commodity issue. The demand for prior acceptance of broad statements of principle, the rigidities of the Group system, and the consequent delay and stalemate have again dominated. Of course there have been some differences that set debt and the transfer of technology somewhat apart from commodities (and from each other), since different interests are affected and a different range of results is anticipated. For example, the Group of 77 has thus far been relatively more moderate in its demands for generalized debt relief and the developed countries have been relatively more adamant in rejecting such demands. These stances reflect the fact that within the Group of 77 internal opposition to generalized debt relief comes from some of the most influential developing countries (who fear the effects on future commercial lending) and that the developed countries fear the potential effects on the private banking system.[69] Transfer of tech-

---

[68] On the effects of the original proposal, see ibid., pp. 291f., and on the effects of delay, see ibid., pp. 294-297.

[69] Note that if doubts about the wisdom of the proposal came from the poorest states, it is not clear that it would have induced moderation: the poorest countries have generally lacked the technical resources to deal with complex issues effectively and as a result have usually been dragged along by the higher income countries and the staff. This is one reason why they have begun to band together as an increasingly influential cross-regional and cross-issue caucus within the Group of 77.

nology, conversely, has not yet become as sharply focused as debt or commodities because the issue itself is more diffuse, costs and benefits are difficult to calculate and may be primarily long-range, and it is difficult to isolate the transfer issue from other issues such as the control of multinational enterprises and the restructuring of the world's industrial geography. Nevertheless, the differences among all these issues are essentially matters of degree, for they are part of the same negotiating process with the same structural, ideological, and procedural characteristics.

I do not want to discuss the debt and transfer of technology issues in depth, for each would require (and deserves) a manuscript of its own. There is one aspect of these issues that I do want to comment on, however, since it provides a somewhat different comparison with the commodity issue. I have noted earlier in several places that the IPC elicited serious technical criticisms from a number of critics, some of whom would be considered genuine friends of the Third World, and that it also raised serious distributional issues. If the same points were to arise on debt and the transfer of technology, this perhaps suggests the need for the Third World to reconsider exactly what it is seeking—and why—in the effort to construct a (or "the") New International Economic Order. Or, alternatively, it raises questions about who puts together the various packages that have become part of the NIEO.

The debt issue seems to be deficient on both counts. Without detailing the arguments, it should be noted that a number of highly regarded and independent experts such as Jagdish Bhagwati and Paul Streeten have expressed great doubt about the wisdom of proposals for generalized debt relief.[70] These doubts seem to be shared by the finance ministers of the Third World: despite UNCTAD's demands for generalized relief, at a recent World Bank annual meeting the finance ministers accepted a resolution without demur that did not even mention the issue. The distributional issue is more ambiguous, for who benefits most is obviously de-

[70] See the comments by Bhagwati and Streeten in Jagdish N. Bhagwati, ed., *The New International Economic Order: The North-South Debate* (Cambridge: The MIT Press, 1977), p. 14 and pp. 78-79, respectively.

pendent on the form of relief granted. Peter Kenen, for example, has argued that most of the proposals generated by UNCTAD and the Group of 77 thus far would help the higher income developing countries more than the lower income countries; consequently, he argues for a form of debt relief designed to benefit primarily the poorest countries, most of whose debt is intergovernmental.[71] While it is not clear that turning the debt issue into an aid issue for the poorest countries is either politically or economically sound, this kind of proposal at least does not provide disproportionate benefits to the already (relatively) well-off countries—or to the bankers who have loaned them great sums.

Demands for a legally binding code of conduct on the transfer of technology (a staple on the UNCTAD agenda for the Nairobi Conference) have also generated substantial critical doubts about effectiveness and equity. Codes of conduct have also been advocated for other issues, some of which overlap in part with the code on technology (for example, the codes on multinational enterprise, on restrictive business practices, and on bribery). On the surface, efforts to codify behavior among and between states and entities of such varying values and levels of development seem bound to fail. Why then have they become so fashionable?

A code of conduct on the transfer of technology might provide some benefits to both exporters and importers. From the point of view of the developing countries, a code might limit the impact of restrictive business practices, it might improve competition, it might improve bargaining leverage by reducing the opportunity of multinational corporations to shift between developing countries with different policies and laws, it might improve data collection and information, and it might legitimize and provide some moral authority for special

[71] See Peter B. Kenen, "Debt Relief as Development Assistance," in ibid., pp. 50-77. Perhaps one ought to add that the SDR-link proposals may also have negative distributional effects if—as desired by the developing countries—SDRs were to be disbursed according to IMF shares. This would give most of the benefits to the richest LDCs. Also, if given automatically, there would be no way to control or evaluate the manner in which the benefits were used. See William R. Cline, *International Monetary Reform and the Developing Countries* (Washington, D.C.: The Brookings Institution, 1976).

treatment of the developing countries.[72] The developed countries (or their corporations) would receive in return something of great value in a very unsettled environment: a higher degree of stability and predictability by virtue of jointly negotiated rules that are either legally binding or morally compelling.[73] The practical question is whether a code that included all or most of these mutual benefits could ever be negotiated, since one side's desire for stability may be directly opposed to the other side's desire for more competition, more bargaining leverage, and a better distribution of benefits.

Negotiating uncertainties are only part of the reason that many observers doubt the wisdom of codes. There is a general feeling among critics that the code can be no more than a very general, nonbinding codification of the status quo and that it will have minimal practical effect on the behavior of multinational corporations.[74] This reflects the judgment that such codes will touch only shadow, not substance—that they fail to deal with the underlying structure of economic and political power and do not significantly affect the internal decision-making criteria or the pricing policies of the corporations that control most technology. In effect, a strict code probably could not be enforced; if it were enforced, it would

[72] These potential advantages are extracted from a number of sources. See especially G. K. Helleiner, "International Technology Issues: Southern Needs and Northern Responses," in Bhagwati, *The New International Economic Order: The North-South Debate*, pp. 300-301; and Karl P. Sauvant, "Controlling Transnational Enterprises: A Review and Some Further Thoughts," in *The New International Economic Order—Confrontation or Cooperation between North and South?* ed. Karl P. Sauvant and Hajo Hasenpflug (Boulder, Col.: Westview Press, 1977), pp. 356-433.

[73] Stability and predictability seem to appear in virtually all commentaries as the potential advantages for developed countries and the MNCs.

[74] See Dieter Ernst, "A Code of Conduct for the Transfer of Technology: Establishing New Rules or Codifying the Status Quo?" in Sauvant and Hasenpflug, *The New International Economic Order*, pp. 297-314; and Constantine V. Vaitsos, "Foreign Investment and Productive Knowledge," in *Beyond Dependency—The Developing World Speaks Out*, ed. Guy F. Erb and Valeriana Kallab (Washington, D.C.: Overseas Development Council, 1975), pp. 75-94. Vaitsos also criticizes the codes for not sufficiently differentiating among firms, industries, or countries.

probably diminish the transfer of technology or engender efforts to bribe and cheat. The most likely result of the interaction of these factors would be a conservative, nonbinding code that would have little positive effect and might even have negative effects if it were to distract from more important measures (many of which are domestic, not international), if it were to harm regional cooperation efforts, or if it were to lead to a code that was actually *weaker* than some current national efforts at control.[75] And, as with the earlier discussion of indexation, it needs to be asked whether it makes sense to codify the existing relationship when the primary aim is to establish new norms and new rules?

The equity issue is difficult to clarify because so much depends on what kind of code is established and whether it is enforced. In general, however, if the code did lead to improved data collection and information and if it enhanced bargaining leverage, a case could be made that the poorest states would be the relatively greatest beneficiaries.[76] But the likelihood that the poorest countries would begin to take advantage of these opportunities (should they be realized) would probably lead to an entirely different outcome: the poorest countries would be sacrificed as the multinationals sought more profitable and more sympathetic locales. At any rate, apart from major technological breakthroughs in food or energy production, very little of great significance would happen to the poorest countries as a result of the existence or nonexistence of a code of conduct on the transfer of technology.

These comments clearly imply that the case study of commodity bargaining has a good deal of relevance in terms of several levels for bargaining on other North-South issues. The quest for commitment to statements of principle, the impact of the idea of unity and of the group structure, the diffi-

[75] See Helleiner, "International Technology Issues," p. 298, for the argument that domestic policies of each developing country are more important than either codes or the policies of the developed countries.

[76] Ibid., p. 303.

culty of arranging trade-offs and compromises, and the acceptance of delay as a necessary and acceptable price to pay for ultimate victory seem to have become conventional aspects of the North-South bargaining environment. The influence of international secretariats and the institutional setting have also been consistently influential in determining the frame of reference for negotiations. And, finally, there has been the same tendency to oversimplify technical issues and to exaggerate the likely gains from any feasible range of external change, especially in relation to the importance of domestic reform. Psychic and ceremonial victories have come to seem more important than genuine progress on the issues, perhaps because of the need to affirm a better vision of the future or perhaps because what can actually be achieved in the international negotiating system seems so insufficient.

I have noted that I do not intend to deal at length with the internal factors that have heavily conditioned the responses the United States has made to developing country demands. I note here only that procedurally the same general combination of factors—ideological, technical, bureaucratic, congressional—seem to play a role in all issues. The result has tended to be a policy that conflicts with Group of 77 demands in rather consistent ways across issues: the case-by-case emphasis versus an emphasis on first principles, an emphasis on efficiency and stability versus an emphasis on equity and redistribution, an emphasis on improving the market versus an emphasis on radically restructuring it, and an emphasis on reforming old institutions versus an emphasis on creating new ones.

The other question I want to discuss in this section, albeit very briefly, is whether the external environment in which the negotiations I have described took place is likely to change so much that any lessons are bound to be irrelevant or misleading. No one who has come of age in the 1960s and the 1970s is likely ever to be able to foresee simple continuities and a world without persistent but surprising "shocks." Still, it is very difficult to imagine developments that will reduce the pressure of the developing countries on the international system, and it is very easy to imagine developments—in energy, food, or the trading system—that will make them increasingly demanding, if not desperate, members of this system. Inevitably, this will keep the bargaining process between North and South on the top of the international agenda. If the result were a repetition of the process that I have described in the last three chapters, the prognosis is grim.

As a result, major reforms of the bargaining process between North and South—and indeed within each group— seem imperative. But reforms are easier to advocate than to implement. The bargaining constraints that have been described thus far are strong; they cannot be overcome or diminished by rhetoric nor is there any magic key that can guarantee quick results—and for many developing countries quick results may be of the essence. Still, we need to do what we can as expeditiously as possible.

We begin this discussion of the reform process in the next two chapters by examining one set of factors that has exerted a profound effect on North-South bargaining. These are the institutional and structural factors that bear a substantial part of the responsibility for generating a particular pattern of conflict, confrontation, and stalemate. The nature of the UNCTAD staff, the role of the Secretary-General, and the arguments for and against the group bargaining process will be examined in more detail than the IPC case study permitted. I should emphasize that these factors are not solely responsible for the current impasse, as Chapter 7 will indicate. What follows is both analytical and prescriptive; moreover, both analysis and prescription draw on but are not limited to the commodity negotiations, as our concern shifts more broadly to the entire North-South negotiating agenda. The key question analytically is *why* the institutional and structural factors have impeded the negotiation of viable settlements; prescriptively, the key question is what possibilities of reform genuinely exist.

PART TWO

Global Bargaining: Reforming

The Process of Settlement

Chapter 5

UNCTAD and
the Institutional Crisis

Declining confidence in the UN system is widespread among the industrial countries. A persuasive indictment of what the United Nations has become is well within reach, and it cites as evidence such factors as: the increasing dominance of a Third World coalition that is occasionally irresponsible and narrowly self-interested; the politicization of even apparently technical issues (that is, differently politicized than when the industrial countries were in effective control of process and outcome); resolutions that patch together everyone's demands, that are masterpieces in the phraseology of ambiguity, and that result in uncertainty about what, if anything, has been decided; the absence of agreed standards by which to evaluate performance; substantial doubts about the competence, the impartiality, the size, and the remuneration of professional staff appointed on increasingly nationalistic grounds; a rigid bureaucratic ethos inevitably accompanied by excessive centralization and documentation; a confusion of responsibility between different institutions and an attempt to legislate or at least declaim on issues that are too complex to be resolved in grand confrontations or open debate; and a pervasive sense that the UN drains increasing amounts of scarce resources from the industrial countries but returns insufficient benefits—to either rich or poor. That the industrial countries have expended little energy in attempting to arrest these developments is generally true, perhaps because the UN has never seemed substantively significant (except for occasional and episodic ventures into peacekeeping). But shared responsibility for the present state of affairs in no way diminishes the force of the indictment itself.

Growing disenchantment with the UN system has coincided with an increased need to discuss and resolve or regulate more and more issues in a process of collective decision making. As a result, a number of analyses have begun to appear that seek to bypass or limit the role of the United Nations by dealing with many issues in ad hoc institutional arenas, or in narrower functional institutions, or in institutions still controlled by the industrial countries. For some issues, this is certainly a sensible and perhaps inevitable development, but it may also engender problems of its own that need to be carefully weighed.

Critics of the prevailing institutional structure tend to share the judgment that international economic issues ought to be dealt with outside the UN framework and that larger, public forums like UNCTAD ought to be limited to discussion and debate.[1] The critics also share a number of other judgments. There is, for example, a sense that the proliferation of functional institutions to deal with specific issues is necessary and wise. Issues will be more manageable when the participants share power and interest, agreement on objectives will be more likely and rhetorical posturing less likely, like-minded expert delegates will communicate more effectively, and blackmail on agenda-setting and on linkage with extraneous issues will be more difficult.[2] In effect, the politicization that inevitably accompanies negotiations in large, public arenas will be diminished, and the possibility of genuine consensus on substance will be enhanced.

Arguments for the proliferation of new institutions also reflect other considerations. The old institutions, even if they could be substantially reformed, always seem anachronistic, especially in periods of rapid change. They remain identified with the configuration of power and the pattern of concerns that prevailed at the time of creation. And, of course, faith

---

[1] The more general criticisms can be found in Seymour Maxwell Finger, "United States Policy Toward International Institutions," *International Organization* 30, no. 2 (Spring 1976): 347-360; and Sidney Weintraub, "What Do We Want from the United Nations?" *International Organization* 30, no. 4 (Autumn 1976): 687-695.

[2] See especially C. Fred Bergsten, "Interdependence and the Reform of International Institutions," *International Organization* 30, no. 2 (Spring 1976): 362-363; and Eugene B. Skolnikoff, *The International Imperatives of Technology* (Berkeley, Cal.: Institute of International Studies, 1972), p. 135.

that they can respond to new problems and new needs has been eroded by several decades of ineffectuality.

The potential benefits from new institutions are thus reasonably clear. But there are some reasons to doubt that these benefits can or will be consistently realized in the years ahead. In part, this reflects the increasing politicization of even apparently technical issues; consequently, the smaller arenas merely duplicate the patterns of conflict prevalent in the larger arenas. Increased politicization can be attributed to two factors. In the first place, many of the technical issues do not have technical solutions or, perhaps more accurately, the choice of a particular technical solution can have profoundly differing effects for the states involved. Moreover, in many cases our doctrines or theories do not even provide reliable guidance about the existence or shape of a technical "solution." In the second place, the developing countries have managed to maintain sufficient unity to carry over the quest for new principles of international order from the grand arenas like the General Assembly to the smaller arenas like the Conference on International Economic Cooperation (CIEC). Comparison shopping between different institutional settings (which has been central to most discussions of alternate institutional strategies) may thus become increasingly difficult or problematic. Finally, other potential or real disadvantages of proliferating functional and ad hoc arenas ought to be noted: costs in time and money, dangers that poor countries with little effective power but great concern for particular functional issues will be left to fend for themselves (a problem in any pluralist system, for not all players can gain access to the game), and the possibility of fragmentation, drift, and incoherence without powerful central institutions.

Bergsten has attempted to avoid some of the dangers of fragmentation and incoherence among so many different decision-making arenas by advocating informal coordination by the "big guys" in "smoke-filled rooms."[3] He has suggested a series of concentric circles, with a small, inner circle of coun-

---

[3] He uses this analogy in a comment in Don Wallace, Jr. and Helga Escobar, eds., *The Future of International Economic Organizations* (New York: Praeger Publishers, 1977), pp. 87-88.

tries coming to an agreement among themselves on an issue, then broadening the agreement through discussions with close associates, and finally more general consultations and actual implementation of agreements in existing institutions. According to Bergsten, this would succeed in performing two critical tasks of the institutional order: the integration of new power centers into the decision-making structure (some, for example Saudi Arabia, in the inner circle; others in the second circle) and the ratification and legitimization of the power structure that results.[4] This is pluralism tempered by oligarchy—or worse, paternalism.

Proposals for inner directorates by the powerful have been a familiar part of the international landscape. The attempt to ensure that those with the power to act also have—and take—the responsibility to act is both inevitable and justified—for some issues. The strategic arms issue is one obvious example, although even here the need to inhibit the proliferation of nuclear weapons may require a sharp extension of the "inner circle." On many other issues, however, especially issues with a direct bearing on North-South relations, the attempt to revive and implement a principle of hierarchical order may neither be possible nor justified.

Informal coordination among the "core" countries may be necessary or useful for effective policymaking on any global issue. But making it a prerequisite for movement seems dubious. One reason is that the process of consultation has not worked very well, primarily because of the difficulty of extracting agreement within each government (and especially the United States) on a common policy.[5] Core group consultation is also a process that leaves global policymaking on crucial issues hostage to the vicissitudes of the domestic politics or economics of a few key countries. This may well be true of any international decision-making system, for few policies can

[4] This scheme is described in C. Fred Bergsten, Georges Berthoin, and Kinhide Mushakoji, *The Reform of International Institutions* (New York: The Trilateral Commission, 1976).

[5] In studying UNCTAD, I was often struck by the failures of consultation—some allies were as uncertain of U.S. intentions as were the Group of 77. Getting a U.S. decision, after which consultations could be undertaken, seemed impossible until some kind of deadline intruded.

succeed without the support of these countries; but closing off the process in this fashion may not only delay agreement and provide a tacit veto to a few dissenters but also diminish the possibility of seeking useful, if partial, agreements among those core countries and other countries that share a consensus on particular issues (that is, not all cores are equal cores). And if the core countries do reach agreement among themselves, consultation with the outer circles may become a euphemism for passing the word on. Only those who believe a few experts from a handful of rich, conservative governments always know what is best for everyone can greet this outcome with equanimity.

Two other problems may be even more critical. The Bergsten proposal implicitly presumes that the most advanced or most critical developing countries can be split from the rest of the Group of 77 by promises of incorporation in the inner circle. He suggests that CIEC is something of a model in this regard, integrating the new powers into the system and reconciling the tension between effective decision making and widespread participation (with nineteen of the developing countries chosen to represent the rest).[6] This seems to me a fundamental misreading of the CIEC experience: in fact, the nineteen were tightly bound by instructions from the Group of 77, and they were frequently forced to be even more extreme than the other developing countries in order to avoid charges of "selling out." But beyond this, given the level of *shared* hostility and distrust toward the developed countries and given the very strong peer group pressure and emotional force behind the commitment to unity, the effort to split the Group of 77 by offering differential favors to a few developing countries is likely to be counterproductive.

In any case, what offer would entice the potential "breakaways" into a new relationship? One doubts that ceremonial incorporation into the inner circle without substantive concessions will suffice. But most of these countries are already the actual or potential prime beneficiaries of most of the items currently on the North-South agenda. Should the developed

---

[6] See Bergsten, Berthoin, and Mushakoji, *The Reform of International Institutions*, p. 28.

countries offer them more, or can they do so without offering others (more in need) even less? In addition, not all of the rich developing countries are conservative: several are demanding more rapid and more politically difficult change (for example, market access for manufactured exports) than the other developing countries, perhaps because they benefit most or because they need help against internal pressures. In any case, a clumsy and heavily publicized effort to bring a few of the anointed into the club is only likely to bring the Group of 77 even closer together: if the developed countries compelled an either/or choice, the results would probably be very embarrassing (both numerically and philosophically).

The other problem concerns legitimacy. Most advocates of inner circle decision making and/or an increased emphasis on narrower, functional settings for the negotiation process concede that this raises an important question: By what right—beyond might—can these smaller bodies decide issues that have an important effect on those outside the inner circle? The general assumption, implicitly or explicitly, is that wider arenas like the General Assembly and UNCTAD will provide the required legitimacy by ratifying results negotiated elsewhere—a rather narrow version of the principle of "collective legitimization." But will the majority of the developing countries play their designated role if they have not been consulted along the way, if they fear that their interests have not been protected, if they have not received some form of special compensation—and if their control over the developing countries who have been invited into the inner circle is not firm? In sum, if legitimization or majority support from the developing countries were necessary to implement a particular outcome, the leverage of the Group of 77 over the inner circle could be substantial.

I have stressed a number of disadvantages and dangers implicit in some recent efforts to devise a coherent institutional strategy. But there are no cost-free institutional strategies, and it may well be that something like the Bergsten approach will become increasingly necessary—if only because the UN system has continued to disintegrate. The results could be an increasing level of hostility with the majority of the Third World, declining levels of legitimacy for attempts at global policymaking, substantial costs in time, money, and personnel to deal with proliferating institutions, and an increasingly fragmented and discontinuous system. Under these circumstances, the UN system would rapidly become a kind of residual forum for rhetorical outbursts and small amounts of technical assistance for the poorest developing countries—the "outer circle."

Is there a viable alternative? There is no simple or conclusive answer to this question. Too many uncertainties exist not only in the sense that international institutions cannot control or dominate the environment in which they must operate but also in the sense that we can only make rough and ready—not theoretical—judgments about the presumed superiority of different kinds of institutional structures. Within these constraints, we can at least suggest the need to seek an institutional strategy that is coherent rather than episodic and ad hoc, that is balanced rather than reflecting an either/or choice between different arenas, and that promises increased degrees of stability and effectiveness. But the extent to which we can approach this ideal depends on what answers we give to two critical questions.

The first question is whether meaningful reform of the UN system is really possible? Most of the proposals for reforms have concentrated on improved management techniques and bureaucratic reorganization. These are without doubt crucial measures, for they bear significantly on the capacity of an organization to operate efficiently. But I mean by reform something more than improved efficiency; I have in mind primarily efforts to diminish the political and structural obstacles that are responsible for much of the UN system's current disabilities. In this sense, efficiency is only a part of the more general notion of effectiveness or the achievement of desired goals. For the UN to be effective, it must be able to achieve its member's goals consistently (and, hopefully, efficiently), which is to say—in the best of all possible worlds—irrespective of changes in the environment or personnel.[7] Approximations of this goal (which is all that is possible but well below what has been achieved) are dependent on basic improvements in the process of decision and not merely on more efficient use of resources.

The second question is, if we were to outline a number of useful reforms of the structure of decision, what possibility is there that they would be accepted by the developing countries or that the developed countries would expend some scarce political capital in seeking support for such measures? In effect, what are the terms of a bargain that would permit both groups of countries to see such reforms as mutually beneficial? I shall discuss possible answers to these questions in a later section. Here I want only to note several attitudes that may exert considerable influence on perceptions of the utility or possibility of institutional reform. The first of these is the attitude, widely prevalent among many developed country officials and experts, that institutions do not really matter and that only the substance of issues is significant. I hope that the preceding analysis of commodities has indicated just why this view is insufficient: the institutional setting had a very crucial impact on both process and outcome. Moreover, on a more general level it needs to be emphasized that improving the process of decision may be more important than achieving agreement on any particular substantive issue. Simply put, the rationale for this is that consistent and dependable outcomes are improbable without a more effective decision-making structure.

Failure to understand the growing linkage between substance and setting will surely diminish the possibilities for effective reform. In addition, in the short run it will diminish the possibility of developing a viable policy toward (and within) existing institutions and exacerbate the tendency toward a kind of random ad hocism. Finally, the pervasive cynicism that now surrounds efforts at institutional reform (so

[7] There are interesting comments on these matters in Paul Diesing, *Reason in Society—Five Types of Decisions and Their Social Conditions* (Urbana: University of Illinois Press, 1962), pp. 3-5.

that they are perceived as a cheap substitute for substantive progress) may well continue to grow. This is especially true if all concerned were to continue to act as if tinkering with mechanics were the root of the problem. Even if tinkering were to reflect the limits of the possible, there is utility in understanding why it is so and in taking it into account in devising policy.

There is another attitude or assumption that may be significant in this context. Existing institutions reflecting earlier power structures and patterns of concern may seem incapable of responding to new imperatives; but in a period of rapid change and great uncertainty even new institutions may be obsolescent by the time they become operational (which may take several years), or they may be seen to have grasped the wrong part of the problem. In common-sense terms, this apparently justifies the belief that institutions are more important in a time of consolidation than they are in a time of change. In the latter, quick and flexible response is central, a fact that necessarily implies indifference to existing institutions and an emphasis on informal or ad hoc patterns of consultation and settlement.

I doubt the utility of a simple distinction between the role of institutions in periods of consolidation or change. At a minimum, one needs to understand what kind of change is underway in what kind of setting. Insofar as there are many issues that require global agreements (or agreements among all the negotiating groups), the institutional question is bound to be important—in spite of, but also because of, the nature of prevailing patterns of change. Even more significantly, in the context of North-South issues, effective institutional decision making is imperative and perhaps indispensable. Many of the developing countries are not yet in a position to articulate their own interests on very complex and rapidly shifting problems, and they need the help of existing institutions not only to identify those interests but also to package them and to seek acceptance and implementation. This is not to say that such help can only come from the existing institutional structure, although the weight of habit and the costs of alternative settings probably make this the most likely choice; it is to say, however, that it is mistaken to dismiss the importance of institutions simply because we are in a period of rapid change.

Neither of the two questions that I have posed can be answered definitively, and even an affirmative answer to both—a doubtful outcome—would not resolve the issue. The reform process and the development of sufficient support are likely to take a great deal of time. This suggests the need for a transitional strategy that combines efforts at reform with an attempt to play the existing institutional game more effectively. In terms of the latter perspective, what seems appropriate is a more carefully defined attempt to implement some parts of the Bergsten approach, more sophistication about how policy is made in existing institutions, and an effort to create only the minimum necessary new institutions. The dangers of the Bergsten approach might be diminished if a serious effort were made to ensure that the expansion of the inner circle(s) of decision making was more representative of all interests, not merely the new and the old rich. Only this will permit the legitimization of decisions made in smaller arenas. Some decision making by the rich seems necessary in order to deal with issues that cannot wait for the creation of a wider consensus and also in order to serve as a spur for serious attempts at reform: the availability of competitive institutions may incite reform more effectively than any other tactic. But some line also needs to be drawn, since promiscuous institutional proliferation may create more problems than it solves.[8]

[8] The developing countries have been the foremost advocates of institutional proliferation, though hardly for the reasons I have noted; rather, they distrust the older institutions, and they hope for more aid (and more positions) and more intellectual support from new forums. And so we have "special sessions," UNIDO, IFAD, and even UNCTAD (now dangerously "aging"). But the argument for new institutions seems to have been carried to its ludicrous limits in a recent report to the Club of Rome by a group under the leadership of Jan Tinbergen. Tinbergen's report, *RIO: Reshaping the International Order* (New York: E. P. Dutton & Co., Inc., 1976) advocates among other things the creation of a World Food Authority, a World Agency for Mineral Resources, a World Energy Research Authority, a World Technological Development Authority (and bank), an International Control Agency (for the environment), a World Disarmament Agency, and a World Trade and Development Authority. The authors also advocate strengthening the existing UN! For what?

It may be useful to make one final comment. The contention that international institutions cannot be major agents of change by themselves but can only register and institutionalize changes that have occurred elsewhere seems amply justified by the commodity case study.[9] Even the hope that institutions might become increasingly effective agents of change over time, either as a result of small but accumulating concessions from the rich or because of the power of resource-control, merely emphasizes the domination of environmental impulses. Perhaps the only important qualification to this argument is somewhat different: for some developing countries, what might seem like minor change from a global perspective can be of major significance locally. In effect, some changes may be major for all and some changes may be minor for all, but there are other changes that might be both at once. Still, in what follows we shall be concerned with reforms that enhance the facilitating function of international institutions (in articulating and establishing agreement on common interests and procedures of dispute settlement) and not with reforms that aim at more autonomous power.

My major focus will be the reform process within UNCTAD, although the analysis should have wider relevance. I shall examine what appear to me to be UNCTAD's major problems, and suggest a number of possible reforms, and then discuss why these reforms might be perceived as mutually beneficial. In addition, some reforms in the manner of playing the existing game during the transitional period (or longer) will be highlighted. I shall then conclude with a brief discussion of some of the implications and consequences of the preceding analysis.

Perceptions of Reform

UNCTAD has never been a very popular organization with the governments of the industrial countries. Accusations of incompetence and ineffectuality have been widespread; even more telling have been assumptions of bias and hostility to-

[9] Barry Buzan makes a similar point in reference to the Law of the Sea negotiations. See Barry Buzan, *Seabed Politics* (New York: Praeger Publishers, 1976), pp. 296-297.

ward the interests of the developed countries. One American official has also argued that UNCTAD "manufactures repetitive crises" and engenders "unilateral demands, and there is really no end to this process." And a former high official of the Commerce Department has concluded that "there are at this moment two international organizations that are quite useless: the UN and UNCTAD."[10] But despite these sentiments and despite a rather general consensus among policy elites in the industrial countries that reform of existing institutions must suffice, UNCTAD and its supporters seem intent on seeking far more profound changes in UNCTAD's power and status.

UNCTAD has been primarily an arena of debate and discussion, a "forum" organization in Cox and Jacobson's terms.[11] But it now seeks to become a central negotiating arena in the international economic system.[12] Moreover, UNCTAD also seeks more explicit authority to offer recommendations on any issue that affects the developing countries, even if the legitimate arena of settlement were elsewhere.[13] On another track, particularly in the transfer of technology and commodities, UNCTAD also seeks wider operational responsibilities. All of these demands inevitably justify claims for major increases in budget and staff.

Demands to increase UNCTAD's power are not new. For example, after UNCTAD-II Haas argued that UNCTAD "ought to become the superspecialized agency with competence over the entire development nexus"—with control

[10] The quotations are both in Wallace and Escobar, *The Future of International Economic Organizations*, pp. 163-164 and p. 174.

[11] See Robert W. Cox and Harold K. Jacobson, "Decision Making in International Organization: A Report on a Joint Project," in *Political Decision-Making Processes*, ed. Dusan Sidjanski (Amsterdam: Elsevier, 1973), pp. 146-147.

[12] Thus a paper prepared for the Nairobi Conference argues for "the strengthening of UNCTAD as the negotiating instrument of the General Assembly," and expects it "to undertake a major share of the responsibility for elaborating and implementing fundamental reforms of the world economy." UNCTAD, *Institutional Issues* (Geneva: TD/194), April 1976, p. 8.

[13] "UNCTAD should be given a clear mandate . . . to make recommendations with respect to questions being dealt with by other organizations." Ibid., p. 9.

over the World Bank, the IMF, UNDP, and UNIDO.[14] And Gosovic has argued that there "is no inherent reason for not having a pressure and policy forum, a research institution, a technical assistance center, a negotiating body and an executive organization all in one."[15] But neither Haas nor Gosovic ask whether UNCTAD has the competence to perform these functions or whether it has the confidence of enough governments: even if we were to grant the need for an "umbrella" organization, the possibility that UNCTAD or any other institution could fulfill the function does not necessarily follow.

UNCTAD has not had a consistent or substantial record of achievement over the past decade or so, and even the developing countries have become increasingly critical (especially after the disastrous Santiago Conference in 1972). Thus demands for an enhanced role for the organization have been primarily generated by external developments—not an unusual occurrence for an international institution.[16] But UNCTAD did have to be alert enough to grasp the opportunities (for itself and for the developing countries) created by recent events.

The institutional paper prepared for the Nairobi Conference (May 1976) notes that measures to strengthen UNCTAD "should not be inconsistent with the objective of establishing a comprehensive trade and development organization."[17] This theme has been in circulation since the failure of the International Trade Organization in 1948, but no one believes a new ITO is on the immediate horizon. Instead, UNCTAD has

[14] Ernst B. Haas, *Tangle of Hopes—American Commitments and World Order* (Englewood Cliffs, N.J.: Prentice-Hall Inc., 1969), p. 293.

[15] B. Gosovic, "Institutional and Decision-Making Traits of UNCTAD," in *UNCTAD-III Symposium Report* (The Hague: Netherlands National Commission for Development Strategy, 1972), p. 242.

[16] For example, see Haas's comment on the ILO: "organizational autonomy grew as a result of later environmental inputs that owed little or nothing to what the Organization had previously done. The ILO was the unwitting beneficiary of changes in the system that had occurred autonomously." Ernst B. Haas, *Beyond the Nation-State—Functionalism and World Organization* (Stanford: Stanford University Press, 1964), p. 443.

[17] UNCTAD, *Institutional Issues* (TD/194), p. 25.

rested its claims for an enhanced role on two other characteristics: the universality of its membership (in contrast to GATT, the IMF, and the World Bank), and its very broad mandate from the General Assembly.[18]

Although these are useful virtues, they are hardly decisive. Universality, for example, might impede the quest for agreement on issues in which only a few have major interests, and a broad mandate can also become a recipe for jurisdictional squabbles with other institutions. In any event, such virtues only suggest that UNCTAD might be a reasonable candidate for a more powerful role in the international system. But judgments about whether UNCTAD should receive more power must rest on other considerations, such as a more careful assessment of its virtues (not limited to procedural issues) and more detailed treatment of its shortcomings.

UNCTAD has itself provided an interpretation of its weaknesses. The primary deficiency is perceived as political: the members, particularly the industrial countries, are criticized for too frequently choosing other institutions to deal with their problems. This is certainly true, but there is no analysis of why it should be so—obviously a key point. Other weaknesses are related to the first point (for example, administrative and budgetary constraints) or deal with internal and external jurisdictional issues (for example, compartmentalized divisions and uncompartmentalized problems and a lack of clarity at the boundary with other institutions).[19] There are, however, more fundamental problems with UNCTAD— some that it shares with most international institutions and some that are a more specific reflection of UNCTAD's unusual role in the international system. I shall now attempt to explore these difficulties by examining staff problems, the role of the Secretary-General, the significance of the group

[18] Ibid., p. 6. UNCTAD's mandate is in General Assembly Resolution 1995 (XIX), December 1964. The original terms of reference are broad enough to allow UNCTAD almost any role in the trade and aid system, as indicated by the fact that demands for new roles have not required any amendments to the 1964 resolution.

[19] UNCTAD, *Institutional Issues* (TD/194), p. 10.

process, and the implications these factors have for UNCTAD's potential as a major negotiating forum.[20]

The UNCTAD Staff

The quality and the reputation of the staff of the United Nations have been diminished by a number of developments: the increasing dominance of the principle of geographic distribution over the principle of merit in the appointment process, the creation of national "preserves" for particular positions, increased use of fixed-term contracts over permanent contracts and thus enhanced fears of national control over seconded staff, internal conflict between staff members with very different political and cultural backgrounds and different levels of technical competence, and as a result of these factors lowered morale and the politicization of the promotion process.[21] UNCTAD has not escaped these problems, but it is my belief that they have appeared in a less virulent form, a fact that should not be surprising for a small organization of well-paid and well-located professionals working on critical and controversial issues.

UNCTAD's major staff problems reflect a somewhat different political factor: the role of the staff caught between divergent views of the world in an ostensibly redistributive organization. In 1976 UNCTAD had 189 full-time professional staff that were distributed in the following fashion:

[20] For background on UNCTAD's early history (which I shall not treat), see Branislav Gosovic, *UNCTAD: Conflict and Compromise* (Leiden: A. W. Sijthoff, 1972).
[21] The best study of these issues is Theodor Meron, *The United Nations Secretariat* (Lexington, Mass.: Lexington Books, 1977). Also useful are Seymour Maxwell Finger and John F. Mugno, "The Politics of Staffing the United Nations Secretariat," *Orbis* 19, no. 1 (Spring 1975): 117-145; and Robert Rhodes James, *Staffing the United Nations Secretariat* (Brighton, England: Institute for the Study of International Organisation, 1970). Thomas George Weiss's work, *International Bureaucracy—An Analysis of the Operation of Functional and Global International Secretariats* (Lexington, Mass.: Lexington Books, 1975), is badly marred by the author's moral pretensions and self-righteousness.

Group B (the Western industrial countries), 111; Group of 77, 57 (Latin America, 16; Asia, 18; Africa-Middle East, 23); socialists, 19; and stateless, 2.[22] The numerical dominance of Group B nationals can be attributed to historical factors (the developing countries' late entrance into the system), or geographical factors (the desire of many European staff to locate in Geneva, paralleling the dominance of Latin Americans in ECLA, Africans in ECA, etc.), or the need for technically qualified staff not generally available in the developing countries.[23] Within Group B, the United States leads the way with 29 nationals, followed by the United Kingdom with 13, and France with 10; in the Group of 77, representation is very scattered, and only Sri Lanka with 5 is noteworthy; and in the socialist group, the Soviet Union has 12 of the 19 positions.[24]

About half of the UNCTAD staff is on permanent contract and half on fixed-term contract (excluding fifteen "other"). But this is deceptive, for there has been a steady increase in the number of fixed-termers: since 1970, for example, fixed-term appointments have accounted for a little over

[22] All of these statistics were derived from an examination of UNCTAD manning tables. Because of the limitations and ambiguities of the latter, figures should be treated as approximations (although they are unlikely to incorporate any major distortions of the record).

[23] It should be emphasized that the numerical split does *not* reflect an internal ideological split: most of the Western staff share the prevailing ideology and have joined the organization for that reason. But problems still arise because many Western staff, especially Americans, feel that they are not taken into the confidence of the leadership or promoted fairly. Consequently, many highly qualified personnel leave in frustration.

[24] Sewell has argued that "secretariat nationalities can for UNESCO, and for other intergovernmental organizations, be viewed as testimony of greater engagement by certain member nation-states and of less engagement by others." James P. Sewell, *UNESCO and World Politics* (Princeton: Princeton University Press, 1975), p. 311. This seems wrong or at least oversimplified to me. For the developed countries, many or most of the staff join because of personal commitment (or locational preferences), and they are neither seconded from governments nor bound by national policies. It would be very difficult to argue that the United States is UNCTAD's most "engaged" member because of twenty-nine staff positions. It should be noted that in the whole UN system a few developing countries are the most overrepresented (those who achieved independence at an early date, such as India, Sri Lanka, and Egypt).

three-quarters of total appointments. These figures are not unusual, and they reflect a general trend within the UN system.[25] Although the increased number of fixed-term staff has altered the intended character of the international civil service, it has also had two potentially beneficial results: it has permitted more Third World nationals to be hired (and, in some cases, trained on the job), and it has allowed a more flexible response to the increased need to hire specialists to deal with development problems.

But it has also exacerbated a number of internal problems. Turnover rates have been quite high. As one illustration indicates, of the 136 staff members in January 1970, slightly less than half were still with the organization five years later. On the average, from 1970 through 1975 about 17 percent of the staff left each year. A perception of flux is reinforced if we examine length of service for the 189 staff members in 1976: 33 percent had joined since 1974 and another 20 percent since UNCTAD-III in Santiago in 1972. Turnover problems have been especially severe for the substantive departments: 52 percent are on fixed-term contracts, but slightly less than 30 percent of the service departments are so appointed.[26]

A rapid turnover rate diminishes organizational memory (perhaps not always a negative result), and it may increase inefficiency. More critically, it affects morale and loyalty, for many of the staff are forced to expend a good deal of energy negotiating their next job. Some resentment against permanent staff who owe their status to historical and geographical accidents is also inevitable. Staff members who might need to seek employment with their own governments after a fixed-term contract expires are also not likely to resist pressures from those governments. A series of interviews with UNCTAD staff indicated that these attitudes were widely prevalent, but that they were also varied: some staff were indifferent and quite willing to move on after a tour of duty,

[25] See Meron, *The United Nations Secretariat*, p. 80.

[26] The primary reason is that the service departments attracted permanent staff from within the UN system, many of them Europeans desirous of living in Geneva. For example, seven of the eight staff members in administration are permanent, and six of the seven are Europeans.

some took it as a spur to increased effort (fixed-term can become de facto permanent appointments by steady reappointment, although this does not regularly happen), others used it as a rationalization for doing little or for doing only their own work, and some felt that the advantages of bringing in new people outweighed the disadvantages. At any rate, although internal resentments against permanent staff may decline as older staff retire and although it is a useful way of hiring specialists and providing flexibility, the general tendency toward fixed-term appointments suggests persisting difficulties in building institutional loyalty and maintaining a consistent standard of professional work.[27]

Morale and loyalty have also been affected by other internal problems. Interviews elicited widespread complaints about a lack of contact across—and sometimes within—divisions, about insufficient consultation or even explanation of decisions, and about a tendency to reward staff on unprofessional grounds. In addition, some staff from both Western and socialist industrial countries criticized a conspicuous waste of financial resources on unnecessary conferences in unnecessary places (to which staff and support have to be sent), on absurd delays at meetings that caused salary and overhead costs to mount, on reprinting large numbers of trivial speeches (publishing a five-page speech costs over $2,000), on research funds wasted on friends and countrymen—and so on. One very informed member of the staff commented that if UNCTAD were to cut these losses in half and if it were to make more effort to get some work out of *all* the staff, sharp increases in budgetary resources would not be necessary.

A major share of responsibility for these problems must fall directly on the Secretary-General, for he has seemed disinter-

---

[27] I do not want to discuss at length other staffing issues because they are not especially revealing. In brief, Group B and the Group of 77 have about the same percentage of "their" staff in leadership ranks (although the Asians are now overrepresented at the top, and in the past the Latin Americans were overrepresented in relation to the Group of 77); women's liberation has not yet struck at UNCTAD; and departmental growth patterns have been generally very incremental, tempered to some extent by a few sharper increases reflecting prevailing fashions (for example, Transfer of Technology is now rapidly increasing, but was not even a separate division until quite recently).

ested in the internal operation of his organization. This has created a leadership vacuum that is filled, if filled at all, by the heads of the divisions. As a result, the divisions run like feudal fiefdoms: when they want to do something they sell the idea to friendly delegations, after which it comes back as a request for the staff to do what it already wants to do. But central direction is weak, coordination erratic, and a long-run perspective nonexistent; thus the minor reforms with which UNCTAD has responded to these problems are not likely to be sufficient. Only a Secretary-General willing to commit time and resources to these issues can begin to reverse the pattern, but even he will fail without government support and government willingness to sacrifice national preserves.

No organization can be run as a democracy. Still, sustaining the morale and performance of professionals working on interesting and important problems ought not to be as difficult as it has been at UNCTAD. More effort to treat professionals as professionals—as colleagues and not inferiors—would do much to reduce internal strains. More seminars, more direct contact with outside experts, perhaps a modification, where possible, in the UN practice of not naming authors of papers (which would give justified recognition to capable people and might energize the lazy), and especially more efforts to explain decisions would all be useful. It is not without interest that the most successful division within UNCTAD—successful in terms of both morale and output—comes closest to being run as a university department.

Most observers believe that the quality of the professional work of the UNCTAD staff has improved considerably in the past decade. Nevertheless, doubts about staff competence still persist. This is a complex but important issue since part of the influence of the staff is directly attributable to the quality of its work and its professional reputation. But objective evaluation of staff competence seems virtually impossible, for standards differ—especially when visions of what is and what ought to be are so sharply at variance—and competence itself, however defined, is not the only value at stake in evaluating staff performance. Still, the difficulty of defining competence does not justify ignoring the issue, for it has important effects not only on the quality of work and professional reputations but also in a narrower sense in throwing an unfair share of the burden on those who *are* competent.[28]

This is an issue that cannot be settled definitively. The UNCTAD staff is clearly not as competent as it *ought* to be, but whether it is as competent as it *can* be, given the political limitations within which it must work, is a much harder question. My own judgment after following UNCTAD closely for almost two years is this: there are indeed some incompetent people at UNCTAD, and there are indeed some people who do not appear to do anything at all, but there are enough competent (and in some cases outstanding) professionals turning out useful work to suggest that the major problems of the staff are not wholly due to insufficient competence.

There are some experienced observers who might challenge this judgment, arguing that the few competent people at UNCTAD generally leave in frustration or are forced to work well below full capacity. There is surely something to this argument, although I believe two important qualifications must be added: as it stands, the argument is clearly exaggerated, for some of UNCTAD's work has been widely praised; and too frequently criticism seems primarily to reflect ideological hostility or a tendency to dismiss a whole body of work on the basis of a deficient part. But the point I want to make is somewhat different, for I am not interested in arguing degrees of competence or incompetence—especially

[28.] I was told by a very respected staff member that one-third of the UNCTAD staff were competent and worked hard, one-third were incompetent, and one-third may or may not have been competent but did no work anyway. In subsequent interviews I could not elicit any major disagreement with these views, although a few staff members (notably from socialist countries) were far more critical. Obviously I do not mean to suggest that this is a satisfactory breakdown, but it is useful as an indication of internal judgments of competence—which may, after all, be the most accurate and important judgments. There are, of course, some analysts with more extreme views. Thus Harry Johnson complains of the degree of error "that one has to learn to tolerate as measuring the economic illiteracy of the UNCTAD economic secretariat." Johnson in Jagdish N. Bhagwati, ed., *The New International Economic Order: The North-South Debate* (Cambridge: The MIT Press, 1977), p. 244. But this is a judgment that seems both inaccurate and counterproductive to me.

without an agreed or meaningful standard of evaluation. What seems more important to me is to ask why competent people are not always hired or why they leave in frustration. To answer these questions we need to examine the political context of the staff's role within an institution like UNCTAD, and we need also to try to evaluate staff performance within the constraints set by the particular demands of this role—and not merely by reference to abstract notions of professional competence.

There is a major ambiguity in the role of the staff in an international welfare organization that seeks to alter the existing distribution of benefits in favor of the poor. In part the problem reflects a fairly conventional conflict between professional roles and advocacy roles: professionals usually trained in the doctrines and techniques of those who currently dominate the system are expected (or required) to produce analyses that challenge the existing order and that justify new standards and a new order of benefits. Tension is minimal if prevailing standards have already been rejected or if a convincing argument for rapid change were to be justified by conventional analysis (as it can be, for example, with trade barriers or tied aid). But tension increases appreciably when the conflict is sharp (as it is, for example, with debates about the terms of trade or the possibility of cartels), and as a result morale can be affected. Perhaps in the light of this, some of the characteristic patterns of staff behavior become more understandable: there are those who become primarily advocates and advance in the organization, those who concentrate on the external professional audience and are ignored internally, and those who seek a viable compromise and become increasingly frustrated. There is also, to some extent, an impact on the availability of the best professionals, many of whom (on both sides) prefer to avoid the inevitable conflicts that an UNCTAD appointment generates.

External confidence in the staff may also be sharply diminished. Thus, in a series of interviews with UNCTAD delegates, I discovered that many Third World delegates thought the UNCTAD staff was not sufficiently biased (in their favor), and many Western delegates thought the staff was already far too biased.[29] In effect, one group wanted the staff to be stronger advocates (of its views), and the other group wanted the staff to be more impartial and professional (according to its standards of professionalism), a thesis and an antithesis without a synthesis.

Perceptions of bias undermine the staff's ability to play a mediatory role: it cannot be an "honest broker" when compelled to develop one side's position while simultaneously being perceived as hostile by the other side.[30] This puts the staff "out front not in-between," a significant problem for an institution that needs to extract agreement from the developed countries for substantial—if unrevolutionary—changes in favor of the developing countries. The problem might be diminished if the Third World created its own "OECD" outside the UN system, for this might permit UNCTAD to improve its professional reputation and to assume a mediating stance.[31] But analyses "uncontaminated" by too much professionalism and too little bias are not likely to be sensible or convincing, either. Moreover, it may be easier to put together a viable global bargaining position within UNCTAD than in a Third World OECD, for the UNCTAD staff is at least relatively more likely to see all the relevant linkages, to resist many of the most self-interested or unsustainable demands, to be perceived as more legitimate representatives of a wider interest, and to temper proposals with some concern for developed country positions.

[29] One thing that gives currency to the charge of bias by the industrial countries is the pattern of staff-group relations. When the socialists meet, their staff members attend the meeting; when the Group of 77 meets, *only* staff members from the developing countries are allowed to attend (with minor exceptions when a technical issue needs explication); when Group B meets, no UNCTAD staff attend, which reflects not only the ability to rely on home experts but also a different interpretation of relations between staff and national governments.

[30] M. T. Adebanjo, an UNCTAD official, has argued that the staff does act as an "honest broker," but can cite no examples. The argument might be more convincing, although not completely so, in relation to the Group of 77. See "Decision Making Process in UNCTAD and Its Relevance for Multilateral Diplomacy" (unpublished speech, n.d.), p. 8.

[31] And the idea has been favorably mentioned by the Secretary-General at various times.

Staff influence in international institutions is usually attributed to the quality of its technical advice and services and to its reputation for impartiality. I have discussed some factors that have affected staff performance in these areas and have suggested a number of minor reforms that might be beneficial. It goes without saying that none of these reforms are likely to be sufficient unless member governments take these internal issues more seriously.

Staff issues need to be taken seriously not only to make UNCTAD a more effective institution but also because the staff has become so crucial a factor in the North-South context. And here we need to extend our analysis, for the influence of the UNCTAD staff cannot be attributed solely to its technical advice or its reputation. Much more crucial has been the central role thrust upon (or seized by) the staff in devising and promoting programs that become negotiating demands of the Group of 77. Staff leverage is very closely related to the style of group bargaining that has come to dominate North-South exchanges not merely in enhancing the need for a central unit to package the Group of 77's demands but also in the sense that the resolutions that tend to emerge from the group bargaining process—resolutions that are masterpieces of ambiguity and permit varied interpretations of what has transpired—allow the staff to shape a good deal of intergovernmental bargaining. This is a very powerful role, but a role with certain intrinsic limitations. The next section will discuss these issues after examining the group bargaining process more closely.

But before proceeding, I want to emphasize very strongly one point about the following discussion: my analysis and criticism of the group system is primarily relevant only for major, controversial issues on the UNCTAD agenda. The "fit" for the commodity issue or the debt issue thus seems quite good to me, but it is somewhat looser for the technology transfer issue, and looser yet for least developed country issues. There are also many habitual or noncontroversial activities that have no relevance to the following discussion. In addition, I am primarily concerned with developments in the last few years; the more benign effects of the group system in earlier years are not at issue. I note this here because I want to avoid the charge that I am exaggerating the effects of the group system or that I am unaware of much useful work that goes on in UNCTAD. Still, analysis of the effects of the group system on the most controversial issues is very crucial, for it is these issues that heavily condition the climate of the North-South arena.

There is perhaps a more important question about the relevance of the group system that requires some comment. Observers from other institutions have occasionally emphasized the extent to which their institutions have prevented or avoided the development of the highly formalized and rigid system that prevails at UNCTAD. One might argue, therefore, that my analysis is limited not only to a particular time period but also to a particular institution. These are matters of judgment, not fact, and thus the degree of relevance cannot be known for some time. Nevertheless, I would argue that the increasing institutionalization of the Third World, the desire to maintain unity and to defeat "divide and conquer" tactics, and the increasing need for external support and for protection against adverse external developments suggest that the group system will become increasingly pervasive in the North-South arena—particularly on the central economic and political issues. I do not mean to argue, of course, that the effects of the group system will be invariable, for quite clearly it is likely to be most severe in an institution like UNCTAD and in a period of great stress. I mean rather to assert my own judgment that intermittent periods of calm in the North-South arena do not imply a secular trend away from group conflict and, perhaps most critically, that unless we seek to reform the existing bargaining system reasonably quickly the results produced may only generate an even more hostile pattern of confrontation.

The Group Bargaining Structure

As I have already noted, UNCTAD has been primarily a forum organization, providing a setting for discussion, negotiations, and "collective legitimization."[32] The creation of new norms in the international trade and aid system that are designed to transfer a greater share of the benefits to the developing countries has provided the central theme of its existence. But UNCTAD has not really been an effective negotiating arena, and its recent demands to become the "focal point for deliberation and negotiation in the field of trade and international economic cooperation" have received little support from the developed countries.[33] Why this has been so has much to do with the environment within which UNCTAD has had to operate, but two other factors have also been significant: the absence of a consensus about what is at stake in the bargaining process and the political and structural factors that have created a particularly dysfunctional pattern of bargaining within UNCTAD (and elsewhere).

UNCTAD has never been a revolutionary organization. There is an apparent paradox here, for the attempt to create and implement deliberately redistributive norms seems to imply much more than incremental change. But UNCTAD has never had sufficient power to achieve its ostensible objectives. Moreover, throughout most of its history, revolutionary goals were primarily rhetorical: in general, the prevailing intellectual climate was dominated by conventional assumptions about trade and aid, and the developing countries were too weak to refuse whatever was offered. In these circumstances the group system did not seem especially pernicious, for major changes were not at stake, and the effective institutionalization of the Group of 77—so that consistent policy in different arenas resulted—had not really begun. In effect, UNCTAD talked big but took what it could get—which was not much.[34]

[32] Recently there has also been some movement in UNCTAD toward enhanced operational responsibilities, particularly in the area of technology transfer and in dealing with the least developed countries.

[33] For the quoted phrase, see UNCTAD, *New Directions and New Structures for Trade and Development: Report by the Secretary-General of UNCTAD to the Conference* (Geneva: TD/183), April 1974, p. 86.

[34] Limited gains reflected not only UNCTAD's lack of power but also the intrinsic limitations of external change, a point to which I shall return.

The context of this issue has obviously been altered by the increasing assertiveness of the developing countries as a result of the OPEC phenomenon, by rising fears of resource scarcities, and by a perception of substantial disarray among the developed countries. Thus a bargaining relationship that has already been complicated by asymmetrical benefits—one side usually demanding, the other usually giving—has been made even more difficult by a failure to agree on what or how much is really being negotiated.[35] In one sense, the developing countries have become less willing to emphasize mutual benefits and accept compromise agreements: the balance between confrontation and the need to take the best available package has been tilted—though hardly completely—in favor of confrontation. In another sense, disagreement about the framework within which negotiations proceed tends to destabilize the settlement process: distrust is very high, suspicion that no proposal can be understood without reading between the lines is prevalent, and the fear that concession will not lead to a stable agreement but only to a new series of unending demands is widespread. Even without these disagreements, the process of decision within UNCTAD is bound to be difficult: aggregating the interests of over one hundred and fifty very disparate countries into a viable and coherent set of proposals would strain the capacity of any system of decision, let alone a system of dispersed and fragmented power devoid of effective central control. What emerged in UNCTAD was a process of group decision making—within and between groups—that emphasized the quest for consensus and that de-emphasized voting.[36]

As I noted in the last chapter, UNCTAD's members are divided into four groups: the Group of 77, the Western industrial countries (denoted as Group B), the socialist countries,

[35] I do not mean to suggest that elements of mutual benefit do not exist, for they usually do. The problem is that most of the benefits for the developed countries are important only in the long run or are intangibles dealing with atmosphere and climate within the North-South dialogue. Current domestic political difficulties and other factors make these trade-offs very problematic.

[36] For a good discussion of the origins of these developments, see Diego Cordovez, *UNCTAD and Development Diplomacy: From Confrontation to Strategy* (Twickenham, England: Journal of World Trade Law, 1972), pp. 62f.

and China as a "group" alone. Each group or subgroup (for example the EEC within Group B or the three regional blocs within the Group of 77) meets and attempts to devise a common intragroup position on an agenda issue; representatives of each group then meet in "contact groups" that seek to develop a common intergroup position; if a consensus emerges, the common position is put before a plenary session to become official policy; if no consensus emerges, the issue is usually left for future resolution or each side makes a public statement of its own position. Some informal coalition-building both within and between groups does take place, but—particularly between the groups—it is less important than one might suspect. The decision-making process within each group has tended to be encapsulated, and the quest for consensus between groups has tended to be left to the contact groups established at various formal meetings. Why this is so and what effects it has had need to be understood.

The group decision-making system has been defended on a number of grounds. For example, many people who have worked in the UNCTAD arena contend that the group system, right or wrong, is unavoidable: it has become so habitual that there is no alternative but to learn to live with it. This avoids the question of whether meaningful reforms are possible. Others have argued that it is a democratic process that gives even the weakest a chance to be heard and to exert influence. This is much less true, however, than might first appear: all are equal at UNCTAD, but some are much more equal than others. The group system has also been defended as the only alternative to chaos. What other way could coherent bargaining packages emerge that "let the many speak with one voice?"[37] This is to argue that the process saves time, not wastes it. While this may well be true, the process still remains extraordinarily cumbersome and time-consuming. Nor is it to say anything about the possibility of negotiating effective compromises once each group packages its own demands. Order and economy may not be worth the price if stalemate is to be the likely result.

An analogy with collective bargaining between trade unions

[37] Ibid., p. 145.

and employers has also been used to defend group bargaining. In this sense, it is a natural tactic for the poor countries to band together to make the whole greater than the sum of its parts. As Mahbub ul Haq has argued:

> One of the essential tactics of the Third World should be to proceed through the process of collective bargaining so that whatever bargaining strength its individual members possess is pooled together. This means resisting a case-by-case approach at the initial policy level while accepting it as an operational necessity once the overall policy decisions are reached. . . . If the process is reversed, the bargaining power of the Third World will be further weakened and it is easier for the rich nations to take advantage of their diverse circumstances and interests.[38]

This position seems so practical that the trade union analogy for the bargaining process at UNCTAD has become something of a cliché. And although the need to maintain a common front has become an article of faith among the developing countries (for which testimony has been provided by OPEC), I shall argue, nevertheless, that procedural unity without substantive unity diminishes the possibility of achieving viable settlements. Or alternatively, it might be said that the process works well if one is not overly concerned with substantive outcomes.

Before discussing these matters, I want to make a brief comment on the trade union analogy itself, if only because the use and misuse of analogies affects perceptions, and thus policies, in critical ways. The problem with the trade union analogy is that it tends to oversimplify, to imply more similarities in kind between UNCTAD and, for example, GM and the United Auto Workers than in fact exist. One obvious difference is that the normative framework wherein domestic bargaining takes place is usually far more settled, "good faith" (with a few exceptions) can be taken for granted, and the negotiations can more easily follow a customary pattern. Thus in most collective bargaining situations in this country the notion of alternative moves (and concessions) in the game

---

[38] Mahbub ul Haq, *The Poverty Curtain—Choices for the Third World* (New York: Columbia University Press, 1976), p. 182.

has become a convention.[39] But this is not so in UNCTAD, for "good faith" is absent, and the pattern of demands and concessions is skewed: one side makes all the demands, it challenges the basic value position of the other side, and its concessions are usually in the form of marginal adjustments in the timing (but not the substance) of original demands. This is an unstable game, at least in part because the industrial countries have strong domestic constituencies that are opposed to such concessions and because it has been so difficult to prove that the benefits given have been used well or that they will in fact prove to be in the general interest over the long run. In sum, the UNCTAD context is more fluid, more complex, more uncertain in terms of actions taken and results expected and less certain in terms of shared interests than the context of domestic collective bargaining. At best, then, the analogy must be with the early and very conflictive period of union-employer bargaining.

Consequently I have found an analogy between group bargaining and religious or ideological political parties in a pluralist system (a system of dispersed power in which major interest groups are too weak to compel but usually strong enough to resist or veto) to be more useful than the trade union analogy. Unions and management usually share a preoccupation with jobs and profits, and they tend to fight primarily about the distribution of gains; union members tend to share values, goals, and—perhaps most critically— benefits. The Group of 77 differs not only in the sense that it is a coalition of interests (some identical, some divergent, some parallel) but also in the sense that the coalition is bound together by common beliefs and a common interpretation of the world. The Group serves to articulate and mobilize interests so that a common package emerges, but it has not been consistently successful in transforming demands into agreed international policy. Something akin to a two-party system (with minority parties) without the cultural and political disposition for compromise and concession that is characteristic of pluralist societies is the result. The Group of 77 is thus both

---

[39] See Richard E. Walton and Robert B. McKersie, *A Behavioral Theory of Labor Negotiations* (New York: McGraw-Hill Book Company, 1965), p. 88.

too ideological, which diminishes the commitment to bargain, and too weak and divided, which diminishes the willingness to test the faith. Some parallels with the coalitions of the left in France and the center-right in Spain are suggestive—but no more than that.

The disabilities engendered by the group system reflect the relationship between process and outcome: how the system operates tends to produce an outcome that makes serious negotiation increasingly problematic and time-consuming. Group B and the Group of 77 contain so many countries at different levels of development with such divergent or conflicting interests that strenuous effort has to be expended to construct a common position. The problem is especially severe for the Group of 77 since the membership is wider and more diverse and ability to accept short-term sacrifices in expectation of future benefits is very limited. A widely shared ideology—if very general—and the very strong commitment to unity exert a powerful centripetal force, but provide no guidance on programmatic details: on a sufficiently broad level, consensus is manageable, but any movement toward specificity creates tension.

A network of staff experts and key delegates who either possess important expertise or represent important countries provide the substantive link between the general agreement to act in a unified fashion and the details of what is to be acted upon. There are few problems if a policy or a program does appear to benefit virtually everyone—for example, the demand that the developed countries transfer a guaranteed percentage of resources each year. But not many issues qualify. On issues where there are substantial or numerous losers within the Group of 77, the staff plays the central role in devising a program that promises as many benefits as possible to as many countries as possible. Only the staff has the legitimacy and the expertise to perform this function—to provide the common policies that the unified Group will promote. Given the limited expertise within many developing country governments (and especially within the delegates assigned to UNCTAD), staff perceptions of what the Group of 77 ought to seek and staff decisions on how to package a set of demands are very critical but not completely determinative.

The staff's role is thus only partially technical. But it must also play a double political role, the first (and most critical) in selling a package to the Group of 77 itself, and the second (which combines the technical and the political and is also shared with the leadership of the Group of 77) in defending the agreed package against the attacks of Group B and occasionally the socialist countries. The key question in terms of the first political role is, who are the dissenters? If they were few in number and small in influence, the facade of unity may still be maintained by appeals to Group loyalty, combined with promises of some kind of compensation (in effect, side payments).[40] On much rarer occasions, countries that are unable to calculate their own interests effectively or are dilatory in analyzing for themselves all the implications of a particular program may not even realize that they have a reason to dissent.[41] If the dissenters were influential countries, however, unity could be maintained only at a very broad and rhetorical level. That the more influential countries have not defected more frequently reflects the fact that they are more continuously consulted by the staff and their interests are more carefully protected in most packages—and indeed in the whole program of UNCTAD. It should also be noted that for both the weak and the strong countries the increasing institutionalization of the Group of 77 (and the developing countries in general) has facilitated the maintenance of unity, for peer pressure to stand behind a common program is maintained steadily and fervently. There is a potential conflict here between loss of face within the Group of 77 and acceptance of profferred concessions that has been easily resolved because the developed countries have not been sufficiently enticing.[42]

[40] For example, support for the GSP was assured only after those countries that would lose from relinquishing special preferential arrangements were guaranteed compensation. And in the Integrated Commodity Program potential losers among the developing countries (those who are net importers of the relevant commodities) have been promised some kind of special treatment as compensation.

[41] This seems true for some of the small African countries in the commodity discussions, and it may also be true for those supporting indexation of commodities that are currently low-priced.

[42] I do not intend to deal with the bargaining process within Group B beyond the comments already made in Chapter 4.

Regional blocs have always existed within the Group of 77. Bitterness between the Latin Americans and the Africans has been particularly intense, but most conflicts have been resolved by addition: that is, the final Group package simply incorporates everyone's demands. More recently, however, the regional conflicts have tended to be superseded—to a degree—by a conflict between "haves" and "have-nots." The OPEC countries do not, of course, meet formally within UNCTAD, but they have been the target of a few rudimentary pressures to restrain oil prices (the Indians at CIEC were especially prominent in this regard). The only nonregional bloc that functions openly at UNCTAD has been the least developed countries. They have been reasonably successful in receiving Group support for their own demands, primarily as a form of compensation for failure to benefit greatly from most of the measures on UNCTAD's agenda. Nevertheless, the appearance of the least developed bloc has not greatly altered the political process within the Group of 77. Most of the least developed are in Africa, which tends simply to reinforce the prevailing regional conflicts. In addition, since there is no means to resolve conflicts (except through persuasion, which has not been very successful), the tendency to merely pile demand upon demand continues. More delay and more complexity have been the most tangible results; less concrete results have included an increase in the tendency in the developed countries to discount the firmness of Group of 77 unity (especially when private comments by members of the Group differ significantly from public stances).

Despite internal and external pressures, the unity of the Group of 77 has bent but not cracked. The attendant costs, nonetheless, have been substantial and—arguably—more than the achieved benefits. The unity produced is usually very fragile, for the difficulties of devising positions that satisfy nearly everyone are enormous, and the forces available to contain dissent are not always sufficient.[43] As a result, there

---

[43] Perhaps it is useful to think of this as a double bargaining process in which the attitudes appropriate for one level are in conflict with the attitudes appropriate for the other level. To reach agreement within the Group, emotions need to be reduced, ambitions moderated, issues treated on their

is a tendency to remain at the rhetorical level—the level of grand principle—where all can agree and where the practical contradictions of simply adding everyone's demands together can be avoided or delayed. Decisions within the international system are forced to the highest political (and philosophical) level but without first clarifying what is really at stake, or what is feasible, or what consequences can be expected. A global framework is imposed for problems that may well be beyond the current state of the art in either politics or economics. In addition, expectations of large external gains divert attention from more critical domestic problems, and excessive ambition is thus built into the process. These are heavy costs to pay for unity, costs that even the rich—on both sides—can no longer afford to ignore. Major improvement is likely only if the developing countries' fears can be assuaged concerning the developed countries' "divide and conquer" tactics, an outcome dependent on more forthcoming policies from the developed countries and a better sense of the limits of external change by the developing countries.

Beginning a negotiation with maximum demands is not always unjustified or unwise, but it creates severe difficulties when the rules of the game are at stake. Commencing with very large demands does have some potential virtues, for premature commitments can be avoided, more bargaining space is available, and information can be accumulated before the point of decision.[44] One major problem with this ap-

---

merits, information freely exchanged, and commitments kept flexible. But to bargain with the other group, support for the struggle has to be generated, emotions need to be raised, commitments have to harden, and philosophical differences must be emphasized. It is difficult to moderate these kinds of attitudes once established, and the result may be stalemate and rhetorical cannoneering. But the Group of 77 has not needed to cultivate the first set of attitudes too assiduously, for simply adding the demands together facilitates intergroup "toughness." The point is that if it seems too difficult to run a two-layered bargaining process when attitudes at each layer conflict, the problem may be finessed by avoiding real bargaining at one or the other level.

[44] The strategy of settling the easy issues first and slowly building trust and confidence before confronting major issues—the "camel's nose" approach—has many advocates in the professional literature. See, for example, Roger Fisher, *International Conflict for Beginners* (New York: Harper and Row, 1969).

proach is that it is difficult to avoid the appearance of defeat with any settlement short of total victory. More critically, stalemate tends to be the most likely outcome of the process. Compromises threaten to unravel one or the other side's package, an obvious or salient stopping point is difficult to discern, and detailed discussions threaten to reveal or exacerbate internal conflicts of interest—thus a holding pattern on initial demands, especially in areas of contention, may well emerge. One side demands broad agreement on vague statements of principle; the other responds with vague statements that permit avoidance of any clear commitment to do anything. The "compromise" that results—normally at a grand conference where the sparring presumably stops—is usually a virtually meaningless verbal formula whose main purpose is to allow everyone to claim victory and the game to go on. The difficulty of compromising principles and the fear of internal defections also puts a premium on efforts to divide the other side by various threats, promises, and entreaties or to await the arrival of a *deus ex machina*—a new administration, a defection, a crisis—that will somehow convert the disbelievers.

Bargaining is also impeded within this structure by the difficulty of arranging trade-offs within and between groups. This has been an especially severe problem within the Group of 77 since most have so little to offer each other and the pattern of winners and losers on different issues tends to be symmetrical (that is, the advanced developing countries and a few mineral producers tend to be winners; the poorest countries the losers or nongainers). The main "trade-off" has thus usually been an agreement to support one position fully in exchange for full support of another (the least developed countries have used this tactic to ensure concern for their problems), and not some kind of substantive compromise within or between issues. The issues also differ in offering different kinds of benefits in different time frames, so that the problem of determining what the trade-off ought to be between, for example, commodities and the debt issue is ex-

---

Which strategy makes more sense (produces better results) is probably impossible to answer in the abstract, since much depends on what strategy the opponent chooses—as well as on many other variables.

traordinarily complex. Adding demands rather than compromising them is easier. In addition, the problem of devising packages that reflect mutual benefits for the developed countries is rarely treated seriously—too much time and effort have to be expended in merely getting agreement on a package that is not impossibly burdened with idiosyncratic or contradictory demands.[45] One notes also that this process tends to give substantial influence to radical spokesmen, for only extreme demands seem to promise something to everyone. Finally, in terms of bargaining between the groups, even if the other problems could be resolved, trade-offs are difficult because the developing countries have had so little to offer— although this problem should diminish with rising fears about resource scarcities and the need for global cooperation on some issues. In sum, one of the most illuminating aspects of the bargaining process at UNCTAD is how little bargaining actually goes on.

Although UNCTAD's bargaining pattern delays and obstructs the negotiation of settlements, agreements on some controversial issues have been reached. However, these agreements are also affected by the negotiating climate and structure within UNCTAD. The developed countries, suspicious of resource transfer mechanisms disguised as trade agreements and worried about continuously escalating demands, have sought above all to maintain control of the process of implementation.[46] This has generally led to two different forms of damage limitation.

In the first, an agreement on a change in prevailing principles may become possible as a result of pressures by the developing countries and realization by the developed countries

[45] The failure to emphasize mutual benefits has been criticized in the past, but the structural reasons for it have not been sufficiently examined. Note also that the point in the text suggests violation of another bargaining principle: choose actions in relationship to how one expects the other side to act. Here the key is how one's own side will react.

[46] Suspicion of disguised resource transfers should not necessarily be taken as evidence of hostility toward the Third World. For some at least, the issue centers on the effectiveness or the equity of giving aid in this fashion, not on the necessity of giving aid. Of course, if aid levels continue to drop, the argument for disguised aid transfers may need to be reexamined.

that costs will be bearable. But to insure that this remains so, the details of the agreement that results—its scope, timing, and duration—are left in the hands of developed country governments. The latter agree in principle to change a pattern of behavior, but decide for themselves what changes to make. The agreement on a General System of Preferences (GSP) is illustrative. Many developed countries agreed to institute such systems, but each decides unilaterally what products to include or exclude and what safety measures are necessary. Generosity has been limited, control has been preserved, and the benefits have gone primarily to a handful of relatively advanced developing countries.[47] A similar pattern is likely to develop if the developing countries succeed in extracting a commitment on indexation to protect the purchasing power of their exports: there will be no agreement on automatic compensation for declines in purchasing power, but rather an agreement to review prices and earnings periodically. In effect, this is a pattern of controlled concession with sharp limits on automaticity or joint decision making.

The second pattern is even more restrictive. General agreements that threaten established principles are resisted, and narrow agreements in which there is some element of mutual benefit are emphasized. The debate on commodities is illustrative, for the more conservative developed countries refused—until recently—to accept a generalized commitment to UNCTAD's Integrated Program for Commodities, in part from fears that the commitment would be transformed into

[47] See Tracy Murray, "How Helpful is the Generalized System of Preferences to Developing Countries?" *The Economic Journal* 84, no. 334 (June 1974): 449-455. Anindya K. Bhattacharya, "The Influence of the International Secretariat: UNCTAD and Generalized Tariff Preferences," *International Organization* 30, no. 1 (Winter 1976): 75-90, traces staff influences on the GSP (which were even stronger than he suggests), and is much more favorable than I have been to the group system and the bargaining process in UNCTAD. Nevertheless, he never examines the very limited and highly concentrated results that ensued (and were predicted at the time) nor does he sufficiently stress the maintenance of control by the developed countries. Finally, I note also that his work refers to a time period in which attitudes and expectations were much different among both developed and developing countries.

an agreement to transfer resources (and not merely stabilize prices) via commodity agreements. Resistance to demands for a legally binding code on the transfer of technology tends also to fall into this pattern. These patterns of settlement, in which one side is perceived as demanding more than meets the eye and the other responds with concessions that yield less than meets the eye, reflect an inability to move beyond a bargaining style that encourages grand confrontations and a "you win, I lose" attitude.[48]

I have already expressed some reservations about the contention that one virtue of the UNCTAD process is its democratic character. UNCTAD has operated as an imperfect oligarchy dominated by the Secretary-General, a number of key staff members, a few key delegates, and the leadership of the Group of 77. This adds two ancillary political factors: the personal ambitions of some of these individuals for wider roles or higher status, and the desire of the staff to protect or enhance UNCTAD's role. I want here, however, to be somewhat more precise about the influence of the staff, for the range and depth of that influence varies considerably with the stages of the bargaining process.

The influence of the UNCTAD staff is very critical in the

---

[48] Students of international institutions may wonder at the lack of parallel between my settlement patterns and those discussed in Haas, *Beyond the Nation-State*, p. 111. Even the least demanding of Haas's patterns—accommodation on the basis of the minimum common denominator—requires "exchanging concessions of roughly equal value," and is thus very distinct from my patterns. Even more distinct are "splitting the difference" and "upgrading the common interests." Professor Haas's patterns seem to reflect a pluralist-incrementalist bargaining universe in which value questions and rules of the game questions are already settled or in which there is pragmatic agreement to avoid divisive questions of principle in order to concentrate on narrower issues of mutual benefit. In this context, one recalls the decision of the founders of the EEC to leave unresolved the major splits (planning versus the market, right versus left, federalism versus unification, the end envisaged, etc.) and to commence with practical agreements. None of these conditions hold to any significant degree in North-South conflicts: principles and rules are at stake, and the benefits from pragmatism and "reasonableness" generally do not seem sufficient to one of the major actors. That actor may (or may not) be right, as I noted in earlier chapters, but it is still possible to question the means chosen to reach the desired goal.

early and middle stages of the bargaining process.[49] Its role in putting together a package for all of the Group of 77 is absolutely essential, and its role over time in selling, defending, and—if necessary—revising the package is also very critical. In effect, it comes close to dominating the Geneva aspect of UNCTAD's existence (the working period between the quadrennial conferences). But at the grand conferences or at any other meeting sufficiently important to attract ministerial level officials from home governments the staff's role is less crucial. Here high-level officials with a different set of essentially political concerns (their primary goals being to obtain some kind of passable agreement) and a different degree of expertise (both more and less than that of the Geneva delegates) come to dominate the process. Thus at UNCTAD-IV in Nairobi after three and one-half weeks of stalemate, a handful of prominent delegates—presumably reflecting, if loosely, group positions—disappeared into the top floor of the Nairobi Hilton to hammer out a settlement of the controversial issues sufficiently ambiguous to avoid an immediate disaster (in terms of public relations and "atmospherics" but also in terms of possibly provoking OPEC into retaliation).

The staff's influence during the early phases of the process also reflects another factor. For many of the developing country governments, Geneva issues do not have very much salience. Indeed many of the governments lack the capacity—and perhaps the interest—to establish individual positions on complex issues like the Common Fund or a code of conduct on the transfer of technology. As a result, there is a tendency (partially verified in interviews) to instruct Geneva delegations primarily to support the Group consensus—the package worked out by the staff and a number of particularly influen-

---

[49] Here, as elsewhere, I am referring primarily to the process on controversial issues. One should note that there are other cases of staff influence that seem to parallel my description, if in a different setting. Thus Thomas G. Weiss and Robert S. Jordan, *The World Food Conference and Global Problem Solving* (New York: Praeger Publishers, 1976), describe the influence of the secretariat on the Food Conference in this fashion: "An international secretariat did not merely influence indirectly the shape of policy but actually *made* policy" (p. 103, italics theirs).

tial delegates.[50] This also provides part of the explanation for the occasional discrepancy between what some developing country governments profess in private, bilateral meetings with developed country officials and what their delegates are saying or doing in Geneva: the home government may be more moderate and more concerned with real gains or with keeping lines open to potential benefactors, while the delegation in Geneva may be more concerned with the need to maintain Group unity or to establish new principles of order. In short, the staff dominates the period before "low" politics issues become "high" politics issues. It should be noted, however, that when key officials from the home governments finally appear on the scene and when UNCTAD issues have become increasingly salient to them, the outcome is only rarely a rejection of the Group package. The symbolic value of unity generally remains too high, and no country or group of countries (except perhaps the leaders of OPEC) has the power to impose a compromise on the others; consequently internal conflicts tend to be resolved by maintaining unity behind the maximum common denominator.

Presumably the influence of the staff should revive in the postconference period. This has not been completely true, however. In the early periods when demands are set and promoted expectations of benefits also begin to rise. These have generally (but not totally, or the game would collapse) been frustrated at the ensuing conference. Consequently, there tends also to be disappointment with the staff and especially with the Secretary-General and a period of uncertainty and vacillation between moderates willing to settle and radicals asserting the futility of moderation. Staff influence could be sustained only if quick victories and real payoffs were negotiable, but the staff does not possess this kind of power. The staff also usually becomes more moderate in the later stages of the negotiating process, either (or both) as a result of

[50] Thus the group system and staff expertise permit some countries to hide their own lack of technical skills behind a common position. But this has also led to the charge that these countries are manipulated by the staff and the more advanced LDCs—"the unscrupulous leading the ignorant" (to borrow a phrase from the Law of the Sea negotiations).

technical challenges to earlier work or because of a desire to salvage something from its efforts. But the Group of 77 may not be in a listening mood: raised expectations followed by frustration may not induce much moderation. Staff influence begins to rise again only when earlier issues are resolved (or there is agreement to disagree) and the need to prepare for the next conference begins to become prominent. This analysis of a decrease in staff influence over time should not be taken to imply that the staff is less central than I have argued; in order to dispel this notion one needs only to emphasize that the agenda the high-level officials are working with and the proposals they are seeking to compromise have been largely set by the staff.

Keohane and Nye have stressed the extent to which possession of information and legitimacy make the staff potential catalysts for the creation of transgovernmental coalitions.[51] This has not occurred very often or very significantly at UNCTAD for at least two reasons. First, the developed countries have their own sources of information and substantial doubts about the legitimacy of a staff perceived as hostile and biased. Thus, so far as I have been able to detect, the coalitions that the staff has formed have been primarily with a few friendly governments such as Norway and the Netherlands, but these governments do not exert sufficient influence to affect matters substantially.[52] Second, even with the Group of 77, most of the staff's influence has been with the Geneva delegations (where information and expertise are at a premium) and these delegations, like the staff itself, tend to lose influence as the point of decision approaches. As a result, the coalitions with the delegations tend to be most critical in the early stages of gathering support.

Perhaps there is another way of making this point. Rising levels of interdependence seem to have transformed many

[51] Robert O. Keohane and Joseph S. Nye, "Transgovernmental Relations and International Organization," *World Politics* 27, no. 1 (October 1974): 39-62.

[52] The Nordics and the Dutch should be able to play an important mediatory role in these circumstances, but they have not done so (for reasons that I have already discussed in Chapter 4).

"low" politics issues into "high" politics issues. But just because they have become high politics issues, critical decisions have to be made at the top—transnational coalitions and transnational bureaucratic politics can no longer provide a substitute for traditional intergovernmental relations. Moreover, the tendency of the developing countries to emphasize general principles and to delay discussion of specifics has also diminished the possibility or the utility of transnational coalitions. Such coalitions are likely to become much more important if agreement on principles were to be reached or if the Group of 77 were to change its negotiating tactics, but for the moment they have had little influence. It may not be inappropriate to add that in many interviews with delegates and staff virtually no one indicated that they had thought very much about interdependence—beyond rhetorical allusions—or that they believed interdependence necessitated or implied new patterns of thought and behavior. In effect, interdependence seemed to create new problems, but it did not seem to generate new answers or new perceptions of proper behavior. For these elites, the first instinct in the face of apparently new conditions was to retreat as rapidly as possible to familiar and comforting patterns of behavior.

In respect to the issues we have just examined, it seems obvious that reforms of the group bargaining process are imperative. But before I discuss a number of reform proposals one other issue needs some comment: What role can or has the Secretary-General played in bridging the gap between group positions?

The Role of the Secretary-General

The mediatory function has not been performed well by UNCTAD's Secretary-General. But whether it can be performed well must remain an open question—especially as it is evident that the political context wherein the Secretary-General works may sharply constrain any effort to become an "honest broker."

The mixture of roles that the Secretary-General chooses to emphasize is likely to reflect the interaction between opportunities created by external developments, his personal pre-dispositions, and the reputation he carries with him. The first factor is likely to be *primus inter pares*. Thus the tenure of the current Secretary-General, Gamani Corea, has been domi-nated by the rising expectations and demands of the develop-ing countries as a result of recent events—by the notion that a New International Economic Order is necessary and possi-ble—and by the disarray of the developed countries who have reacted to fears and uncertainties by assertions that reform will suffice and major restructuring is neither necessary nor possible. Questions of internal administration and institu-tional effectiveness have not been major issues for Corea, ex-cept in the general sense that he has sought to enhance UNCTAD's influence in the system—but by external political maneuvering. Finally, Corea has not been a charismatic intel-lectual leader (like Prebisch). He is clearly an intelligent and competent man, but he has not been identified with new ideas or principles: he has been the cutting edge of the current conventional wisdom, but not one of its major theorists. As a result of these cross-currents, Corea has become a major spokesman for the effort to construct a New International Economic Order, a role that seems personally congenial and politically inevitable (to insure the support of the constituency that he must serve).

Sophisticated analysts have stressed the mediatory and transformational role of executive leadership in international institutions. Understanding the environment and what it permits, isolating aspirations common to all groups and sys-tems, building consensus behind common objectives, creating an organizational ideology that is widely shared, and altering the expectations and preferences of his constituency—reedu-cating them in the art of the possible—are familiar impera-tives.[53] Building the foundation for what cannot be done today but may be necessary and possible in the future is also emphasized. But these are extraordinarily difficult, perhaps even contradictory tasks, for the head of an organization like

[53] See Haas, *Beyond the Nation-State*, pp. 97-103; and Robert W. Cox, "The Executive Head: An Essay on Leadership in International Organization," *International Organization* 23, no. 2 (1969): 205-230.

UNCTAD: so many resources have to be expended in keeping his primary constituency together and so many promises have to be made and expectations raised that efforts at constructing a wider coalition have floundered, and support from the primary constituency has gradually eroded. Consequently the time horizon wherein UNCTAD operates is very short, the range of the possible has been misperceived, and consensus on program, ideology, and future directions is still minimal. Not all of this, however, is directly the fault of the Secretary-General.

The problems confronting the Secretary-General reflect two of the central dilemmas in North-South relations. No complaint can be legitimately raised about the Secretary-General's effort to extract a range of change in the trade and aid systems for the benefit of the developing countries; this is, after all, UNCTAD's major purpose. But when too much is sought too quickly (for example, in terms of political feasibility and genuine intellectual uncertainties about what must be done) the Secretary-General rapidly alienates those from whom changes are sought, and he increasingly diminishes his own credibility. Also, his credit is likely to run out very quickly with the Group of 77, for whatever results he manages to achieve are very likely to be perceived as insufficient—the "what have you done for me lately?" syndrome.

The dilemma arises from the fact that there is no way in which any feasible range of external change can deal with the problems of most developing countries, for such changes only create opportunities that can be grasped by a minority of these countries. Nor are there any programs—except perhaps a universal development tax—that promise immediate benefits to all the developing countries or that allocate benefits in an equitable fashion (both within and between countries). The quest for external salvation may be a result of commitment to oversimplified ideologies, or of the unwillingness of corrupt elites to risk necessary domestic changes, or of the problems created by inappropriate development theories that cannot be altered quickly by poor and inflexible economies. But it also needs to be strongly emphasized that there *are* numerous cases in which external actions have been taken by the rich countries and their corporations that have ignored the interests of the developing countries or made them the first victims of policies chosen on narrow national grounds. International change can and should diminish these problems, but it cannot eliminate them; that can only be accomplished slowly and painfully, by a concentrated effort to increase the ability to cope domestically so that external effects are relatively more controllable and external opportunities are relatively more easy to grasp. The recent effort to move development theory toward a basic needs and redistribution strategy is a very critical step in the right direction, but it is still not widely accepted and is even less widely implemented.[54] In the meanwhile, the Secretary-General is caught between rising demands by the developing countries and insufficient response by the developed countries.

The second dilemma is institutional, and it reflects the difficulty of establishing a record of success without prior agreement on principles and procedures. It seems a commonplace to assert the need for the Secretary-General to articulate and stand for the commonly shared values of an organization; indeed, doing so provides him with his most effective leverage against narrowly self-interested proposals. But what role can he play in an organization with very minimal value consensus and with sharp disagreement about what rules need to be changed to produce a different distribution of the world's goods? I merely want to emphasize a fact that seems to have been forgotten in much current discussion: the role of the Secretary-General of a deliberately redistributive institution such as UNCTAD is not identical with the role of the Secretary-General in organizations that are less dominated by conflict and more oriented toward regulation of shared interests. There are differences in degree that need to be taken into account.

There is more at issue here than the simple proposition that the Secretary-General is not a dictator. More critically, the absence of shared values and a shared vision of the or-

[54] For discussion and analysis of the points in this paragraph, see Robert L. Rothstein, *The Weak in the World of the Strong: The Developing Countries in the International System* (New York: Columbia University Press, 1977).

ganization means that none of the membership groups are willing to allow a truly strong Secretary-General to emerge—that is, an authority with autonomous powers. In essence, weak is safe. A weak Secretary-General is hardly unique. Thus Ernst Haas noted that while his study of the ILO permits "no flat and sweeping generalization about who 'runs' the ILO and whose wishes prevail, this much at least can be said: the leadership, by itself, can do almost nothing."[55] This is true, but insufficient. The Secretary-General may be weak, but he is far from powerless—in UNCTAD or elsewhere.

The central element of the power of the Secretary-General and of UNCTAD rests on the Third World's need to create and control a forum to initiate, coordinate, and negotiate Group of 77 policy packages. Only UNCTAD has been in a position to respond, for no other institution provides the necessary kind of staff and resources. UNCTAD's concern with trade and development has no obvious boundary lines, which means that the right to speak on almost all issues can be justified. Perhaps more significantly, only the UNCTAD staff has been in a position to see the "whole problem" unconstrained by particular national interests or a limited and essentially technical domain. As a result, the Secretary-General, in control of (some of) the staff, inherits a unique leverage and a special perspective that may permit him to speak for all of the developing countries or to appear to reflect a broader, more global interpretation of Third World interests and needs. Translated into policymaking terms, it gives the Secretary-General and his key staff members great influence in setting the agenda of discussion and in determining what options will be considered and in what form.

Except for the direct, deliberate, and pervasive dominance of the North-South conflict, these considerations do not seem to set UNCTAD widely apart from several other institutions in the international system. But differences begin to appear when we contrast judgments of how a Secretary-General of an international institution "ought" to act with judgments of how UNCTAD's Secretary-General must act in order to sur-

---

[55] Haas, *Beyond the Nation-State*, p. 194.

vive. For example, Robert Cox has argued very sensibly that the leader of an international institution cannot allow himself to become prisoner of any coalition.[56] But under the present circumstances, the Secretary-General of UNCTAD has no choice but to be the prisoner—which is to say the leading exponent—of Group of 77 views. His role seems more reminiscent of the role of the Secretary-General of the UN during the height of the Cold War than the role of a Secretary-General of any of the functional institutions. As in the Cold War, the common interests of the institution are difficult to define (except in broad abstractions), the numerically dominant side seeks to use the institution as the cutting edge of an effort to implement its own view of the world, and the Secretary-General either loses the support of a powerful minority if he supports the majority or he loses the support of both sides if he seeks to represent a vision of the common interest that is shared by no one.

The role of the Secretary-General in UNCTAD is thus inherently unstable, and will remain so, at least until there is a wider consensus on values and purposes. What power he has in these circumstances rests on the interaction between his personal stature (great for Prebisch, less so for his successors), his political skills in putting together an acceptable program and establishing sufficient support for it, the nature of the developed country regimes he must deal with, and the play of external events. Only the second factor—political skills—is amenable to much short-run manipulation, but the key is that the Secretary-General is likely only to have the power of persuasion, not the power to compel and dominate. He can make promises to have the staff take particular interests into account, he may use some elements of patronage, and he may even threaten to resign, but he can neither guarantee nor impose intended results. The package is always threatening to unravel, especially when a compromise proposal from Group B seems acceptable to the more powerful members of the Group of 77; and only the symbolic glue provided by the idea of unity has prevented fragmentation. As with the staff, the

---

[56] Cox, "The Executive Head," p. 178.

Secretary-General is gradually likely to lose influence as issues reach the stage of political decision and as the number of unachieved expectations rise—like many "radical" regimes in the Third World, the Secretary-General can be undermined or outflanked by more "radical" leaders promising more future benefits for all.[57]

The constraints discussed thus far clearly suggest that the Secretary-General is unlikely to play a true mediator's role between the two groups. His bias is too apparent, and his ability to guarantee membership performance is too limited. This still leaves him with some important tasks. Perhaps the most critical of these tasks has been the least performed: the Secretary-General can run his organization more effectively, especially in terms of developing proposals that are strong enough to resist the criticism of independent experts. Politically, the Secretary-General could play a useful if necessarily private role by indicating certain areas where compromise might be possible and where the line between rhetorical and real goals—or aspirations and expectations—might be struck. This is important because the exchange of principles fails to reveal obvious stopping points and because the absence of trust ensures that the developed countries suspect even moderate demands and fear that concession only generates new demands. A strong Secretary-General might also seek to press against the constraints within which he must operate, and he might seek to educate and not merely stand in front of his followers. In short, he might risk his position as well as defend it. The Secretary-General has not performed these tasks well, at least according to most informed judgments, perhaps because of pressures from the Group of 77 to satisfy everyone or perhaps because the constraints have appeared too powerful.

Would reforms be successful in transforming the Secretary-General's role so that different tasks—especially mediation and the representation of common interests—could be accomplished? The creation of a Third World "OECD" to

---

[57] This is especially so because the developing countries have become more assertive, expectations of the benefits of change have risen, and the need for external help is growing—in part as a consequence of domestic failures (and, lately, of the actions of OPEC).

prepare positions for the Group of 77 would probably not change matters greatly, at least as long as unity around the highest common denominator remained the norm by which internal disputes were "settled." It might, however, be a useful first step, for the Secretary-General and his staff could be relatively more critical of proposals that they had not developed, and it might be easier to improve the quality and reputation of the staff. A Secretary-General more perceptive about the political systems from which he seeks concessions and more willing to risk his own political capital in dealing with his supporters would also be helpful—although this probably puts too much faith in the accidents of personality and the selection process. Perhaps an agreement to limit the Secretary-General to one longer term in office (six or eight years) would also be useful.[58] This would eliminate or diminish the need to build support for reelection by promising more than can be delivered or by not opposing demands that may be excessive, unjustified, or premature.

None of these measures are critically important nor are they likely to have much short-run significance. They constitute tinkering, which is useful only if the basic framework is functioning effectively. This suggests that reforms of major significance are likely only if the bargaining environment between rich and poor were to change markedly and if structural reforms of the group bargaining system were to become feasible.[59]

[58] Would a Secretary-General from the developed countries be more effective in extracting support—as McNamara has been with the World Bank? The possibility is too remote (currently) to make this an interesting question. Even so, one is doubtful that it would make much difference.

[59] These topics shall be discussed in Chapters 6 and 7, respectively.

Chapter 6

Institutional Reform:
Is What is Possible
Sufficient?

The Reform Process in UNCTAD

The group system is unlikely to disappear because it responds rather well to two imperatives: the need to aggregate and order individual demands, and the psychic and political need for unity on the part of the developing countries. I shall thus suggest only two kinds of reform, the first dealing with measures that might diminish the likelihood of persistent stalemate and confrontation after and while group unity is established, and the other suggesting a few tactics designed to help play the game better. The latter rests on the presumption that the reforms may not be undertaken or, if undertaken, will require some time before effective implementation can occur.

The forces arrayed against reform are quite strong. Opposition is traditionally ascribed to inertia, to the power of vested interests, and to the comforts of habitual behavior. Equally important now are intellectual uncertainties about what should be done, particularly when the environment changes so rapidly and conventional doctrines seem to consistently produce unforeseen consequences. The reluctance of the rich to accept changes that diminish their own control, especially when it is unclear where the challenge to control will stop, is also apparent. Finally, the UN system has never been taken very seriously by Western political leaders, and lip service to periodic calls for reform joined to institutional improvisation have been the normal patterns of response; the political costs of full-scale support have seemed greater than the expected results. In these circumstances, hopes for fundamental reform seem utopian. Still, some discussion of major reforms is useful, if only to suggest a direction of effort should circumstances alter or to keep some momentum behind a reform process that seems always on the verge of becoming a charade. There is also an implied judgment here: discussion of better means of playing the existing game is more likely to be immediately significant than discussion of reform.

The reform issue could be conceptualized in terms of four interlocked levels of change. The first level, which tends to be the most frequently discussed, is administrative. Here would fall such measures as improvements in the budgetary process, staff recruitment and selection, internal coordination, and the demarcation of organizational responsibilities. A second level is political, by which I mean efforts by national governments or groups of governments to better understand the existing policymaking process and to take advantage of whatever opportunities are present to move that process in particular directions. I describe this as playing the existing game more effectively, and I shall discuss a number of relevant measures (but only from the perspective of the developed countries) later in this chapter.

A third level of reform is institutional or structural. What is implied here are major efforts to deal with the formidable obstacles that impede the negotiation of acceptable agreements—for example, efforts to restructure the group bargaining system or to clarify UNCTAD's role in the international system. It bears some emphasis that these are difficult tasks not only because each country or group cannot or has not defined a coherent institutional strategy in an environment of great uncertainty but also because success at this level ultimately requires agreement and cooperation between the different groups. Some of these problems will be discussed shortly. Finally, the fourth level of change is conceptual, altering the way each side perceives, thinks about, and responds to the North-South arena. This facet of reform shall be discussed in Chapter 7.

The four levels of reform are interconnected to the extent that concentration on any single level of reform is not likely to be sufficient; success at playing the game better or improving existing operations, for example, would yield few benefits if major structural and conceptual reforms were avoided. But it needs also to be noted that success at any level may facilitate (but surely not guarantee) success at other levels. This connection, or possible connection, provides part of the rationale for taking administrative or political reforms seriously—for doing what one can as quickly as possible. Thus playing the game better may only be a tactic for particular countries or groups, but it also has the potential for becoming a useful first step in a very difficult and very long-term process of reform.

A number of reforms of the group system have been suggested. Particularly prominent is the idea of some form of majority voting to diminish the power of dissenters.[1] This has been unacceptable to the larger and more advanced developing countries who fear that the interests of the many poor countries will come to dominate Third World concerns. Conversely, some form of weighted voting is unacceptable to the majority who fear domination by various local "great powers." Agreement on either of these changes seems improbable because in each case either the few or the many would have to relinquish a major benefit of the quest for consensus: leverage to ensure that interests will be protected. Stalemate at the intergroup level seems preferable to sacrifice at the intragroup level.

In an attempt to reach agreement on stalemated issues, a more recent reform proposal has emphasized the creation of small negotiating groups with a carefully defined mandate and specific time frame.[2] Small groups of negotiators working

[1] According to some observers, Prebisch had this kind of reform in mind after UNCTAD-II. It is not clear whether he intended voting to work only within each group or between them as well (for example, with some form of concurrent majorities). In any event, this runs against the trend to avoid voting in favor of various forms of conciliation, which is an additional factor in the ambiguity of UNCTAD resolutions, for dissenters frequently permit resolutions to be passed without protest but then register disagreement or qualifications in postresolution speeches. Who is bound by what is not always easy to disentangle—which, of course, may be the end in view.

[2] This is discussed in *A New United Nations Structure for Global Economic Cooperation* (New York: United Nations, May 1975, E/AC 62/9). UNCTAD has taken up the suggestion in *Institutional Issues* (Geneva: TD/194), April 1976, pp. 18-19.

without the glare of publicity and the short deadlines of UNCTAD might well improve the prospect of agreement. Taken by itself, however, a procedural reform such as this is not likely to work well, for concentration on the intergroup confrontation is insufficient without reforms of the intragroup process. Under the present circumstances, the smaller negotiating groups are likely to continue to be bound by the positions of the major groups; indeed, it is unlikely that agreement on the smaller group would be possible without fairly explicit control by the parent group (as happened at CIEC after some struggle). The representatives in the smaller group might even feel compelled to be firmer and more demanding for fear of accusations of "selling out" or for fear that the agreement would be disavowed by its own constituency. Repetition of the intergroup stalemate would be the most likely outcome, engendering further bitterness and cynicism about the possibility of meaningful settlements. In effect, this kind of reform can only work well where there is already consensus between the groups on the proper intellectual framework (on the cause of conflict, if not on the specific solution) and consensus within each group on priorities and specific policies and positions.

Successful reform must begin, I believe, with the process of demand formation (or, for Group B, demand response) within each group. The central problem for the Group of 77 has been the split between the advanced, semiindustrial developing countries and the rest of the Group. This is far from the only split, but in terms of specific programs it has had the most influence.[3] There is no easy way to compromise these conflicts, since interests are so disparate and unanimity so prized. In addition, there has been growing bitterness among the poorest countries (mostly African) over an agenda dominated by proposals that seem most likely to benefit the advanced developing countries, a result that can be largely at-

[3] That is, many of the internal fights have reflected disputes about what to give the poor countries in exchange for support of programs that primarily benefit the advanced developing countries and/or a few mineral exporters. These splits only partially and only on some issues reflect a conflict between Latin Americans and Afro-Asians, since each regional group has its own (relatively) rich and poor.

tributed to the fact that the latter are more technically skilled, more aware of their own interests, and more influential within the Secretariat. The question is whether there is a feasible reform that would permit each group of countries to protect its own interests (that is, to ensure that they would get a fair hearing in the bargaining process) but that would also diminish the tendency to simply add demands together and to prefer philosophical confrontation to practical results. Stated somewhat differently, can the bargaining process (and especially the process of demand formation) be restructured so that there is an alternative to confrontation and stalemate over vast packages of complex and perhaps nonnegotiable demands?

This is a very difficult issue to clarify. As we shall see momentarily, the absence of alternatives is not the problem: restructurings based on common interests or on developmental levels are not difficult to articulate. It is much more difficult, however, to explain how to move from present patterns that are strongly engrained to new patterns, or to explain why the new patterns will elicit sufficient support to generate an effort at reform. To illustrate this we shall first examine an alternative that seems sensible (as it deals with the interests of the more advanced and the less advanced developing countries in different arenas) then discuss the factors that make acceptance by the developing countries unlikely.

The interests of the two groups of developing countries can be articulated at UNCTAD, but it seems much more unclear whether they can be negotiated there. Perhaps we could diminish the problem by dealing with the substantive concerns of the advanced LDCs in other arenas or by other means. Many of their concerns (for example, more access for manufactured exports or more access to private capital markets) fit rather well into existing institutions such as GATT and the IMF. Other issues might be dealt with by regular consultations in the OECD or by the creation of specific institutions (either permanent or transitory). Assurance that interests would be protected in other arenas or by other means might diminish the need to rely on the bargaining process in UNCTAD.

While it is apparent that there are different problems confronting the two groups of states, it is perhaps not quite as evident that there are very different political patterns activated by these problems. The demands of the more advanced countries for more access for manufactured exports, more access to private capital markets, sharp controls on the transfer of technology, and increased political power in existing institutions tend to generate substantial difficulties for the industrial countries—especially in the current environment. The additional support that the advanced developing countries amass for their demands in the UNCTAD context as well as the extension of the demands themselves as more countries need to be satisfied do not enhance the prospect of settlement. A smaller arena may do so. Trade-offs might also be more feasible since many of the advanced developing countries do have something of value to barter. Finally, I emphasize that I am not suggesting that these countries leave UNCTAD: on some issues their interests will still be involved, and on all issues their support will be useful and their commitment important for legitimacy. But for substantive negotiations that primarily affect only the advanced developing countries, better results are likely elsewhere.

Movement in this direction might well strengthen UNCTAD by more effectively matching its capacities with national needs. In this perspective, UNCTAD would become increasingly an organization devoted to four major tasks. Dividing lines between these tasks are hardly precise not only because the issues are too complex and interconnected to be arbitrarily distributed between very rough categories but also because this is a dynamic system and changes within and between categories are highly probable. But precision and stability are not my main goals here. Instead, I want merely to suggest directions and intentions, not rigid guidelines, and to encourage a degree of awareness that institutional roles and behavior can be usefully altered.

UNCTAD's first role would be very familiar. As there is neither need nor possibility of depriving it of a central role as an arena of discussion and debate on the whole range of North-South issues, it would retain this role—criticizing old ideas, developing new ideas, holding a watching brief on progress in other arenas, and emphasizing the multiple interdependencies that condition or determine the fate of the developing countries. The recent creation of a Committee of the Whole by the General Assembly may challenge UNCTAD's preeminence as a forum organization, but the resulting competition may be salutary, for UNCTAD might begin to perform more effectively if it were to realize that failure to do so would only strengthen a rival arena.

What should be done about issues or areas in which UNCTAD has gone beyond discussion and debate? UNCTAD's recent analytical work in commodities and the transfer of technology seems valuable enough to justify its continuation. For those who deny it's competence, the argument could be made that UNCTAD fills the need for a forum in which to discuss and analyze these issues certainly as well— if not better—than any currently available alternative. The more difficult question is whether UNCTAD's responsibilities should be broadened to include a wider role in the negotiation and implementation of agreements. The record does not seem to justify more than a conditional answer.While UNCTAD's competence is growing, it is also too dependent on the work of a very small group of experts (who may leave or lose influence). Furthermore, the prevailing pattern of negotiations, as we have seen, has hardly worked very well. Consequently it seems prudent and in the interest of both sides to limit UNCTAD's role to discussion and analysis until the negotiating process is reformed and until UNCTAD has convinced more of its detractors that its work is competent and fair. Perhaps in the interim a useful compromise would be to give UNCTAD some role in determining when substantive negotiations are appropriate in these areas but not to give it the power to control the negotiations themselves. The latter power would remain with more functional arenas (such as individual commodity organizations), except for specific proposals that (like the Common Fund) cut across several narrower arenas.

The last point suggests UNCTAD's second task: it could become or remain the primary setting for the discussion and analysis of certain proposals that seem to reflect a widely

224 / Reforming the Process of Settlement

shared interest in all of the Third World or that seem to require some kind of central institutional setting. The recent emphasis on collective self-reliance illustrates the first case, as does the general effort to extract more aid from the developed countries. Perhaps the attempt to negotiate codes of conduct illustrates the second case, but only if the codes were meant to be guidelines and not legally binding. In the latter case, a setting closer to those most directly affected might be more appropriate.

UNCTAD's two other tasks are probably even more critical. It's operational focus (but only *part* of its analytical focus) would shift increasingly toward the problems of the "unblessed" developing countries, not only the least developed or the "most severely affected" by the oil crisis but also those who fall somewhere between Chad and Brazil and were not born geologically blessed. Most of these countries need and will continue to need every kind of help for decades, and UNCTAD could be immensely useful as a center of analysis, of implementation through technical assistance, and of evaluation of policies and programs. And in contrast to countries such as Brazil, Mexico, and India, which are well able to provide their own analytical capacities and can receive sophisticated operational help from other sources, the very poor desperately need the services the staff can provide—as well as an institutional forum to keep their concerns on the agenda.

The fourth task is more controversial and uncertain. Legitimization is a very crucial function within any political system; it is no less so here. For it is apparent that there is a need to legitimize decisions affecting the Third World that are made in narrower institutional settings. Without legitimization, the decisional system will remain unstable, the temptation to pursue narrow and selfish ends will rise, and the dissatisfaction and desperation of most of the developing countries will escalate. But the gap between the desirable and the possible in international relations is very wide, which is to say that legitimization may be desirable, but it is far from clear that it can be meaningfully achieved in the context of sharp ideological conflicts, great uncertainty about effective patterns of behavior, and rapid changes in a number of key variables. In these circumstances is it possible to suggest that UNCTAD might play a small but important role in legitimizing certain decisions?

A simple affirmative answer is not possible. The problem is that UNCTAD currently has neither authority, which must rest on respect or power and which would guarantee that decisions would be obeyed, nor legitimacy, which must rest on the perceived lawfulness or "rightness" of its decisions. Perhaps no organization designed to redistribute benefits to the advantage of poor countries (especially in a world divided about the means of implementation or the responsibilities for action) can ever do more than approximate values such as authority and legitimacy. Minimally, this suggests two points: UNCTAD can take actions to improve its record so that the approximations are less distant from the desired end; and for the moment the areas of concern must be carefully circumscribed wherein UNCTAD might be given some role in legitimization.

The area in which UNCTAD could most reasonably assert a claim to provide legitimacy for decisions would relate to the least developed countries. Here UNCTAD could not only provide legitimacy for its own consensus decisions but also seek to question decisions taken elsewhere that could adversely affect the least developed. In the latter case, while a formal veto is probably not feasible, the call to reconsider or to delay implementation might very well be effective—at least as long as the Third World continues to value unity and as long as peer pressure and reputation for keeping the faith remain important. On decisions that do not directly affect the least developed countries there seems little justification for giving UNCTAD more responsibility than to pass resolutions of approval or disapproval. This is not to imply that decisions on other matters should be taken without reference to their legitimacy; rather, it is only to acknowledge that some decisions need to be taken by the states most directly concerned, even if present circumstances were to make the achievement of system-wide legitimacy unlikely. Perhaps the most one can hope for in these cases is that decisions will be authoritative (that is, obeyed by those who have participated in making them) and that all who are significantly affected will be consulted.

Movement in the direction that I have been describing might also make the other procedural reforms of UNCTAD work more effectively. With institutional responsibilities more clearly defined and with more effort to emphasize negotiating arenas that reflect power and interest in an issue, procedural reforms would seem less threatening to countries who fear their voices will not be heard. There would also be less need to blackmail because each group of countries would have a guaranteed hearing for real concerns. Perhaps even a GATT approach to the settlement problem might be worth considering in this situation: the unanimity principle has not been applied within GATT, and only those states that sign an agreement are bound by its provisions.[4] This diminishes the power of dissenters, a result that would be more acceptable if the dissenters could remake their case in the wider UNCTAD forum.[5]

If the developed countries believed that reforms such as this made sense, they could begin to articulate their views and to seek patterns of implementation. They could, for example, be far more adamant (and precise) about which arenas they are willing to make what concessions in: discussions can go on anyplace, but substantive negotiations can only go on where they seem likely to be successful. This effort to treat the problems of the advanced developing countries separately should move in tandem with an effort to reform UNCTAD and to work seriously with it in its areas of concern. A two-track

[4] See Kenneth W. Dam, *The GATT: Law and International Economic Organization* (Chicago: University of Chicago Press, 1970), p. 380.

[5] Implicit in these and earlier comments are practical reasons for trying to determine the principle of equity: only a widely accepted principle would (or might) diminish the tendency to demand that all the poor be helped by any measure (which usually means tacit or explicit promises of side payments), for all would be assured of help from some source. Perhaps only those significantly injured by a proposal and without countervailing advantages (such as oil) should have the right of compensation: this would at least limit the blackmail leverage of those countries neither much hurt nor much helped by a proposal. Anyway, we need to think seriously about this issue, for Christmas tree proposals may be the hardest of all to negotiate.

strategy, which must in the beginning be a mixed strategy, moves toward a compromise between the views of those who want increasingly to deal with substantive issues outside of the UNCTAD framework and those who believe that procedural reforms of UNCTAD (or the UN in general) will suffice. This strategy attempts to deal with different problems in different arenas (but *not* always the smallest, since some problems are clearly left within UNCTAD's domain and others may gradually be placed there), but it simultaneously seeks some coherence and direction by defining institutional responsibilities more clearly, and it seeks some control over the results by providing a means to limit illegitimate intrusions of self-interest or indifference to the interests of others. It also seeks to help UNCTAD by not overburdening it before it can carry the weight. The availability of an alternative decisional track may also provide a useful catalyst for reform (as the World Food Conference apparently did for the FAO).[6]

What might induce the Third World to accept these reforms? Not the argument that the developing countries are the ones who will be most injured by either an increasingly inefficient and ignored UNCTAD or by the failure to reach viable agreements. The Third World elites at UNCTAD do not seem overly concerned with the issue of implementation—rhetorical victories seem more satisfying—and they at least do not suffer from current patterns of behavior. Even the threat of withdrawal (as with the ILO) seems only to elicit bravado about going it alone. When one value in the trade-off is the creation of a new order, calculations of the gains from reaching pragmatic bargains are not likely to count for much.

There are other reasons to doubt that the developing countries would take these proposals seriously. For one thing, the richer LDCs have hardly been altruistic (and probably cannot afford to be), and they are not likely to give up the opportunity to use UNCTAD for their own purposes—which is not to say that they would also reject participation in other, more exclusive forums. For another thing, the thrust of these re-

[6] See Thomas G. Weiss and Robert S. Jordan, "Bureaucratic Politics and the World Food Conference: The International Policy Process," *World Politics* 28, no. 3 (April 1976): 422-439.

forms is toward more careful delineation of UNCTAD's role—for more power and legitimacy in certain areas but at the expense of little power and legitimacy in other areas. In short, the exercise of limited but real power would replace an indiscriminate grab for massive but illusory power.[7] One must doubt that the majority of the developing countries would accept this exchange or see it in quite this fashion. The effort to delimit UNCTAD's power would more likely be seen as part of a plan to undermine the institution—a not-so-clever attempt to return to divide and rule tactics. The argument that UNCTAD lacks the capacity to deal with all issues is also unlikely to be very persuasive. What for the developed countries is an only partially competent and trustworthy organization is for the developing countries the most competent and committed supporter of their views.

The likely outcome, I believe, is that serious efforts to reform UNCTAD will probably repeat a familiar pattern: confrontation, stalemate, futility. Neither side can impose its own views without the cooperation of the other side—but cooperation is unlikely because the common ground is so small. We need, therefore, to consider ways of playing the existing game more effectively. This can be accomplished through efforts by the developed countries to moderate the worst effects of the existing bargaining system.

The relationship between the foregoing comments and those that follow could be stated more optimistically. Reforms will take time, and they can only be discussed and implemented slowly; what has proceeded could thus be taken as a mid- and long-term statement of direction. What follows is more short-run in intent. But the two kinds of reform can and should go on together.

Playing the Game Better

There seem to me to be several areas in which the approach of the developed countries to the policy process in UNCTAD could be usefully reformed. One key to understanding

[7] Some have argued the need for a central institution with responsibility for the whole development nexus, but no one has indicated how to negotiate it or why it would function effectively in present circumstances.

UNCTAD is a heightened awareness of the staff's enormous influence in setting the agenda and establishing the frame of reference for discussion. I do not mean to imply that this is an illegitimate role. It is, however, a role that has been performed without sufficient contribution from the industrial countries. This is one reason why there has been so little concern with proposals that reflect mutual interests or even with stressing mutual interests in proposals that are not zero-sum.

The developed countries can begin to alter this situation only if they make an effort to assert their views in the early stages of the process. By doing so, they may deflect or dilute the creation of frozen packages of group demands. This would be in the interest of *both* Group B and the Group of 77, for the only ones who benefit from the current stalemate are the extremists of both sides.[8] Getting into the process early— and not merely reacting after the package has been set— hardly guarantees that legitimate Group B interests will be integrated into the package or that technical disagreements will be resolved, but it does mean that they will have to be considered and weighed along the way. This is as much as effort to induce early self-consciousness in the staff and the Group of 77 about developed country interests and political constraints as it is an effort to develop a consensus package. More clarity about where areas of agreement and disagreement fall may also result.

The costs implicit in simply reacting to proposals that have

[8] The socialist countries are in a difficult position within UNCTAD because so many of the issues in conflict seek to provide the developing countries with a better stake in the existing system. Thus the Soviets might have to join various institutions and agreements that are politically or ideologically unacceptable if they want to maintain a major role in the North-South dialogue. Of course, they have also protested bitterly about being lumped together with the industrial countries, and they have argued that they are too poor to give much aid or other help. The result is a low profile with some rhetorical support for Group of 77 demands, a number of fairly minor proposals of their own, and a very limited practical commitment to issues on the UNCTAD agenda. If some of the latter issues were ever to reach the point of substantive agreement, the socialists would need to make some hard decisions about their own role. The United States ought to be thinking of ways to influence that decision toward cooperation, for increased socialist trade with the LDCs *might* diminish some pressure on the United States and other developed countries for difficult concessions.

been developed by the UNCTAD staff under the influence of only a few powerful developing countries have been obvious to many observers of the North-South dialogue. The most important cost reflects the structural rigidities of the policymaking process within the Group of 77: once a set of proposals has been accepted, compromise—short of acceptance of the whole package—becomes increasingly difficult. In turn, this makes the developed countries even more reluctant to offer concessions for fear of "salami" tactics: there is only reluctant yielding to "perhaps" and then to "yes, but" because of fears of harming the dialogue politically and of losing the good mixed in with the bad economically. Finally, in addition to the difficulties of negotiating a package that may not reflect mutual interests, there is clearly no guarantee that the staff's judgment of Third World interests is always the wisest or that all the interests within the Third World will (or can) be effectively represented. The irony of fervent Third World support for programs that may be either unsound or a reflection of misconceived priorities should not be treated as a kind of occasional aberration—it has happened too frequently.

As I have noted, several observers have commented on some of these problems, but they have not been very helpful in suggesting what to do about them. Simply asserting the need to get into the policy process earlier is not sufficient. One key to improvement that almost everyone recognizes is the need for the developed countries to determine their own policy preferences earlier—not five minutes before the next deadline—and to consult with each other more seriously. There is also a need for more effective bilateral consultations with various developing countries on North-South issues. These are self-evident needs, for without them there is no alternative but ad hoc and perhaps incoherent reaction. But this is an area of concern that I do not intend to discuss, because my primary focus is elsewhere.

Another useful reform for the developed countries concerns representation in Geneva. Getting into the policy process earlier will require that there be delegations in Geneva sufficiently competent both to understand technical issues and to offer substantive comments on the way in which the staff is dealing with them. More qualified representatives can intervene in a number of ways: informally by consultations with staff and delegates or by requests to see research results before publication; formally (that is, via requests from capitals or as a result of resolutions) by requests for new studies on controversial issues or for special meetings of outside experts. The goal would be not only to make developed country views known and to determine opposing views in more detail but also to force earlier consideration of practical matters or earlier clarification of technical disagreements (more about this shortly). Perhaps more consideration should be given to assigning professional economists to Geneva (not simply diplomatic representatives)—even economists working on a one- or two-year appointment.

There are other measures that seem particularly crucial to me in tactical terms. They are measures aimed at diminishing the direct group versus group confrontations, inducing earlier concern for empirical questions and reducing the suspicion that any concession will only generate new demands. The fear of making small concessions, especially in the prevailing environment of distrust, has been especially disabling, since even the more liberal developed countries worry that the momentum for more change will rapidly outpace the ability of their political institutions or the willingness of their populations to respond. To contend that this problem can only be dealt with by creating an agreed intellectual frame of reference (an agreement on what is just, on the causes of present disabilities, and on the rules by which reform will be guided) wherein real bargaining can take place is probably true on some level of exhortation, but it is not helpful in terms of what to do before the millennium arrives.

The first reform would be aimed at the role of the staff. The developed countries should expend much more effort at preventing the staff from devising a *single* package of demands that henceforth becomes the negotiating agenda. What the developed countries should seek—that is, should accept—is a resolution on an issue that requests the staff to set out a series of proposals from which governments will then choose. The initial stage of the process is very critical because the process itself is so cumbersome and inflexible; thus great care must be taken to insure that more than one option is proposed so that premature foreclosure is avoided and all countries are at least given the opportunity of weighing costs and benefits in different proposals (or combinations of proposals).

The second reform would stress the need for impact statements for all UNCTAD programs. The primary aim would be to establish a relatively more precise sense—where it is possible to do so—of which countries are likely to gain what range of benefits (or losses). The deliberate attempt to avoid such an accounting in the commodity negotiations was a serious mistake, for the issue was bound to surface: the attempt to suppress it could only be sustained by private assurances (that could not be fulfilled), and it merely left the field open for rumor and misunderstanding. Impact studies might help to keep expectations from being unrealistically raised by tacit promises of more than can be delivered. Poorer countries with weak analytical skills might also understand their own interests more clearly, diminishing the effect of the "unscrupulous leading the ignorant." This effort might also encourage the discovery of cross-bloc common interests and thus the creation of new coalitions. All of this could help to reduce the salience of the grand conflicts of principle insofar as the achievement of real benefits is actually of concern—a supposition that cannot be taken for granted in the case of all the elites on the international development circuit. In addition, since some of the impact statements will surely indicate to many developing countries that external salvation is not imminent, perhaps concern for domestic performance—for salvation by (one's own) acts—will rise.

The third area of reform concerns the nature of the proposals that the developed countries agree to accept. Normally, these have been minimal or qualified acceptances of developing country demands. I believe it would be useful, however, to seek concessions on issues of interest to the developed countries themselves (as with access to resources or investment rules in the IPC debate). This is not meant to imply the need for reciprocity in all cases but rather to increase awareness of mutual interests and interdependencies—to stress genuine bargaining rather than unilateral demands and unilateral concessions. More critically, since insufficient attention to implementation and indifference to what makes even accepted proposals work effectively have too frequently characterized negotiations at UNCTAD, I believe the developed countries should insist on regular evaluations of the effects of programs and of the efforts of the developing countries to implement them. Such "intervention" is now sanctioned by the developing countries only in reference to *their* evaluation of compliance by the developed countries; the same right must now be demanded in reverse. Refusal cannot be justified by invocation of a mystical right of "nonintervention," a virtually meaningless term in this international system. At any rate, refusal to treat this issue seriously—to seek to establish mutually acceptable rules about kinds and limits of intervention—merely indicates that both developed and developing countries prefer to continue a dialogue that is more charade than substance.[9]

Before proceeding, an earlier point needs to be restated. For the developing countries, rising pressures on the institutional structure are largely a function of domestic failures.[10] This makes a commitment to a basic needs strategy very crucial, for it seems the best way to steadily increase the ability of the developing countries to cope for themselves and to deal more effectively with the pressures of the external world (which will in turn hopefully decrease the rising demands for external salvation). At any rate, whatever the development

[9] I should reemphasize that these reforms are not meant to go on in isolation, but rather that they should be joined to other efforts to improve UNCTAD's competence, administrative efficiency, and decisional processes.

[10] Developing and developed countries need an effective institutional structure for different reasons: the developing countries because of domestic deficiencies and rising dependence on external support, and the developed countries to deal with rising levels of interdependence that erode the capacity of autonomous national decision making to achieve national goals. And both groups of countries need the institutional structure to deal equitably and effectively with truly global problems like the oceans.

strategy, the interconnections between domestic failure and overburdened institutions needs to be recognized.[11]

A Role for UNCTAD

Objective assessment of UNCTAD is difficult. Performance standards are ambiguous because the objectives sought by organizations with wide and disparate membership cannot be stated in any clear or specific fashion: and if the task cannot be specified, the assessment of how well or how badly it is being done is nearly impossible.[12] Evaluation is thus largely philosophical.[13] The difficulties are compounded in UNCTAD's case, since many of the goals of a redistributive organization are bound to be controversial: giver and receiver are not often likely to agree on the quality of performance. In addition, tests of performance for an organization that has emphasized discussion and debate as well as the generation of ideas are especially uncertain: today's failure may be tomorrow's conventional wisdom. Finally, an obvious point needs to be restated: UNCTAD is not autonomous, and much of its performance is heavily conditioned by external developments beyond its control. Even a nominal standard of some sort—good performance is performance acceptable to members; bad is unacceptable—is not much use, even if governments were in agreement, since it merely shifts the question "why" back one level.

[11] As already noted, I do not mean to suggest basic needs as a panacea, for it is far from that. Rather, basic needs will remain a critical element in a coping strategy that will take different forms with different countries. For further comment, see Robert L. Rothstein, *The Weak in the World of the Strong: The Developing Countries in the International System* (New York: Columbia University Press, 1977).

[12] On this point, see John White, "International Agencies: The Case for Proliferation," in *A World Divided—The Less Developed Countries in the International Economy*, ed. G. K. Helleiner (Cambridge: Cambridge University Press, 1976), p. 276.

[13] For a discussion of the evaluation problem for specific projects that stresses the philosophical element in many current evaluation efforts, see Dennis A. Rondinelli, "International Assistance Policy and Development Project Administration: The Impact of Imperious Rationality," *International Organization* 30, no. 4 (Autumn 1976): 573-605.

Subjectivity is thus unavoidable, but its most dangerous effects might be diminished if the judgment of performance were perceived as a relationship and not a single standard. Thus the issue is not simply whether UNCTAD has performed well or badly or whether governments are pleased or displeased but rather the nature of the gap between what the organization has accomplished and what—subjectively— seems to have been within its reach as a result of external opportunities and existing internal capacities. The complexity of this calculation is just the point, for it requires both thinking contextually and widening the circle of praise and blame.

The outcome of the calculation depends on which of UNCTAD's tasks we choose to emphasize. As a forum organization in which discussion and debate and the creation and legitimization of new norms are the central tasks, UNCTAD has been generally effective. This is true not so much in terms of immediate policy success (where the GSP stands pretty much alone and very limited in its effects) as in terms of ensuring that persistent attention and analysis will be devoted to Third World problems, that a sufficiently inclusive perspective will be adopted, and that necessary information will be collected and disseminated. These may appear insufficiently heroic tasks in a world that values great operators, but what requires emphasis is that they are necessary tasks that have been accomplished in an environment—until recently— hostile and/or indifferent.

UNCTAD is also a relatively democratic forum. Everyone has a right to speak out and to withhold support and assent. Nevertheless, the right to speak is not equivalent to the right to be listened to or to be taken seriously, and oligarchy combined with peer pressure toward unity suggest the limitations of the democratic process. Still, UNCTAD's utility as a forum organization is far greater than its critics have conceded, a fact that can be illustrated by the discontent engendered by its aggressive intrusions into the development debate. The forum function is also not undermined by UNCTAD's internal problems, and it might be enhanced by the unity produced by the group system.

This conclusion needs to be reversed in response to

UNCTAD's current efforts to become a central negotiating arena for international economic problems.[14] A perceived bias on the part of the staff and doubts about its competence diminish the chance that it (or the Secretary-General) can serve as a relatively impartial mediating force. And the structural rigidities created by the group bargaining process diminish the chance that viable agreements can be negotiated or, at best, that they will be negotiated as quickly or as efficaciously as possible.

The bargaining process in UNCTAD may be particularly deficient in current circumstances. Bargaining in a domestic context has seemed to work best when each side respects the central power position and the key values of the other side. Settlements thus tend not to stray too far from familiar patterns, and suspicions about the motives and the aspirations of the opponent are not exaggerated. This is also the kind of moderate system in which pressure group tactics are likely to be most effective. In the international system, however, one side seems to be directly assaulting the other's position and values, and even acceptance of moderate gains (or private assurances about the irrelevance of public rhetoric) does not diminish suspicions about real intentions. Without agreement on principles, even concessions on specifics can look or be interpreted very differently by each side. Implied meanings are rarely read in the same fashion.

Agreement on principles is obviously not imminent. Nevertheless, the change in tone (and to a much lesser degree, in substance) between administrations at least suggests more possibility of movement toward each other. This makes it more feasible that the distributive bargaining pattern of North-South relations in which one side's gain is perceived as the other's loss could slowly be altered toward a more integrative bargaining pattern in which problem solving and the

---

[14] I shall bypass discussion of some of UNCTAD's other roles because they are not yet critical. I note, however, that regulatory action of ongoing programs has not been very effective, in part because UNCTAD cannot compel the developed countries to perform and in part because UNCTAD is unable (or fears) to intervene in the developing countries to check performance. The operational function at UNCTAD may become increasingly important, especially for the least developed countries, but it is as yet very limited.

quest for mutual gains becomes the norm.[15] In practice, of course, there is already a mixture of these two bargaining styles, although it is inclined too sharply toward distributional conflict on major issues. And while it is doubtful that a movement toward integrative bargaining will ever be completely achieved, it is crucial that movement in the desired direction be sought.[16]

I note these matters only to emphasize how difficult it would be in the present circumstances for UNCTAD to facilitate any movement toward problem solving and mutual gains. In the choice between "soft" and "hard" stances, conflicting ideologies and divergent principles combine with the structural rigidities imposed by the group bargaining system to compel a choice of hard strategies by both sides—from which neither really gains—presumably in the hope that the other side will choose a soft strategy (in which case the hard option makes sense). As a result, the tactics that dominate the UNCTAD arena ("blue sky" proposals, a refusal to move from principles to specifics, a failure to communicate freely or to exchange information, and a failure to think about the other side's problems and perspectives) tend to exacerbate

[15] These bargaining styles are analyzed in Richard E. Walton and Robert B. McKersie, *A Behavioral Theory of Labor Negotiations* (New York: McGraw-Hill Book Company, 1965).

[16] Insofar as the developed countries do have a genuine commitment to making a number of structural changes in North-South relations, they may be making a mistake in not seeking to discuss and analyze the proposals in the New International Economic Order more objectively. I do not at all mean to suggest that they should or can accept many of these proposals but rather that demystifying them—seeking to discover and articulate who gains what and when—is a useful first step toward improving the quality of the current dialogue. Finally, in terms of actual settlements, it seems clear that agreement would be possible only if the developed countries were to alter their discount rate on the future. One way to do so is to accept the fact that they are locked into a continuing and probably permanent bargaining relationship with the developing countries in which short-run sacrifices to improve the quality of the long-term dialogue may be sensible. The developed countries can hardly ignore calculations of efficiency in their decisions, for all are too poor to do otherwise. But they also need to be more sophisticated about these supposedly "neutral" judgments by recognizing that they implicitly favor the already rich in various ways and by recognizing that a longer time horizon may alter calculations.

the difficulties of moving past confrontation and stalemate. The response of UNCTAD and many Group of 77 spokesmen to this is that on the part of the developed countries only political will is necessary to break the stalemate, by which is usually meant surrender to Third World demands. This is not especially helpful, although to UNCTAD and the Group of 77 it is surely soothing.[17]

Can UNCTAD be successfully reformed? We need to understand that this is as much a question about government intentions as it is a question about institutional performance. Governments have been more willing to complain about the deterioration of the institutional system than to pay the costs of reform. In current circumstances, it may well be that values and principles are too disparate and internal decay too advanced to permit more than cosmetic reforms. But if more effective reforms were to become possible, governments would need to begin to take institutional problems more seriously not only because where one seeks to settle issues may have considerable impact on what can be settled but also because an ad hoc proliferation of institutions puts great strain on all sorts of scarce resources and opens up increased possibilities of institutional buckpassing. Moreover, the decline in the authority and legitimacy of the central institutional system could generate more and more national willfulness—especially on the part of those countries who need the central institutions to help them protect their interests. In sum, a simple point: reform of UNCTAD begins at home—in Washington, and Moscow, and New Delhi.

This suggests that given government support, a better personnel policy, improved management, and clearer lines of responsibility are possible. But they will amount to little without

[17] The absence of "will" as an explanation for failures to agree has become an incantation—or a substitute for thinking. The term should be banished from serious discussion, for it obscures all the enormously difficult practical problems that inhibit the operation of "will" (such as congressional or public support, intellectual uncertainties, effective consultation with allies, allocation priorities for scarce resources, etc.).

substantial reforms of the bargaining process and an effort to determine where and what can be dealt with in different institutional contexts. I have suggested one direction that these more fundamental reforms might take—a direction that the UNCTAD hierarchy will surely resist, for they seek far more responsibility than these reforms would allow. But I believe that what I have suggested is in UNCTAD's interest, for continuation of present patterns will only accelerate the tendency to seek other institutional settings. Moreover, if the need for major changes and a central negotiating forum becomes increasingly apparent, a reformed UNCTAD might well be a logical and sensible choice. It will not be so if it continues to lose the confidence of the developed countries; indeed, the worst thing that could happen to UNCTAD now would be for it to get what it wants.

This also suggests the need to employ or develop alternate arenas for questions that cannot or should not be dealt with (at least at present) by UNCTAD. This needs to be done carefully, with a serious effort to justify why other arenas are necessary in some cases (and not simply as an effort to reimpose traditional and obsolescent patterns of hierarchy) and with full awareness that actions taken in smaller arenas need to be justified in wider ones. This double-track strategy reflects more than a judgment about the virtues of smaller, functional institutions. It also reflects the judgment that the UN system cannot be repaired if it is continually overloaded and if it becomes a dumping ground for every intractable problem that confronts the international system.

Chapter 7

The Quest for Rules
In the North-South Arena

The Nature of the Game

The quest for settlements in the North-South arena has been markedly unsuccessful. This is not a judgment that reflects the manifest failure to implement the New International Economic Order (NIEO) or to convert all the players to a shared vision of proper ends and acceptable means. Rather, the judgment reflects even more costly failures: the failure to attain ends in reach, or to diminish obstacles that were not immovable, or to reduce unnecessary suspicions and uncertainties. Success on either side's terms has never been probable; even so, the gap between what might have been achieved and what has been achieved has been far too wide. Stalemate, increased distrust and bitterness, pervasive cynicism about whether anything meaningful could be accomplished in North-South negotiations, and indeed substantial doubts about whether the ends in view are proper or wise were not surprising outcomes. But they were (or are) at least partially avoidable outcomes.

There were times during the commodity negotiations when the presence of different individuals in key positions or different governments in key countries would have had an appreciable effect on atmospherics (style, tone, climate), but whether the effect would have been extended to substantive outcomes is far less clear. The difficulty that the Carter administration has had in converting improved atmospherics into acceptable agreements is probably symptomatic: something more than "good will" is necessary. Changes in personality or regime can be important, but they are not likely to be important enough to eliminate structural and institutional obstacles that are deeply engrained and that seem to protect important interests and values. And even if the structural and institutional obstacles could be significantly diminished (for example, by a serious effort to implement the measures and policies described in the last chapter), more favorable outcomes for North-South bargaining would hardly be assured. Thus we must also restructure the way we think about the North-South arena in an effort to alter the intellectual environment wherein bargaining takes place.

A concern for the intellectual framework of the North-South arena is imperative for a number of reasons. For one thing, the structural and institutional obstacles are also, in part, intellectual obstacles: the way process and setting are perceived and employed is significantly affected by judgments about what "stands to reason" or what "goes without saying." Without reexamination, reforms of process and setting may yield some marginal benefits in efficiency but very few substantive and persisting benefits. Furthermore, procedural improvements provide no guidance for the choice of goals. Thus failure to seek some understanding of where we are going and where we want to go virtually guarantees the triumph of drift and inertia.

In Chapter 1, I have already noted another factor that justifies increased attention to how we think about North-South relations. Intellectual uncertainty seems to me to be one of the most critical behavioral characteristics of the current international system. The validity of traditional doctrines or of any of a number of alternatives seems increasingly problematic, and the likely consequences of acting or not acting are far from clear. The injunction to act to protect the interests of the state, or the coalition, or the system itself has a certain comforting familiarity. But how should the interests be defined? The staggering uncertainties engendered by different values, different systems of interpretation, and different discount rates on the future are only part of the problem. The vast number of variables that may affect particular decisions, the possibility that the growth rate for external "shocks" and unforeseen consequences is on the rise, and the fear that the effects of external developments now resonate further and in a less controllable fashion are also influential. What is "right" to do in these circumstances is frequently obscure—unless one chooses to define progress as simply accepting or rejecting the other side's proposals, irrespective of the merits of the case.

A good part of the uncertainty can be attributed to the failure of existing concepts or approaches to provide satisfactory explanations for behavior in the North-South arena. I have already noted, for example, a number of anomalies produced by attempting to employ the concepts devised by bargaining theorists or conventional interpretations of organizational behavior, and we shall shortly see another anomaly in the use of collective goods theory to explain coalition behavior within the Group of 77. Simple attempts to extrapolate from patterns of bargaining within pluralist political systems tend also to obscure as much as they reveal. But these failures are even more consequential when we move from specific concepts to the paradigms or intellectual frames of reference (theories would be far too strong a term) that we use to provide guidance and predictability in the current international system.

None of the prevailing paradigms appear to provide an adequate explanation for the results of the negotiating process in commodities. Perhaps one problem is that if interdependence has decreased the autonomy of national decision making, it has also decreased the autonomy of the intellectual constructs that attempt to explain such decisions. Realist approaches, for example, have been undermined by the increasing salience of domestic factors in external decisions, by the increasing ambiguity and complexity of calculations of power, and by the increasing influence of states, institutions, or individuals unschooled in the ancient traditions of statecraft. Neither calculations of relative power nor traditional perceptions of the national interest, for example, adequately explain why some members of the Group of 77 fervently support proposals from which they are unlikely to benefit—or, indeed, why some developed countries oppose proposals from which they are likely to benefit. But the dictates of Realism are far from completely irrelevant—as we shall shortly see.

Similarly, studies of bureaucratic politics are useful and informative, but they also tend to ignore the importance of secular trends and the nature of the international environment. In effect, such studies are helpful, indeed indispensable, in explaining why particular policies are chosen, but they are less helpful in explaining the range of policies that is considered appropriate and barely helpful at all in explaining why policies succeed or fail.

Explanatory paradigms based on the notion of rising levels of interdependence have also not been of much use in explaining these negotiations. Part of the problem reflects the familiar fact—a staple of analyses of international trade in the past fifteen years—that interdependence (as measured by trade flows and financial transactions) has actually decreased between the developed and developing countries and between the developing countries themselves. In this sense, the explanation for the behavior of the South might be more accurately ascribed to these relative declines and to the resulting fears of the developing countries that they are losing leverage and access in the international system. Insecurity, a degree of desperation, and a tendency to overreact to temporary alterations in the configuration of economic and political power would thus constitute predictable reactions. This is especially true (although absolute levels of interdependence have risen—that is, trade and other indices have increased for most LDCs, but at a less rapid rate than such indices among the developed countries) because so many Third World elites tend to measure progress in terms of closing the "gap" between their countries and the developed countries. Nevertheless, while insecurity and overreaction surely occurred, they influenced the climate or environment of decision more than they influenced the specific decisions themselves.

The conceptual ambiguities of the idea of interdependence have also diminished its power as an explanatory paradigm. As one group of authors has recently noted, the use of the term merely to indicate increasing sensitivity to what other states might do "is quite unsatisfactory for analytic purposes."[1] Interdependence has clearly affected the conditions that confront decision makers; rhetorically, at least, it seems

---

[1] See R. Rosecrance et al., "Whither Interdependence?" *International Organization* 31, no. 3 (Summer 1977): 425-472.

also to have affected their perceptions of what patterns of behavior seem likely to achieve desired or expected outcomes. But the range of choice in responses remains very wide, for interdependence does not dictate specific responses, and the conditions it has generated are not so dominant that all other influences on the decision-making process sharply recede in influence. Consequently, as I noted in Chapter 1, the tendency of the decision makers to retreat into familiar patterns of behavior is very strong—as in the commodity negotiations when ritual allusions to interdependence did not inhibit some efforts to base decisions on narrow calculations of interest and power. The real importance of interdependence, however, may manifest itself over time when (or if) responses increasingly fail to produce expected outcomes or when they produce outcomes that reduce *both* national and global welfare.

The practical effects of explanatory confusion and uncertainty seem particularly important to me. Earlier I noted some of these effects on the developed countries: hedging, keeping options open, an emphasis on the familiar and the short run. The tactical emphasis can be very strong, for under the circumstances it is very difficult to invalidate established policies or to prove the superiority of alternatives. Vested interests do not find it difficult to protect prevailing patterns and to counsel delay or the authority of precedent. Powerful leaders with strong (or simple) views may be able to cut through the uncertainty, but whether this will lead to successful outcomes is far from clear. Premature or specious clarity may be more disabling than uncertainty. Conversely, on the part of the developing countries a "grand design" to eliminate uncertainty or to turn it to their own advantage has resulted. My understanding of the commodity negotiations, however, suggests that these responses may be primarily surface manifestations of a more profound psychological malaise. Thinking about what this might mean may help us to understand the dynamics of this negotiating universe more effectively than concentration on the adequacy or inadequacy of one or another theoretical or quasi-theoretical construction. What I shall be concerned with here is why particular courses of action seem justified to decision makers; I shall leave until later a discussion of what kinds of actions might be more effective or appropriate.

What happens when decision makers apply conventional approaches and rules to problems and the outcome is anomalous or a violation of expectations? On the one hand, persistent failure to produce foreseen consequences is likely to generate a search for new approaches and rules, especially among theorists. On the other hand, the practitioner is unlikely to renounce prevailing approaches, even when anomalies result, unless a convincing alternative is available. As Kuhn notes of scientists confronted by a "paradigm crisis," what they tend to do is to "devise numerous articulations and *ad hoc* modifications of their theory in order to eliminate any apparent conflict."[2] Reaffirming the faith takes precedence over conversion to a new faith—particularly when, as in the present case, there are several new faiths, none completely persuasive.

In psychological terms, the process at work may bear some analogy with "theories" of cognitive balance. When there is a disequilibrium between beliefs and actions or when the actions produce consequences that seem to threaten beliefs, psychological pressure is generated to restore equilibrium or consistency. The effort to reduce the gap (the "dissonance") between beliefs and actions can focus on either side of the balance—beliefs can be altered or actions can be adjusted.[3]

A familiar example may help to illustrate how dissonance can be reduced and consistency restored. Smoking is harmful and dangerous; nevertheless, I smoke. The dissonance here can be reduced in a number of ways, for example by giving up smoking (changing the action) or denying that it is really harmful (changing the belief) and by selectively "filtering" the acquisition of information to bolster whatever choice is

[2] See Thomas S. Kuhn, *The Structure of Scientific Revolutions* (Chicago: The University of Chicago Press, 1962), p. 78. The comments in this paragraph obviously draw heavily on Kuhn's familiar argument.

[3] My treatment is obviously superficial, but I hope at least suggestive. For a sophisticated exposition of the various dissonance and disequilibrium approaches, see Roger Brown, *Social Psychology* (New York: The Free Press, 1965), pp. 584-604.

made. In the North-South context, Realist practitioners in the developed countries have tended to respond by asserting that the conditions that seem to invalidate some of their beliefs are transient or less important than they appear—in effect, nothing much needs to be changed. Conversely, UNCTAD and the Group of 77 have tended to respond that new conditions have created a new universe—in effect, much needs to be changed. The developed countries concentrate on and emphasize information that indicates why traditional practices and principles must be reaffirmed and restored (and reformed, if necessary). The developing countries, by contrast, emphasize information that seems to invalidate the conventional wisdom and to justify a quest for a new order. There are two problems with this: first, each side seems to be partly right and partly wrong (or their conclusions are insufficient); and second, the bargaining system that they have developed to seek resolution of their conflicts seems to be constructed to guarantee that neither side needs to question its beliefs or tactics or to seek some meaningful middle ground. This is, in short, a bargaining system that values resolutions more than results. Or, to maintain the analogy, this is a bargaining system in which each side seems to find the costs of reducing dissonance more profound than the costs of living with it.

The unsettled intellectual or conceptual environment seems amply to justify a concern with clarification—but too much cannot be expected from such a venture. And while a clear and definitive resolution of the uncertainties and ambiguities that I have discussed is well beyond my means, it is my hope that the recommendations that follow will lead to an increased awareness of the need to take these issues seriously and to carefully think through the implications of different ways of perceiving North-South relations. My concern shall not be with specific policies but rather with the characteristics of the policies under consideration. In this sense, perhaps some narrow but potentially important gains are within reach, especially in generating a clearer notion of what goals we can sensibly seek, in diminishing unrealistic expectations, and in reducing the tendency to obscure uncertainty behind fervent avowals of statements of faith. In short, my purpose here is to discuss factors that affect the conceptual environment wherein bargaining takes place and to suggest reforms or reorientations that help to establish a relationship that is more stable and productive. I emphasize, however, that these are ends sought, not ends achieved.

Choosing Policies

The policies of the developed countries suffer from a number of familiar afflictions. Two in particular stand out because they exert a very negative effect on efforts to reach settlements with poor and weak countries. The first is an excessive concentration on the short run; the second, which is connected to the first, is an excessive concentration on the efficiency aspects of bargaining. The problem is not that these are wrong emphases—it would be absurd to ignore the short run and we are too poor to despise efficiency—but that they are insufficient.

Perhaps another way of making these points is to note the failure to think in a broad enough context. I do not mean to assert that either side fails to think contextually but rather that the relevant context for each is too narrow: for the developed countries, especially the United States, the domestic political process frequently determines not merely what is possible but also what is "right," and for the developing countries, the internal politics of the Group of 77 performs a very similar function. While a failure to consider these contexts would be irresponsible and ineffectual, to make them more than *primus inter pares* only guarantees stalemate and misunderstanding. The practical question, then, is how to broaden perspectives.

The difficulties created by a failure to take the future seriously are hardly unrecognized. What is particularly critical is not only the incentive given to random and ad hoc policymaking but also the failure to provide some kind of standard to establish current priorities. In the North-South context, the most important effect may be the creation of inhibitions against understanding that North and South are in a *continuing* relationship with each other, a relationship that is not merely episodically important but rather (in rough parallel with domestic collective bargaining) so inescapable that an effort needs to be made to institutionalize decision making, to establish *joint* rules, and to encourage the attitudes and behavior associated with cooperative problem solving.[4] As Shackle has noted, we need to consider "anticipated future occasions of bargaining" in each specific encounter.[5] These are obviously utopian goals, but the effort to move toward them is not utopian, and the felt sense that we are seeking to do so may do more to improve the bargaining environment than any particular concrete action.

An emphasis on efficiency does not necessarily imply excessive preoccupation with the short run. Indeed, a more efficient solution for a problem presumably saves resources that can be beneficially invested for the long run. Nevertheless, the developing countries have viewed efficiency as a political as well as a neutral principle. For countries intent on creating a transfer of resources, the apparently sensible injunction to treat each issue on its own terms or to seek the optimal short-run allocation of resources—on the assumption that everyone's welfare will be improved in the future—seems disingenuous or cynical. The key for the developing countries, of course, is not merely what resources are maximized but whose resources are maximized.[6] And the problem is that most of the developing countries tend to lose in the short run (when they can little afford to do so either politically or economically), as a result of efforts to adopt a supposedly neutral "best" choice. This choice tends to become a euphemism for

---

[4] On adding problem solving and persuasion as aspects of the bargaining process, see James March and Herbert Simon, *Organizations* (New York: Wiley, 1958), pp. 129-131.

[5] G.L.S. Shackle, "The Nature of the Bargaining Process," in *The Theory of Wage Determination*, John T. Dunlop, ed. (London: Macmillan and Co., Ltd., 1964), p. 294.

[6] For an interesting comment on this, see Fred Hirsch, "Is There a New International Economic Order?" *International Organization* 30, no. 3 (Summer 1976): 527. But of course concentrating on equity may diminish the amount of resources to be shared.

maintaining the status quo, and it does not usually or consistently result in the transfer of resources (especially when the developed countries renege when they discover that the best choice just might tend to do so).

Metaphysical and practical considerations merge on this issue, and both need to be dealt with before a truly effective resolution becomes possible. At this point, however, I want only to discuss practical effects, with the additional hope that practical improvements will also reduce metaphysical pressures to treat efficiency as a biased or inequitable principle. Compromise has been especially difficult on this issue because each side's argument is correct, as far as it goes. The developed countries quite rightly fear the political and economic consequences of the intrusion of noneconomic factors into the economic decision-making process—consequences such as a decline in efficiency and a loss of welfare, a continued overemphasis on external change, and a potential political backlash in the developed countries against concessions that yield little except to the already rich. There are also undoubtedly some who use the efficiency argument merely to disguise a *realpolitik* desire to maintain the existing configuration of economic and political power. The developing countries are thus probably quite right in suspecting the motives of *some* of their opponents and surely right in believing that they (as a group) are not likely to get much—at least soon enough—from arguing the economic merits of the case in isolation.[7]

What might provide the grounds for a mutually beneficial compromise? The answer must rest, I believe, on a creative compromise and not on an agreement that simply splits the

[7] These comments indicate why I doubt the value of Fishlow's suggestion that the system can be effectively restructured by returning to liberal economic principles and seeking to make markets work more efficiently—even if the LDCs were granted greater participation in rule making and policing markets. This is a "reform" that benefits only the richer LDCs and exacerbates the suspicions of *all* of them. I believe that a better trade-off between conflicting principles is necessary, not merely improved implementation of one or the other—which would only be helpful if the wider agreement were negotiable. See Albert Fishlow, "A New International Economic Order: What Kind?" in *Rich and Poor Nations in the World Economy*, Albert Fishlow et al. (New York: McGraw-Hill, 1978), pp. 9-83.

difference between the two sides or that merely devises another formula for agreeing to disagree. The need for creativity reflects the fact that the current impasse cannot be resolved on its own terms. That is to say, there is no way to negotiate stable agreements that are efficient and protect the general welfare, on the one hand, and that redistribute substantial amounts of resources to one particular group of states, on the other hand. There may be a few exceptions to this economically—I am not certain—but I believe that there are no exceptions politically. This suggests that an agreement that responds to felt fears about efficiency and equity probably cannot be negotiated for, say, commodities or debt alone. I do not mean to assert that better or worse mixtures of efficiency and equity cannot be incorporated into particular agreements. What I do mean to assert is that such agreements would be inherently unstable (since the result is unlikely to satisfy either side) and that more stable agreements would be possible only if the bargaining context were broadened.[8]

Broadening the bargaining context would require another bargain (a system bargain) concerned with how to deal with specific issues—in effect, a bargain about how to bargain. One suggestion that has been advocated by a number of economists attempts to deal with trade and aid issues in a separate fashion: trade according to the principles of efficiency; aid according to the principles of equity. In the abstract, this makes a good deal of sense. In addition, there are a number of other reasons not often considered by economists that make this suggestion especially attractive in present circumstances. Nevertheless, this is a system bargain that is not likely to be negotiable not only because of the difficulty of making a pure separation of the issues in the North-South context but also

---

[8] Thus, I agree only with the first part of Diaz-Alejandro's comment that "present international arrangements are far from efficient; there is plenty of room for restructuring these arrangements so as to make them both more efficient and more equitable." In the abstract, room for restructuring may exist, but whether there is a reasonably stable "contract zone" within the room seems more uncertain to me—especially in light of the negotiating system that must provide settings and procedures for agreement. See Carlos F. Diaz-Alejandro, "Delinking North and South: Unshackled or Unhinged?" in ibid., p. 159.

because of existing political and structural constraints. Illustrating why this idea is appealing and why it is likely to remain impractical is still useful, however, for it reveals a great deal about what can and cannot be done in this international system.

Trade concessions have become the primary focus of Third World demands for a number of reasons: "Trade, not aid" seems less demeaning than constant demands for charity, about three-fourths or more of the Third World's foreign exchange already comes from trade, and aid levels have declined steadily for a number of years. But there have been a number of problems with the concessions demanded by the developing countries. Most of the benefits have gone to a small number of relatively advanced developing countries, it has been presumed that temporary concessions will become permanent, and demands have escalated at each round in an effort to compensate for earlier failures or to enlarge the number of (potential) recipients.

The developed countries have thus had great difficulty in dealing with demands for these concessions. The reasons are familiar. Despite advocating an open-economy, export-orientation for the developing countries, the developed countries have had political problems in containing protectionist sentiment or in diminishing economic fears about generating new inefficiencies and rigidities in the trading system. As a result, increased amounts of direct aid have been suggested as a cheaper and more effective way to help most of the developing countries.[9] In exchange for an agreement to permit trade negotiations to be dominated by a quest for the most efficient solutions (with only carefully limited exceptions), the develop-

[9] The emphasis on the superiority of the aid alternative goes back a number of years. See, for example, Raymond F. Mikesell, "Commodity Agreements and Aid to Developing Countries," *Law and Contemporary Problems* 28, no. 2 (Spring 1963): 294-312. For a more recent statement, see C. Fred Bergsten, "Access to Supplies and the New International Economic Order," in *The New International Economic Order: The North-South Debate*, Jagdish N. Bhagwati, ed. (Cambridge: The MIT Press, 1977), pp. 199-218. See also M. E. Kreinin and J. M. Finger, "A Critical Survey of the New International Economic Order," *Journal of World Trade Law* 10, no. 6 (November-December 1976): 493-512.

ing countries who were injured by such solutions or who did not benefit from them would receive official development assistance as compensation. Most of the assistance would go to the least developed countries and to various other categories of the very poor—in effect, to the great majority of Third World countries—as an inducement to refrain from using numerical leverage within the Group of 77 to construct trade packages that are nonnegotiable or to blackmail other kinds of concessions. From a less political perspective, a commitment to compensate those who do not benefit from trade agreements bears a loose similarity to the domestic welfare principle that those who pay some price for the progress of others should be recompensed.[10] Finally, if the trade agreements do increase the general welfare, the benefits to the rich are likely to far outweigh the cost of the aid, and the benefits to the poor will likely increase even further as prosperity in the developed countries engenders (hopefully) more openness and more generosity.

These are not the only benefits of seeking to treat trade issues on their merits and of using direct aid to diminish inequities and to respond to cases of need. The implicit bargain is also not difficult to understand: if the developed countries would like cooperation in implementing general welfare outcomes (outcomes reflecting mutual benefits), they must offer something of value to those who do not share in the benefits. In addition, while the politicization of the trade issue is hardly eliminated, at least one of the more difficult and complex kinds of politicization may be reduced. What seems especially important to me, however, is that an agreement such as this might also have a beneficial effect on a number of the obstacles that currently impede the negotiation of North-South agreements. For one thing, the effort to limit substantive negotiations to states with a clear interest in an issue might be facilitated, since the other states would have less need to seek gains in any and all arenas. I have already commented in a number of places on some of the deleterious consequences that result from the Third World's commitment to unity. The

[10] See Richard N. Titmuss, *Commitment to Welfare* (London: George Allen and Unwin, Ltd., 1968), pp. 130-133.

maintenance of unity among so many disparate states reflects more than shared values and some shared interests: it also reflects the failure of the developed countries to make sufficiently attractive offers to the Group of 77 as a whole. Why sacrifice the admittedly limited gains that unity has brought for the even more limited gains (except to a minority) that disunity will bring? The trade and aid agreement that we have been discussing will not eliminate the ideological or political utility of unity, but it might help to reduce its most negative consequences. If all are guaranteed a fair hearing and a right to compensation for injury, bargaining proposals need not be grab bags or shopping lists for everyone's demands, practical discussions may take precedence over philosophical conflicts, and smaller arenas might not need simply to repeat and reinforce the fault lines of larger arenas.

Unity might have become a relatively more effective weapon for the developing countries if it had truly reflected common substantive interests or if the richest and most powerful developing countries had been willing to make more sacrifices for the sake of the majority. Public goods theory has suggested that the largest states in a coalition tend to earn the largest benefits from it, and thus should be willing to pay a more than proportional share of the costs.[11] But, oddly, the larger states, and not their smaller allies, have been closer to being the "free riders" in the Third World coalition. The most powerful and the richest LDCs have indeed earned the largest benefits from the Third World coalition, but they have not been willing to pay a disproportionate share of the costs.[12]

[11] See Mancur Olson, Jr. and Richard Zeckhauser, "An Economic Theory of Alliances," in *Economic Theories of International Politics*, Bruce M. Russett, ed. (Chicago: Markham Publishing Company, 1968), pp. 25-49.

[12] There have been many instances of selfishness on the part of the richer LDCs: for example, in the reluctance to allow the creation of a category of "least developed" countries at UNCTAD because of the fear that aid would be diverted to these countries; or in the reluctance to agree to preferential regimes for the African countries; or in the recent refusal by the richer countries to give up their share of the profits from the IMF gold sales for the benefit of the desperately poor (like Bangladesh). But the fact that most of the richer LDCs do finally pay their proportional share keeps this from being a "pure" reversal of public goods theory—and some *may* pay more in the future if, like Saudi Arabia, they were to greatly fear isolation.

Conversely, among Group B, the Nordic countries and the Dutch—the ostensible free riders in the commodity debate—were generally providing more than their proportional share in aid and debt relief. Perhaps this reflects the fact that "powerful" and "rich" in the Third World context are exceptionally relative terms, for most of these countries are still too poor to risk sacrificing any potential gains. Or, again in relative terms, perhaps they have been able to impose their views not only because of greater analytical competence but also because they are more likely to be able to negotiate acceptable agreements without the support of all their allies. In effect, the joint gains open to the Group of 77 have been reduced by the pursuit of individual gains by the more advanced developing countries. Until this situation is altered, the development of a meaningful package for the Group of 77 is likely to be impeded by internal conflicts—conflicts that cannot be or have not been resolved by sacrifices by the leading states. This suggests the utility of seeking more limited agreements that do not require specific gains for all, especially when all are not concerned.

A number of other potential benefits are also conceivable. The role of international staffs, for example, might be more easily limited to technical and educational tasks, without the additional complexities introduced by the staff's pursuit of its own institutional, ideological, or political interests. Again, this would obviously be a relative and not an absolute shift in focus. In the North-South context, the international secretariats have increasingly come to attempt to fix or determine the outcome of the bargaining process. One sees this not only in the commodity debate but also in other areas such as the effort to negotiate particular kinds of codes of conduct for the transfer of technology or multinational corporations. At the present time these staffs—with, of course, some notable personal exceptions—do not have either the technical competence, the political power or skills, or the reputation for impartiality that justifies such intrusions. I do not mean to imply that the international staffs should not or cannot have a very influential role in the North-South arena but rather that it is likely to be in everyone's interest—including the staffs—if they were to shift the focus of their concern to affecting the environment of the bargaining process rather than to seeking to determine its outcome. I mean by this that they should seek to improve the skills of the Third World negotiators, that they should attempt to provide as much reliable information and to do as much honest research as possible, and that they should lay out a range of policy choices rather than a single policy.[13]

Throughout this work I have been emphasizing the interrelated consequences of uncertainty and an excessively short-run perspective. Treating trade and aid issues according to different principles will not eliminate these deficiencies, but it might have some effect on diminishing them. The technical uncertainties that make resolution of specific issues so difficult will still persist, but the need to provide benefits for all developing countries on every issue might be reduced. Perhaps more importantly, the generic uncertainty that the international system is simply drifting without control or direction might be decreased by evidence of the ability of the members of the system to reach agreement about how to negotiate in two critical areas (although the "what" of the negotiating process will still remain very indeterminate). As for the need for a long-run perspective, there is no way to guarantee that specific outcomes will reflect a proper discount rate on the future or indeed any concern with the future at all. I shall shortly argue, however, that an agreement to treat the trade and aid issues in this way is impossible without a clearer sense on the part of the developed countries of what goals they seek in the North-South arena and what goals are likely to be available. Thus the effort to think about these issues may impose a need to widen and deepen perspectives. Since practitioners seem indifferent to the issue or are too overwhelmed by the pressure of events to devote more than passing atten-

[13] See also my comments in the last chapter. After writing this I discovered a piece with generally similar views on the role of international institutions in the bargaining process. See Michael P. Mazur, "The Developing Countries in the World Economy: A Question of Bargaining Power," in *American Foreign Policy in an Interdependent World*, David Baldwin, ed. (Hanover, N.H.: University Press of New England, 1976), pp. 145-146.

tion to it and since institutional reforms to insure that a long-range perspective is built into the policy process have been unsuccessful, perhaps only the asking of questions that require some thought about goals and directions can compel a degree of concern about the future.

A decision to seek only the most efficient solutions in the trade arena and to use aid to transfer resources or to compensate losers from particular trade agreements is probably not the only system-wide bargain that would improve the prospects for more effective North-South negotiations.[14] I believe, nevertheless, that it makes a great deal of sense in analytical terms. The central point, wholly apart from the details of the bargain, is that it seems very unlikely to me that the present stalemate can be broken unless some effort is made to place the conflict between efficiency and equity in a wider context. A continuation of the prevailing pattern of interaction in which one side preaches efficiency and warns of the consequences of the diminished resources that result from inefficiency and in which the other side preaches equity and warns of the consequences of merely reforming the status quo generates only self-righteousness and a dialogue of the deaf.

Having said this, it needs also to be strongly emphasized that negotiation of a systemic bargain—a bargain on the standards by which different issues are to be judged—seems improbable. Perhaps only a major crisis (something equivalent to the oil "shock") would engender the kind of analysis that would compel consideration of the need for new approaches and new perspectives. Short of that, the obstacles that impede a major change in the bargaining arena are very powerful.

One major obstacle is the likely attitude of the United States

[14] The use of aid as compensation for trade restrictions has also been suggested recently by Jagdish N. Bhagwati, "Market Disruption, Export Market Disruption, Compensation, and GATT Reform," in Bhagwati, *The New International Economic Order: The North-South Debate*, pp. 172-174. A different argument suggesting the general superiority of aid (plus internal reform) over trade can be found in Thomas Balogh, "Failures in the Strategy against Poverty," *World Development* 6, no. 1 (1978): 14-15.

Congress to foreign aid or other resource transfers.[15] The developing countries are surely unlikely to agree to treat trade issues on their merits unless they are *guaranteed* increased amounts of aid. This would presumably require a commitment to meet the widely articulated target of 0.7 percent per year in official development assistance or even, as some have argued, an agreement to institute some kind of international development tax. Additional resources might also be provided through other measures such as taxes on seabed resources, fishing, or the use of nonrenewable resources.[16] The latter have the virtue of transferring new resources rather than a larger share of existing resources.

Congressional attitudes to such measures, especially anything that involves an automatic transfer, are generally negative—and executive branch images of congressional receptivity may be even more negative. In addition, Third World issues (except oil) are not of sufficient salience for this or previous American administrations to justify expending many scarce resources on altering congressional (or public) attitudes. Furthermore, there are genuine doubts that extend well beyond Congress about the wisdom of automatic transfers that indiscriminately provide support for both the needy and the obnoxious, without any effective controls on how the resources will be employed.[17] Finally, the poorer developing countries may object that they will be frozen out of the trad-

---

[15] One notes also that declining aid levels bear part of the responsibility for seeking aid through trade concessions: "trade as aid," rather than "trade, not aid." There is not much point in stressing the superiority of aid or in complaining about the tendency to seek aid in disguise when aid levels are sinking.

[16] Various proposals in this regard can be found in Bhagwati, *The New International Economic Order: The North-South Debate*.

[17] I have made this argument myself in reference to an automatic development tax. It seems to me that the moral and practical objections to any measure that provides aid for corrupt and depraved regimes (Uganda, Equatorial Guinea, etc.) might be allayed only if the aid were given in a form that guaranteed that a substantial part of it would actually benefit the populace at large. I am not sure how to do this, since even food aid can be used for profiteering (as in the Ethiopian famine a few years ago), but it does not seem impossible to devise programs that are relatively more rather than relatively less acceptable in this regard.

ing system and left dependent on perpetual charity—an accusation that has little force for the least developed countries since they share only nominally in the benefits from trade.

The issue in this discussion has been the nature of a possible trade-off between two values. Since neither efficiency nor equity is absolutely superior, a trade-off could only be justified if diminishing one seemed necessary to increase the other. But under the present circumstances this has been particularly difficult: countries that sacrifice on one value tend not to be compensated by gains on the other. Advanced developing countries tend to gain from efficiency (qualified by temporary and limited preferences), and the least advanced developing countries tend to benefit from increased aid. And neither group can afford or is willing to accept sacrifices without equivalent compensation. Consequently I have tried to suggest a trade-off in which both groups of developing countries gain but in which the implicit bargain is that neither seeks to enlarge its own benefits by trespassing on the benefits of the other. The previously noted obstacles to such an agreement are formidable, but in addition another must be noted: although the analytical distinctions between efficiency and equity and between relatively advanced and less advanced developing countries are clear, the practical world is far less clear. Efficiency agreements tend to have an aid component (as with preferences), and the aid agreements need to be evaluated by some standard of efficiency. In addition, some of the advanced developing countries need and receive aid, and some of the poorest countries receive important benefits from trade concessions. And, finally, the question of how much of an increase in aid is justified as compensation for not receiving other benefits has no easy or obvious answer.

What this seems to imply is that the quest for a system bargain is at least premature. But unless there is some kind of agreement to seek to overcome or diminish the obstacles that impede genuine bargaining, what we are likely to confront is an increasingly dangerous repetition of past patterns: demands by the developing countries for both aid and trade-as-aid concessions, increasing resistance by the developed countries, and continued stalemate in the negotiating system, tempered by intermittent crises and shocks. Perhaps it makes sense under these circumstances to move down one level, from a concern with the nature of a probably unrealizable system bargain to a concern with the nature of the rules that might make the existing system function more effectively. Such rules, which must be essentially procedural, do not resolve conflicts, but they may prevent deterioration and keep open the prospect of substantive progress.

Rule Making: Guides for the Perplexed

In a stable system rules presumably reflect common interests (and usually, but not always, common values), and they are implemented by institutions that function effectively and are perceived as legitimate. Rule making in the North-South context thus suffers a double burden: common interests are dominated by divisive interests, and the existing institutions are neither effective nor wholly legitimate. This sets sharp constraints to what we can reasonably expect from any venture into rule making, and it raises serious questions about what ends we can sensibly pursue.

Rules obviously cannot function in a vacuum. Consequently what seems to be implied is an effort to limit the rule making enterprise to domains with a sufficiently strong sense of common interest where the institutional structure seems reasonably effective. The limitations would apply to the scope of the rules and to the range of state coverage. This immediately raises the question of adequacy: Are limited rules sufficient or are only global rules likely to be sufficient?

There appears to be a kind of systemic bias toward global rules and global solutions. Perhaps this reflects the literature on the "global village" and the shared consequences of environmental degradation that seems inevitably to lead to calls for "global compacts" or "planetary bargains" and other such ecumenical solutions to present difficulties. Interpretations of the Bretton Woods system established after World War II may have also contributed to the assumption that global rules were both necessary and possible, although in fact the "global" rules and institutions that were created were primarily the rules of the dominant subsystem of the international system. The very peripheral role of the developing countries (and the socialists) in that system has only led, however, to a demand for a differently structured global system, not a different kind of system altogether. The rationale for this has been essentially political, since the developing countries feel that movements away from the global focus reflect efforts by the developed countries to "divide and conquer." Nevertheless, whatever the justification, the tendency to seek global rules and global solutions is intensified. Finally, there is the apparently pragmatic argument that only a global focus can satisfy all the interests at play in the current system. Thus Hirsch and Doyle argue that

> although the diversity of interests itself would make such a negotiation difficult, the same diversity adds to the necessity for a comprehensive multilateral negotiation in preference to piecemeal and/or bilateral deals. . . . the scope of mutual agreement increases as the range of bargaining is widened.[18]

The objection to the global focus is not conceptual but practical. It may well be that a system based on a set of global rules would operate more effectively than a system based on more modest rules. It may also be that there are issues for which *only* global rules make sense, although I can think of no issue at the moment for which this is genuinely true.[19] And there may be some issues for which the negotiation of global rules suddenly becomes possible, perhaps as the result of a crisis or

[18] Fred Hirsch and Michael W. Doyle, "Politicization in the World Economy: Necessary Conditions for an International Economic Order," in *Alternatives to Monetary Disorder*, Fred Hirsch, Michael Doyle, and Edward L. Morse (New York: McGraw-Hill, 1977), p. 64.

[19] There is an element of "manner of speaking" in reference to the idea of "global" issues. In fact, even apparently obvious global issues like the Law of the Sea debate tend to have very little practical significance for some states and tend not to require nearly universal consensus to implement effective settlements. Surely the more that agree the better, but this is not to say that states with little at stake should be allowed to hinder progress. When I suggest that not every state needs to participate or be consulted on every issue, I definitely do not mean to exclude the weakest states—only those who are little affected (and many of the poorest *are* heavily affected and have both moral and practical rights to participate).

a conjunction of unusual circumstances. In the great majority of cases, however, I believe that the quest for global rules is bound to be futile: the clash of interests and values is too profound, the intellectual uncertainties are too great, the probability of "shocks" is too high, and the available institutions are not capable of the kind of quick and flexible reactions that are necessary in a very unsettled world. The pursuit of global rules may only deflect attention from the pursuit of less dramatic but more practicable alternatives.[20] Moreover, and not so parenthetically, global rules are likely to be loose, indicative, and qualified—characteristics that will not provide much protection against violation or much help in planning for poor and weak countries.

There is, of course, a problem with this argument. As I have already noted in the last chapter, the quest for comprehensive, global solutions has been attacked on many grounds: the increasing costs associated with increasing numbers and kinds of decision makers, the difficulties of dealing with complexity and uncertainty, and the loss of flexibility and responsiveness as the decision makers become more distant from the arena of concern. Nevertheless, simply shifting the locale or scope of decision making to narrower or more functionally specific settings has its own costs, since drift, inertia, and the accumulation of problems may result. As with the earlier discussion of institutions, then, what we seem to need are rules that are set by those most directly affected by an issue, with some means to assure that such rules are not excessively self-interested or destructive of broader values and interests and that they do not preclude more general legitimiza-

[20] Radical spokesmen will reject my emphasis on rules that do not promise either massive restructuring of the system or massive resource transfers. But I doubt that the real choice is between radical restructuring or reform of the status quo. Rather it is between reform rules and stabilization rules that at least keep open the possibility of steady but meaningful change (for the benefit of all) and continuation of the movement away from a system based on agreed rules. In short, for the developing countries the choice is between getting something (with a potential for getting more) and getting nothing (except for the lucky few, who may get a great deal). At the same time, I believe that there is utility in talking about the need for global rules—as a normative exercise and as a reminder of the limitations of lesser rules.

tion at some stage. Here we intersect with the earlier discussion of the difficulties of legitimizing decisions taken in narrower institutional settings: the rule-making process in particular areas or between particular groups of countries should also be sanctioned and approved by more general bodies. The difficulties are obviously enormous, but it should at least be noted that rules jointly agreed upon by those most directly affected may have more chance of being both acceptable and effective than rules imposed from above. In what follows we shall leave aside the legitimacy question and concentrate on the characteristics of the rules themselves.

We ask, then, whether it is possible to devise and implement a set of effective operational rules that fall somewhere between global rules that are desirable but impracticable and *realpolitik* rules that reflect only brute force (as with the "justifications" for attacking a few Middle Eastern oil producers) or a grudging effort to integrate the "new rich" into the old order.[21] There is no simple answer to this question, for even if such rules were judged to be necessary, the factors that impede the negotiation of global rules may still exert a strongly negative force. One needs only to recall that the effort to move negotiations out of large, public forums into smaller, relatively private forums has been undermined by the tendency of the smaller forums to continue the behavioral patterns that dominate in the larger.[22] Perhaps we can attain a better perspective on this issue if we were to begin by asking what we seek (or can seek) from the operation of a set of rules and within what context they can be implemented.

The context within which rules are to be implemented could be dealt with by devising a series of models of possible alternative future international systems. This is not very useful, however, for model building in such circumstances tends to follow a very familiar pattern. Four alternatives are usually offered: one describes an increasingly centralized system dominated by a handful of the most powerful states; a second

---

[21] I do not mean to imply that there is any moral or political comparability between these very different efforts—the only comparability is in the probability that they will not succeed.

[22] See Chapter 6.

describes an increasingly decentralized system dominated by no one; a third describes a compromise between increasing regional centralization and global decentralization; and a fourth describes a system incrementally adapted from prevailing patterns. Since there is no clear way to indicate how to move (or not move) from the present (in which elements of all the models exist) to any of the first three models and since there is no way to guarantee that any of the first three models will be more stable or just (or less stable and just) than the present system, the outcome tends to be predetermined: incrementalism seems the only feasible alternative. Thus the point of going through an elaborate exercise to reach the conclusion that we must seek rules for the existing system or for minor adaptions of it seems of doubtful merit.

The most obvious deficiency of settling on a quest for rules within the existing context (beyond the fact that the context may be rapidly altered by unforeseen events) is that the developing countries are bound to find it inadequate. This does not mean that they have any clear idea of how to implement a new order but rather that they can impede efforts to improve the existing order by refusing to cooperate. What this implies, I believe, is that while we must seek rules for improved performance within the existing context those rules must also be tilted so that the developing countries can feel that, *faute de mieux*, they will at least receive an increasing share of the *joint* benefits and that more substantial movement is not being permanently foreclosed. This may make them amenable to taking less than they want and to accepting rules that do not reflect massive change for their benefit, especially if the alternative were correctly perceived not as a New International Economic Order but rather as an order in which the strong do what they want. Rules somewhat tilted for the benefit of the developing countries do not seem wildly improbable since the commitment to development has already been accepted (to an admittedly varying and uncertain degree) by the international community. But I believe such rules will be much easier to implement in a less than global context.

Efforts to establish operating rules for the international system before establishing an agreement such as this are unlikely to be successful. This is clear, for example, not only in reference to suggestions that the new rich be incorporated into the decision-making process but also in reference to suggestions for "managed incrementalism."[23] Legitimacy is problematic in the first case and effectiveness in the second. As I have argued elsewhere, incrementalism without some effort to provide central guidance about direction and consistency is likely to work only in stable systems with substantial spare resources.[24] In any case, the developing countries will not accept operating rules that do not guarantee significant benefits. We need, therefore, to be clearer about the kind of rules that might be generally acceptable in a context where the conflict between efficiency and equity persists but in which there is some agreement to provide continued benefits to the developing countries. In what follows I shall be concerned only with the nature of acceptable rules in this context and not with detailed or specific rules.

An ordering principle needs to reflect a very wide degree of consensus. Neither efficiency nor equity qualifies, since the attempt to establish the dominance of either will only generate increased conflict. As I have argued in the last section, however, while a sensible compromise between the two seems conceptually justified, political factors sharply diminish the probability of agreement. Another alternative, as some analysts have argued, would emphasize the necessity of stability in a system that seems to be changing too rapidly for prevailing institutions or ideas; conversely, arguing from the same perception of rapid change, others have stressed the need for radically restructuring the existing system. But we are not in sufficient control of events to guarantee stability, and we are not sufficiently intelligent to know how to revolutionize the system or to know what promises to be revolutionary, equitable, and effective.

The exception seems likely to be the rule in the emerging international system. A continuing breakdown of the line be-

[23] The term is from Ernst B. Haas, "Turbulent Fields and the Theory of Regional Integration," *International Organization* 30, no. 2 (Spring 1976): 195.
[24] See Robert L. Rothstein, *Planning, Prediction, and Policymaking in Foreign Affairs* (Boston: Little, Brown, 1972), pp. 22-31.

tween domestic and international economics and politics, increasing demands for special treatment by the developing countries, numerous efforts to protect domestic producers, more ad hoc and informal decision making (in the midst of and partially as the result of a persistent quest for global solutions), and an increase in attempts to enhance national welfare, probably at the expense of the general welfare or a concern with the stability of the system itself—all of these developments are possible and some highly probable.[25] The result will be not only an extraordinarily complex system but also a system with great potential for conflict and disintegration into hostile fragments.

In these circumstances, the integrity of the decisional system—the heart of the political process—is likely to be under severe attack. The import of decisions will be very hard to calculate, legitimacy will be minimal and enforcement infrequent, and the commitment to maintain agreements in the face of temporary adversities will decline. The threat to the system of decision—that no one will take commitments seriously enough—is critically important, since whatever chance we have of working our way out of present difficulties will require a decisional process that produces intended effects and has earned the confidence of its actors. This suggests, I believe, that the ordering principle that might be most valuable in this and the emerging context is dependability.

Dependability might seem a trivial or irrelevant response to a very difficult and complex negotiating environment. In context, however, it may have some virtues that are not sufficiently appreciated. Dependability—keeping arrangements, fulfilling promises, honoring obligations—has occasionally been discussed as a principle of justice.[26] But in the present system it is clearly inadequate in that sense, for there is no

[25] Hirsch and Doyle, "Politicization in the World Economy," forecast a considerably looser international system in the 1980s and raise the question of how to keep the loosening under control—although they do not seem to provide an answer. At any rate, the same question is also important in the analysis that follows.
[26] There is a very useful discussion in Paul Diesing, *Reason in Society—Four Types of Decisions and their Social Conditions* (Urbana: University of Illinois Press, 1962), pp. 166-167.

prior agreement on the criteria by which to judge whether what one is being asked to be dependable about is just or wise. This deficiency could only be remedied in a very stable order reflecting widespread consensus on values and interests. Nevertheless, dependability may be a very valuable operating rule in a system dominated by uncertainty and fears of instability—provided it is properly understood.

To simply assert in the abstract that freely negotiated agreements must be honored, or that exceptions must be justified by resort to agreed procedures, or that sanctions must be available against deliberate and unjustified malfeasance is, of course, a venture into well-meant fantasy. Acceptance of any operating rule must rest on an implicit premise about the nature and purposes of the game itself. But under the present circumstances this requirement cannot be adequately satisfied, for there are obvious and profound disagreements about the viability of the game (the reform versus revolution debate) and about the ends sought (rapid growth, the reduction of poverty, closing the "gap," the primacy of the political or the economic, etc.).

The severity of these constraints might appear to justify the argument that negotiations are bound to be futile. Zartman, for example, has argued that agreement on "referents" or principles of justice are necessary before bargaining on details can proceed.[27] But this is a counsel of perfection: the absence of desired conditions limits what can be legitimately expected, but it does not (or should not) imply that beneficial outcomes are precluded. We *must* negotiate without agreed referents, for the consequences of not negotiating may well be worse than the consequences of negotiating, whatever the difficulties. Merely keeping the process going may be a minimal virtue, but it is a virtue nonetheless. One needs also to emphasize that the absence of common values and an agreed frame of reference has not always prevented successful negotiation—even in the midst of war and indeed in the North-South arena itself. So long as mutually perceived common in-

---

[27] I. William Zartman, "Negotiations: Theory and Reality," *Journal of International Affairs* 29, no. 1 (Spring 1975): 71.

terests are present, the possibility of agreement—although limited—is likely also to be present. What needs to be carefully specified are the enabling conditions that might facilitate such limited agreements. These conditions must attempt to work with and around each side's central fears and concerns, and they must help to concentrate attention on what can be negotiated—that is, on issues where mutual benefits (now and in the future) are salient and the metaphysics of disagreement can be bypassed.

Dependability would be easy to establish as an operating rule if an agreement on efficiency and equity (such as the one discussed in the preceding section) were feasible. Short of that, the implicit premise underlying the acceptance of dependability in the prevailing situation is a willingness not only to keep the negotiating process going but also to maintain at least the existing degree of openness. Threats to pull out, to proscribe discussion of certain issues, or to establish private decision-making channels that are indifferent to the question of system-wide legitimacy are unacceptable. Minimally, one seeks to establish the grounds for moving forward by agreeing not to move backward. The developing countries, fearful of losing place and leverage in the international system, are thus guaranteed an important right: a significant role in a continuing process and a process in which their concerns will not be shunted aside or treated as an addendum to the concerns of the rich. This does not guarantee outcomes but rather attention; as such, it is necessary but not sufficient (a point to which I will return shortly).

As I have already noted, the developing countries are also guaranteed the legitimization of a persisting "tilt" toward their interests, something considerably less than a radical redistribution of benefits but at least something consistently more than is implied by a mere commitment to efficiency. The trade-off for the developing countries is clear: surrendering the notion that there can be no viable compromise short of acceptance of new and radical principles of order in exchange for acceptance of the notion that the wisest current tactic is to take the best offer available—so long as it does not foreclose greater change later. Dependability in this context has another virtue for the developing countries that could be very important: the developed countries would also have to make a greater effort to obey the principles they ostensibly support. That is, dependability is not a one-sided virtue, and the gains from diminishing the tendency of the rich to violate their own principles whenever it is convenient could be substantial. The developing countries have apparently already begun to see this more clearly, as indicated by their rising protest against "voluntary" export restraints, "orderly marketing arrangements," "organized free trade," and other such euphemisms for discrimination in favor of noncompetitive domestic industries. The key point is that effective rules either do not exist or are ambiguous in these cases, and as a result individual outcomes tend to be largely determined by the economic power of the different parties. These outcomes might be somewhat more favorable for the developing countries if dependability were widely accepted as an operating rule. The increased stability would also be beneficial in the sense that improved efforts to plan would be facilitated.

For the developed countries, commitment to a continuing relationship characterized by increasing degrees of dependability also offers a few potentially significant benefits. There is, for example, some virtue in *joint* recognition of the fact that what is at stake in a particular negotiation is not the constitution of a new order but a building block that involves mutual benefits and that may increase the possibility that the outlines of a new order will become more clear. But even more critically, this may encourage a decisional context in which the rhetoric of confrontation depreciates and in which the pattern of concerns begins to focus on practicalities, not principles. This may diminish the tendency to ignore questions of implementation or of the gap between the generalities of global policymaking and the practicalities of local decision making. And, finally, since two of the most salient fears of the developed countries are that demands will continuously escalate and that concessions will merely generate new demands, the increased probability that both sides will maintain agreements—that is, be dependable—may slow the process of demand formation, at least until the consequences of particular agreements become more clear.

I noted earlier that the developing countries will want more than a guarantee of concern; they will also seek more tangible benefits. These benefits must be substantial enough so that failure to achieve them is a strong disincentive to violations. Clearly, once again efficiency must be diluted by some degree of equity, but perhaps the costs are more bearable in this context because agreements themselves are more workable and because the two sides accept both rights and duties.

There are two reasons that I believe this argument points strongly away from a completely global focus. The complexities on the global level are too vast, the trade-offs too uncertain, and the benefits too dispersed and contingent to provide enough developing countries with the sense that they will in fact receive enough compensation for altering present tactics. I believe we must begin with the more precise rules and the more easily perceived benefits that might emerge from narrower agreements and settings. And in the same sense a movement away from the quest for immediate global solutions is relatively more likely to engender a concern with implementation, to diminish the effects attendant upon maintaining unity among large numbers of very disparate states, and to encourage a spirit of compromise. It need hardly be added that the attempt to navigate through current difficulties with the aid of an operating rule like dependability can never be more than an imperfect approximation of the ideal, but successively more effective approximations seem more probable if ambitions and expectations were to be sensibly moderated.

I do not mean to imply that all global approaches are necessarily wrong but rather that the direction of effort should be upward from those directly concerned, not downward from general principles of order. Thus, even where a global focus seems built into the negotiating process (as with various codes of conduct for the transfer of technology or the control of restrictive business practices) such efforts should not seek to determine specific outcomes; what can be established on the most general level is only a better environment of decision or a more just boundary between the permissible and the impermissible. Agreements on access to resources or rules for the protection of investment that may seem to require global rules are only partial exceptions, for even here different rules or interpretations may be necessary for countries at different levels of development or for different industries. In any case, these rules would be good illustrations of dependability, for both sides are likely to benefit from consistent implementation.

There are three global subsystems for which different sets of rules seem appropriate:[28] developed country-developed country interactions, developed-developing country interactions, and developing-developing country interactions. Other subsystems obviously exist, and some are actually or potentially significant: for example, East-West and East-South interactions. But the three that I have noted are dominant, and they tend also to incorporate most of the characteristics that can be found in lesser subsystems. In what follows I shall comment briefly on each of these major subsystems.

The developed countries' relationship among themselves is beyond my immediate concerns. Nevertheless, since prosperity among the developed countries may provide the developing countries their largest gains and since the reduction of external shocks and the threat of protectionism are critical needs for poor, exposed, and inflexible economies, a very brief comment seems appropriate. The interplay of domestic and external factors suggests the importance of seeking joint optimization rules for developed-developed relations. What is implied are complementary domestic rules to facilitate adjustment to external changes: in trade for example, as Harry Johnson has argued, adjustment assistance to increase the speed with which a change can be absorbed and safeguards to control the speed of the change that has to be absorbed should go hand in hand.[29] At any rate, some direct effort to connect internal and external change is necessary to enhance dependability and predictability.[30]

[28] I note again two prior assumptions: the first, that there is general agreement that some "tilting" for the developing countries is justified; the second (already noted in Chapter 6), that efforts to legitimize in wider forums will be undertaken.

[29] See Harry Johnson, *Technology and Economic Interdependence* (London: Macmillan, 1975), p. 158.

[30] Another way of seeking to connect internal and external policy might be

For the relationship between the developed and the developing countries, different rules need to be applied to the advanced, semiindustrial countries and to the great majority of very poor countries. The richer developing countries should be treated as potential or emerging members of the bloc of developed countries. Preferential and exceptional treatment is still justified, but it needs to be carefully limited. Thus such rules should not be open-ended, but rather should contain specific time provisions. In addition, a form of reciprocity seems justified not only in requesting the steady dismantlement of the many tariff and nontariff barriers that these countries have established but also in assuring that they do not attempt to freeze trade patterns so that the poorer developing countries have great difficulty in expanding their own trade. The familiar injunction that shared goals and mutual interests should be emphasized in the negotiating process makes a good deal of sense in this context, provided that the need for exceptional if limited treatment were also recognized.

The poorer developing countries need an entirely different set of rules. Neither the demand for reciprocity nor the effort to set time or volume limits on exceptional treatment seems justified. Here the *first* goal should not be the quick integration of these countries into the international trading system but rather an effort to provide a decent standard of living for all the populace as rapidly as possible and only a gradual and piecemeal integration into the trading system. The rules need to be perceived as the basis for a social welfare system that will persist for many decades, not as transient exceptions to the rules of the trading system itself.

The developing countries have talked increasingly of improving ties among themselves—of "collective self-reli-

---

by a "fair weather" rule: a country agrees to reduce tariff and nontariff barriers when its balance of payments is favorable, but it is *not* permitted to increase them when the balance of payments is unfavorable (since another country will now be in surplus and thus have to reduce its barriers). All barriers would disappear in time. A rule that diminishes the possibility of withdrawing concessions in this way is an attractive stabilization mechanism—and increases dependability. I am not sure whether it is feasible, but it does seem that we should be seeking this kind of rule more intensively than we have.

ance."[31] And while the potential for important mutual gains from cooperation surely exists, thus far only talk—or rhetoric—has resulted. It is true that the developed countries can do little to encourage more substantive outcomes since the impetus must come from the developing countries themselves, but it is equally true that the developed countries can do a great deal to discourage or harm such efforts, and therefore a self-denying ordinance seems necessary: no effort to undermine cooperation by offering special inducements to particular developing countries to stay within a "sphere of interest" is justified. The rules that the developing countries should establish among themselves should probably take the form of scaled down versions of rules in the larger trading system: wider exceptions, longer time periods, more generous safeguards. Two dangers need to be carefully watched: the gradual replacement of dominance by a few developed countries with dominance by a few developing countries; and the creation of a permanent pattern of protection that makes integration within the wider trading system increasingly doubtful. The aim should be to facilitate integration on fairer terms and not to prevent it.

In an environment of conflict and uncertainty, separate systems with different but interlocking sets of rules may be more realistic than the quest for global rules. The more specific rules may enhance dependability and reduce uncertainty, they may make the possibility of seeking shared goals more realistic, and they may make it easier to balance short-run imperatives against potential long-run needs. In particular such rules may also be incorporated more effectively in binding agreements that would permit the weaker countries to apply an important degree of pressure if they were violated, and the emphasis on mutual interests should in itself lower the probability of violation. More specific rules may also provide more certainty about details (duration, precise content, in-

[31] See UNCTAD, *Economic Cooperation Among Developing Countries, Report of the Group of Experts* (Geneva: TD/B/AC.19/1), December 1975, which is a good place to begin examination of this issue.

creased information), a factor of some significance for the developing countries. In short, these are likely to be rules that respond more effectively to both the domestic and international bargaining weaknesses of the majority of the Third World.

One other potential virtue ought to be emphasized: as I have noted in an earlier chapter, the international decision-making system is very distant from the world it seeks to regulate. This seems an almost inevitable outcome of a global focus and of a negotiating system dominated by diplomats in quest of political and ideological "victories." The more differentiated focus that I have advocated does not guarantee that these deficiencies will be remedied, but it should at least increase the possibility that problem solving and negotiation can be moved somewhat closer to the individuals, the sectors, or the countries most significantly affected by a decision. More rapid evaluation of consequences and a more flexible system of response may ensue. To some extent, a differentiated focus may also reduce escalating pressures on the institutional system. The syndrome that has developed (in which weak and derivative institutions are handed problems that they cannot resolve—and then are blamed for the results) needs to be resisted. The rule of thumb should be that solutions are first sought at the lowest level that incorporates all those directly concerned, and global institutions should only be a last resort for problems that cannot be settled elsewhere.

An argument for a decisional setting that reflects the pattern of substantive interests on an issue does not imply indifference to wider concerns like equity and legitimacy. A narrower institutional setting may increase the probability that efficiency will receive its due; a more global institutional setting, conversely, may increase the probability that equity and legitimacy will receive their due, if at some potential cost to efficiency. The precise trade-off in this familiar conflict of values cannot be established by any technical rule. But the key point is that there *is* a trade-off involved, not an either/or choice. In practical terms, the most pressing need is for the articulation of an indicative or normative rule that might provide some guidance—but not a blueprint—for where the trade-off should be made. Perhaps something akin to the economist's notion of external effects should be considered. An agreement negotiated only by those most directly concerned could thus be considered legitimate only if it did not generate negative external effects for states not party to the agreement. From this perspective, global institutions would have something of a watching brief for external effects— which is to say for a proper balance between efficiency and equity. In the nature of the case, distinctions of this kind are more easily stated than precisely specified, but even the effort to articulate a rule that is widely acceptable may be important when the alternative is ad hoc improvisation.

Dependability is a modest and essentially procedural goal in a world where sharp conflicts of value and interest threaten to undermine the possibility of achieving or even discovering the common interests that do exist. The quest for such limited gains—for at least getting the most out of a very difficult environment—may seem decidedly unheroic or insufficient, especially in comparison with "planetary bargains" or "global compacts." Nevertheless, while such gains may not always help the right countries or groups and while they are surely insufficient, it remains difficult to argue that no gains are better than some gains—unless one has a rather naive faith in either the likelihood of revolution or revolution as a panacea. Perhaps above all, dependability may help to create islands of stability and (limited) progress that might provide the necessary base for more profound and enduring changes.

What does it mean in practical terms—in terms that make sense to policymakers barely able to stay abreast of the daily flow of papers, meetings, and deadlines—to suggest the need to seek such rules in existing circumstances? There is no easy or simple answer to this question, since specific policy choices can rarely be read directly from a conceptual exercise (the latter obviously leaves out the details that may be crucial in particular cases). What a clearer conceptual structure may do, however, is provide a large element of consistency and coherence so that specific policy choices in different areas are integrally related and so that a standard by which to evaluate current policies is available. These may be exceptionally important benefits in periods dominated by high degrees of uncertainty.

A conceptual exercise can also be important in an educational sense. This is clearly true for the participants in such an exercise, since the question of why things are being done is likely to become as important as the question of what is to be done—especially since the latter is too frequently answered reflexively in terms of doing what has habitually been done. But the attempt to devise acceptable concepts and approaches may also be educational in another manner. The question of educating others in the new views—in explaining to them why a new orientation seems appropriate or necessary—is bound to arise. This may create a more effective dialogue (perhaps even the beginning of a dialogue with elements of a common language) than simply repeating ever more fervently what has stood to reason in the past.

There is an analogy here that is worth noting. The attempt to devise working rules in a context dominated by sharply conflicting values and interests seems to bear some resemblance to Cold War efforts to achieve mutually beneficial agreements with the Soviet Union in areas of common concern. While there are clearly important differences between the two cases, there are also at least two equally important similarities. The first similarity would be in the decision to set aside certain insoluble issues, to avoid challenging the other side's central value and power positions, and to concentrate on negotiating narrower issues where mutual interests dominate—because the mutual interests are important enough on their own terms and because successful outcomes might facilitate wider agreements. In this sense, it would be all to the good to set aside the debate about how much change is necessary and about who has the right to what order of benefits and to emphasize settling what can be settled—as the first order of business. The second similarity is in the educational process. I have in mind especially the effort begun during the Kennedy administration to seek to initiate the Soviets in a new style of thinking about nuclear strategy and to do so not only by publicizing strategic theory and doctrine but also by deliberate and careful use of official actions and declarations. The need to persuade the other side and to build areas of common understanding is no less imperative in the present case. In this sense one hopes to make the Cold War analogy increasingly inappropriate.

Many will reject this analogy, including radicals who believe it will delay necessary revolutions, conservatives who believe that we owe nothing and need fear nothing from the developing countries, and liberals who believe that common interests between rich and poor are now so salient that more profound changes in the system are possible. I have already indicated in Chapter 1 the extent to which I agree or disagree with these views, and I want only to reiterate that the common interests that do exist will not be transformed into meaningful agreements without very critical changes in the process of settlement and in the conceptual views that both sides hold. Insofar as the analogies we use both reflect and influence the way we perceive a relationship, the educational process implicit in the quest for conceptual clarity might usefully begin by emphasizing an analogy that currently bears some resemblance to what *is*—and not to what divergent analysts and publicists think ought to be.

Conclusions

Without the kind of agreement on procedural rules that I have described, bargaining and the negotiation of meaningful settlements between North and South are likely only to result in continued stalemate and increased bitterness. But agreement is likely to be extraordinarily difficult not only because the structural, institutional, and intellectual obstacles are so formidable but also because both sides must make concessions from beliefs and principles that are very firmly held. The North must recognize that the need for dependable rules cannot be met without cooperation and that cooperation will not be given without some guarantee of consistent and increased benefits for the South; and the South must recognize that a new order must be built carefully and will not emerge more quickly by merely asserting its need. If such a compromise were to be negotiated, the outcome would not be a very efficient system or a system that was rapidly on the way to solving its equity problems but perhaps a system in which the necessary compromises would become gradually more effective approximations of what each side seeks.

Pessimism that either or both sides will see the need for a new perspective is surely justified. For the developing countries the warning is clear: what is necessary is to scale down expectations of what can be gotten from the international system, to concentrate increasingly on improving domestic performance and providing a degree of protection against external "shocks," and to take seriously the movement toward collective self-reliance. For the developed countries the warning is also clear: what is necessary is to calculate the potential long-run dangers of policies that may generate an increasingly fragmented, hostile, and poorer international system (for all). Short of both sides rethinking what they are doing and where they are going, we may drift into a series of desperate confrontations—at least some of which might have been avoided. There are no magic policies by which the North-South arena can be—or will be—transformed into an arena of cooperation and trust, but the confrontations can be contained, deflected, and perhaps even resolved (in some cases) if *both* sides alter prevailing patterns of behavior. Both sides, however, seem content to assert that only the other side needs to change.

Optimists will assert that I am far too pessimistic and that the patterns of behavior that I have described are no longer relevant. Indeed, as I write (in the spring of 1978), spokesmen for both developed and developing countries are happily congratulating each other that the "period of confrontation" is now over.[32] I do not believe it, for if the pe-

[32] Thus Fishlow argues that the "euphoria of 1974 has given way to greater pragmatism within the South. Developing countries are prepared to bargain and to respond to a comprehensive program offered by the North. But instead of a large list of initiatives, what will be more productive is agreement on principles and implementation of priorities." I disagree that a fundamen-

riod of confrontation were over, it came to an end without solving a single problem that first generated it. Even the existence of increasingly important (and increasingly recognized) mutual interests may not generate new attitudes and policies on either side. This is so not merely because of the obstacles described in previous chapters but also because the mutual interests occur in very asymmetrical patterns (with only some countries gaining and others on both sides losing) and because successful agreements may well require substantial and politically difficult domestic changes in both developed and developing countries. In addition, as I noted in Chapter 6, I believe that there is a kind of cyclical effect imposed by the structure of the bargaining system: thus we see periods of grand confrontation as global conferences loom on the horizon, followed by periods of moderation and stocktaking in the immediate aftermath. And in 1979, we see scheduled among others such global meetings as UNCTAD-V, the conference on science, technology, and development, and the Havana summit of the Nonaligned Movement.

Forecasts of slower growth, increased protectionism, potential energy and food shortages, and rising arms spending—all of which are likely to diminish the resources available to deal with developing country problems—must also be set against national and international policymaking systems that seem increasingly dysfunctional. The temptation to look for the "quick fix" (for example, a return to gunboat diplomacy) may once again become very attractive, the futility and the danger notwithstanding. Or perhaps the optimists will continue to hope that the Group of 77 will break apart, thus facilitating the negotiation of "sensible" agreements with the "moderates." But the price exacted by the moderates may be very high (in trade and aid concessions, increased roles in decision

tal shift has occurred, not in the sense that some agreements are not possible but rather in the sense that the agreements will be unstable because they are only momentary stopping points in a continuing quest for very radical changes; and I disagree that the way to seek agreement is *either* by large lists of initiatives or by a quest for broad principles that are mutually acceptable. Such principles, even if negotiable, are likely to be virtually meaningless verbal formulas. See Fishlow, "A New International Economic Order: What Kind?" pp. 81-82.

making, and perhaps political and military support against various opponents), and the desperation of the other developing countries may indeed generate more and more radical, if not irrational, actions. In short, if the developed countries were to attempt to deliberately split the Group of 77, they are likely only to drive the members closer together, thereby incurring a repetition of past patterns of sharp confrontation between North and South. But if the Group of 77 were to begin to splinter because of the operation of internal and external forces that neither side has dealt with successfully, the institutional structure may crumble, conflicts and tensions will escalate, and the opportunities for dangerous mischief and meddling will increase. Taking the reform option seriously in these circumstances surely seems prudent, but that enough will do so and that it will succeed is far from clear. Consequently, the optimists may not have much time to savor the joys of moderation, and the pessimists may come to wish that they had done more to avert an outcome that was foreseen— but not inevitable.

Index

Haas, Ernst B., 180, 181, 205n,
210n, 213, 264n
Hasenplug, Hajo, 34n. 163n
Helleiner, G. K., 103n, 163n, 164n
Henderson, P. D., 84
Hirsch, Fred. 248n, 260n, 265n
Hoffman, Stanley, 9
Hopkins, Raymond F., 13n

ideology, impact of, 81, 97, 124, 126,
139, 143
implementation, 18-20, 85, 146, 233,
269
incrementalism, 15, 18, 57, 263
indexation, 58, 78, 100-101, 204
India, 104, 113, 114, 115-116, 118,
129, 200
inflation, 64, 71-73, 78, 100, 121n
"inner circle" decision making, 171-
174, 178
institutional strategy, 21n, 109, 171,
218, 226-227, 239
institutional structure, 27-28, 169-
179, 233, 238
institutions, 36n, 109, 169-179, 238,
273. See also institutional structure
Integrated Program for Commodities (IPC), 43-57, 58-102,
138; commodity coverage, 87-89,
111, 123; objectives, 61-81; origins, 43-57; principles, 60-61; as
staff creation, 69, 104, 109-110,
121-122; techniques, 81-102. See
also Common Fund
intellectual climate, 106-107
interdependence, 11-13, 121n, 209,
243-244; conceptual ambiguities,
243-244; and the LDCs, 11n, 243
international policy process, 16, 19,
30-31, 57, 172-173, 278
International Resources Bank, 62,
134n
Iran, 104
Iraq, 113
Islam, Nurul, 77n
Ivory Coast, 23

Jacobson, Harold K., 180n
Jamaica, 23, 104
James, Robert Rhodes, 183n
Japan, 23, 58, 123, 125, 133
Johnson, Harry G., 55n, 188n, 270
Jordan, 113
Jordan, Robert S., 206n, 227n

Kaldor, N., 47n, 71n
Kallab, Valeriana, 163n
Kenen, Peter, 162
Keohane, Robert O., 208
Kissinger, Henry, 86n, 141
Knudsen, O., 64n
Kreinin, M. E., 251n
Kuhn, Thomas S., 245n
Kuwait, 113

Lal, Deepak, 84
Laursen, Karsten, 65, 66n, 72n, 73n,
82n, 92n, 96
Law, Alton D., 41n, 63n, 66n
Law of the Sea Conferences, 157-
160
leadership role in international institutions, 210-216
learning process, 107-108
least developed countries, 116, 158,
160n, 200, 202, 220-222, 224-225,
252, 258, 271
Lebanon, 113
Leff, Nathaniel H., 33n, 74n
legitimacy, 174, 224-225, 261-262,
267
Libya, 113
Lindblom, Charles E., 18n
linear concession rate, 131
Lipton, Michael, 33n, 117n
Little, I.M.D., 65n

MacAvoy, Paul, 66-67
McBean, Alasdair, 64n, 68n
McKersie, Robert B., 122n, 197n,
237n
McNicol, David L., 42n, 43n, 63n,
64n, 71n, 75, 84, 89, 96
Malaysia, 23, 129

LIBRARY OF CONGRESS CATALOGING IN PUBLICATION DATA

Rothstein, Robert L
    Global bargaining.

    Includes index.
    1. Commodity control.   2.   United Nations.
Conference on Trade and Development.   3.   Commercial
policy.   4.   International economic relations.
I. Title.
HF1428.R59   382'.3   78-70316
ISBN 0-691-07610-3
ISBN 0-691-02190-2 pbk.

Date Due